The New Era
in Religious Communication

The
New Era
in Religious
Communication

PIERRE BABIN
with Mercedes Iannone

Translated by David Smith

FORTRESS PRESS   MINNEAPOLIS

THE NEW ERA IN RELIGIOUS COMMUNICATION

Interior and cover designs by Publishers' WorkGroup.

Library of Congress Cataloging-in-Publication Data

Babin, Pierre.
   [Ere de la communication. English]
   The new era in religious communication / Pierre Babin with
Mercedes Iannone; translated by David Smith.
     p. cm.
   Rev. translation of: L'ère de la communication.
   Includes bibliographical references and index.
   ISBN 0-8006-2437-8 (alk. paper)
   1. Communication—Religious aspects—Christianity. I. Iannone,
M. II. Title.
BV4319.B213   1991
261.5'2—dc20   90-40129
                                                                 CIP

Manufactured in the U.S.A.   AF 1-2437

95   94   93   92   91   1   2   3   4   5   6   7   8   9   10

CONTENTS

Illustrations   ix

Preface   xi

Introduction: The Birth of Conviction   1

  Youthful Conversion   1
  The Audiovisual Turning Point   3
  The Encounter with McLuhan   4
  The Medium Is Christ   7
  Other Transforming Ideas of McLuhan   8
  The Age of Information   11
  Encountering New Cultures   15

1. Religious Education from Gutenberg to the Electronic Age   18

  Communicating Faith in an Oral Culture   19
  Faith by Immersion   20
  Communicating Faith in the Age of Print Media   24
  The Catechetical Way   27
  Communicating Faith in the Age of Electronic Media   29
  The Audiovisual Way   31
  A Radical Change in the Church's Policy   33

2. A New Approach to Moral Life   39

  "E" Is the Formal Cause   41

The Breakup of Structures   41
The Emerging Affectivity   44
The Subdued Inner Life   45
Everything Is in the Eye   46
The Awakening of Interiority   48
Affinity Communities   51

3. The Impact of Electronic Media on Faith   54

A Long-Term Mark   54
The Framework of Faith   56
Testing Two Approaches to Faith   66
Believing Is Being "In"   67

4. A Christian Approach to Communication   70

Communication Is the Core   70
  Revealing the Reality of Communication   71
  Christian Feedback   73
  The Aim of Religious Communication   75
  A Christian Look at Schemes of Communication   76
The Schemes of Language   77
  Scheme 1: Communication of Modulation   77
  Scheme 2: Alphabetical Communication   84
The Schemes of Affinity   90
  Scheme 3: The Communication of Friendship   91
  Scheme 4: The Communication of Spirit   94
The Schemes of Christian Faith   100
  Scheme 5: The Communication of the Poor   100
  Scheme 6: Communicating the Christian Faith   106

5. The Way of Beauty   110

Sounds and Images Revealing God   114
Fundamental Distinctions   115
The Ingredients of What Is "Religious"   116
The Religious Dimension   118
Ways of Expressing the Christian Dimension   132

6. The Symbolic Way   146

Symbolic Language   149
An Experience of a Break   156

Conviviality   158
Religious Education and the Symbolic Way   163

7. The Family: The Cradle of the Symbolic Way   168

Interpersonal Relationships   168
Ritual, Symbol, and Story   171
The Physical Environment of the Home   173
The Family and Television   174
Family and Television: Vehicles of Religious Images   175
Television as a Stimulus   175
The Ability to Make Relationships   176
Strategies for the Use of Television   178

8. Stereo Catechesis   182

Channel 1: The Symbolic Way   183
Channel 2: The Catechetical Way   184
New Formulas   185
The Stereo Way of Functioning   186

9. Media for Evangelization   188

Mass Media, Group Media, or Self-Media?   188
The Self-Media—Unobtrusive and Pervasive   192
What Is the Way Forward?   192
Programs and Media for Evangelization   194
What Programs?   197
The Christian "Happening"   197
The History of Our Christian Heritage   199
Parables, Stories, and Testimonies   201

Epilogue: Formation Comes First   203

How Are Our Teachers to Be Convinced?   205
Formation by Immersion   205
Ways of Formation   207

Appendix: How to Evaluate Audiovisual Texts   211

Notes   222

Index   230

ILLUSTRATIONS

1. The Rails 118
2. Veronica (Georges Rouault) 126
3. Indian Child in a Bombay Slum 127
4. The Laughing Christ 134
5. Seventeenth-Century Religious Print 138
6. Poster for Priesthood 139
7. The Face of a Thai Buddha 142
8. Christ the Pantocrator 143
9. The Peruvian Christ 145

PREFACE

In recent years, many of my students and colleagues have asked that I make available in English my thoughts regarding the new media culture and religious communication. In response, I have prepared an original manuscript, which is a synthesis of my recent books in French with considerable interpretation and updating for people in various parts of the English-speaking world.

I have gone back to a work that for me was seminal, *Another Man, Another Christian in the Electronic Age* (*Autre homme, autre chrétien à l'âge électronique*). Many of the ideas in that volume grew out of conversations with Marshall McLuhan, and my interviews with him were included in the book. The organizing framework of this volume, however, is my 1986 publication, *The Era of Communication* (*L'ère de la commmunication*).

This volume was the result of many exchanges and working sessions with American, Canadian, British, and French colleagues, among whom I would like to mention a few in particular. First and foremost were Joe and Mercedes Iannone of the Institute for Pastoral Ministry at St. Thomas University in Miami. They were the first to urge me to produce the present version of my work for an English-speaking reading public. Mercedes Iannone also made a special contribution by preparing the chapter on the family as the cradle of the symbolic way of faith. Another member of our work group at St. Thomas University was Anthony Scannel, O.F.M., former president of UNDA International and the director of Franciscan Communication Productions in Los Angeles.

I also owe a great deal to Robert A. White, S.J., professor at the Center for Interdisciplinary Studies in Social Communication at the Gregorian

University in Rome, for his valuable and loyal editorial advice and help in bringing this volume to publication.

I owe a special debt of gratitude to Michael Traber and Philip Lee at the World Association for Christian Communication, for arranging a major part of the translation costs through WACC and for their assistance to the translator, David Smith.

The members of the Faculty of Theology of the University of Lyon provided an important stimulus for me with their research into the theology of communication. My associates at the CREC-AVEX group, involved with training in social and religious communication, helped me with their practical expertise as well as their international vision and missionary experience.

Finally, I owe a debt of gratitude to Barbara Bauer of Toronto; Norbert Fournier, C.S.V., of Montreal; Henri de Halgouet, O.M.I., of Lyon; and Marcel Patry at the Communications Institute of St. Paul University, Ottawa. All of them have encouraged me in this research and have helped me with the translations.

—Pierre Babin

THE BIRTH
OF CONVICTION

It is almost impossible to present a view of the world and educational options without revealing one's own life history. As I expose these personal experiences, I often feel like a child first attempting to stammer the name of God. At the same time, that stammering conceals a number of beliefs that have developed from my personal history and in the course of my constant and often painful movement between contemporary culture and my perception of the presentation of the gospel in an earlier age.

I shall first explain my various positions by retracing the path I have followed and by showing the lasting impressions left on me. I feel the need to convey something of this before I try to explain or justify the spiritual realities these impressions point to. I am convinced that it is a great mistake to speak about faith and communication without putting one's thinking, indeed oneself, within quotation marks, so to speak.

YOUTHFUL CONVERSION

I have always been drawn to young people. What has inspired me, both in the work of educating youth and in promoting new technologies of communication among them, is that I have seen such potential in the seeds planted in young people. In these budding possibilities, I have caught a glimpse of the future flowering. There is a need to proclaim the "new earth," not by fulfilling vague longings, but rather by continually compromising between these longings and the real possibilities for communicating faith that are opened up by new technologies.

Like so many others, at the age of twenty or so I went through a crisis of questioning and rejecting everything that I had hitherto learned about Christianity. The problem presented itself to me in this form: I wanted to live fully and I wanted to find or create a more fully alive modern society. As I began my studies, my head was spinning with contemporary philosophy and the search for a new humanism. I was caught up in debates about communism and the brutality of Nazism, as well as the Christian objections to these ideologies. But out of these debates came one clear conviction: the Christianity that I had learned and experienced as a child did not free me. Indeed, it fettered me: it was a burden that did not allow me a full life.

Because my decisions in those days were based on only one criterion—my determination to live more fully—I drew an imaginary circle in my mind and said to myself, "I cannot stay surrounded by doubts and hesitations. I must live, and that means first deciding to break out of the circle." Eventually I freed myself by a great act of faith, which meant adopting the following two attitudes that have become, in the course of time, the driving forces of my life:

1. The gospel is "good news." Everything that diminishes a person and makes him or her sterile and lifeless is the opposite of the message of Christ.
2. At any cost, I must set myself and others free from the prison of pessimism and formalism, which is the result of a certain type of religious upbringing. If a particular aspect of Christian dogma—for instance, the presumption of hell—or if one part of Christian precepts, however insignificant, is not presented in a way that makes a person generous and free, we should cease to teach it. To continue formalistic traditions is to be unfaithful to Christ.

I had to make a fundamental decision and enter into a fuller life. That great decision, which I have never revoked, was to renew the presentation of Christianity in terms of truly "good news." So I turned with enthusiasm to humanistic studies and, in particular, to psychopedagogy.

I also began to be involved with summer camps for young people, which were called "Gospel and Mission." Sharing in young people's idealism and hope was an extraordinary experience of gospel community, a "gospel paradise." In those sessions, I began to be aware of the power of gospel symbols and discovered the symbolic way of faith. The key to religious education lies in providing, from the very first steps toward faith, an experience of the kingdom of God. Undoubtedly, for many young people, this is a naive experience, but it leaves an indelible mark, which deepens in the lives of those called to be Christians. Wasn't this the experience of the disciples with Jesus in the very beginning of their following in Galilee?

It was during those camp sessions in the early 1960s that I was inspired to write my first two books, *Crisis of Faith* and *Faith and the Adolescent*. They were soon followed by a number of works on catechesis and religious education.[1]

THE AUDIOVISUAL TURNING POINT

It was also during the 1960s that I first experienced what I would call "the discovery of the audiovisual." My innate taste for music, images, and stories undoubtedly opened me to this new approach, but I was nonetheless shocked when Pastor A. Wyler, then the director of the Protestant Office for Catechetical Research in Geneva, Switzerland, told me, "The books on religious education you have written have helped us enormously, but nowadays people speak a different language—the audiovisual language."

Since that time, one question has continued to preoccupy me: What affinity does the audiovisual language have with the gospel? My search for an answer has led me to identify three stages of discovery about audiovisual media: (1) realizing the power of audiovisual methods as an *aid to instruction*; (2) recognizing that audiovisual materials are not simply "aids," but are a *language* in themselves; and (3) understanding that the audiovisual media bring with them a new, all-encompassing *culture*.

The first stage, using audiovisual materials simply as instructional aids, I soon found to be insufficient. The process consisted of using audiovisual media to strengthen the power of written words and, consequently, to reinforce traditional catechisms. Adding audiovisual methods to conventional forms of teaching amounted to sugarcoating the pill, making it more pleasant to swallow. It assisted religious instruction and made it more enjoyable. But I soon discovered that such a method did not relate such instruction to young people's lives.

Young people spend six to seven hours a day watching television and go through the streets with Walkmans in their ears. They dance to rock music and find peak enjoyable moments in discos. They immerse themselves in the sounds and images of music videos, and they find computers fascinating to the point of addiction. These activities change their life routines drastically, and they are no longer attuned to abstract doctrinal formulas.

They are attuned to messages that vibrate with their sensitivities, that speak to their hearts, and that awaken their desires.

The problem with simple audiovisual communication, then, was not the audiovisual media themselves, but a radical change in the culture of young people that called for an equally radical change in forms of communication. A new type of human functioning, a new type of school, family, and society was being born. The real question seemed to be: What are the new languages of communication? I began to see that going no further than adding audiovisual aids to existing forms of education—sprinkling in a few slides and films—was only a palliative and might even become dangerously illusory, preventing us from seeing the real changes in contemporary culture and communication.

The real insight into the second stage began with my encounter with the work of Marshall McLuhan and the way I experienced the 1967 Universal and International Exhibition in Montreal. When I first read McLuhan's *The Gutenberg Galaxy* in the mid-1960s, I did not understand much of it. Like many of my colleagues in education, I was accustomed to thinking of media as external instruments. But McLuhan's convictions kept returning to me. Little by little, rays of light penetrated and illuminated my very conventional understanding of media and audiovisual methods.

The visit to Expo '67 was, for me, an experience that shattered many of my presuppositions. In the Labyrinth exhibit, I became conscious, for the first time in my life, of the possibility of understanding things not through words but through the effects produced in me by visual and aural stimuli. Gradually and unknown by me, a Copernican revolution took place in my thinking. The written—or spoken—word could no longer give meaning to everything. Audiovisual is another mode of communication, one that brings out in us quite different aspects of our understanding and personality. Audiovisually oriented people were being born, and we could no longer speak to them as we had spoken in the past. The church's educational and pastoral work had to change. I recognized three characteristics of modern life that we must keep in mind in our approach to the younger generations: the resurgence of the imagination, the importance of affective relationships and values, and the dissolution of national and cultural frontiers.[2]

THE ENCOUNTER WITH McLUHAN

My repeated meetings with Marshall McLuhan gradually led me to rethink thoroughly my traditional view of the function of communication, including the communication of faith. McLuhan received me, with a few students and friends, outside his home near the great trees of Wychwood Park in Toronto, Canada. Fortunately, I had remembered to bring along a tape recorder.

What ensued was less a leisurely conversation than it was his penetrating to the heart of every issue and overturning assumptions with the message of a prophet. I had time for only a few brief questions, but his replies were well-landed blows, striking at the core of my thinking and destroying the foundations of all its patterns. He was a genius for me at that moment, and I am still convinced of the importance of McLuhan's ideas for our times. He had the capacity to lead us to completely different ways of combining ideas and new processes of learning. He gave us a taste for forming different connections with everyday realities. With an insistence that was sometimes difficult to bear, he managed to make us understand how technology or, more specifically, the audiovisual medium of communication, is the key to interpreting our contemporary culture.

The edited transcript of my dialogues with McLuhan over several summers has been published in my book, *Autre homme, autre chrétien à l'âge électronique*.[3]

What, then, was McLuhan's contribution to my thinking? Briefly, he turned upside down the ideological structure of my religious training. Like many of my generation, my life was governed by the aphorism that "ideas rule the world." McLuhan opened my mind to the fact that the crucial factors in changing culture and human behavior are not just ideas, philosophies, and religions, but more fundamentally are the technological innovations of the era, especially when they touch on communications.

For some, McLuhan's view is debatable. Nevertheless it helped me to look at the world in a different way. I began to see how technology had changed my town over the past fifty years. For example, what would New York be without electricity? Others have commented on the importance of technological change, but McLuhan's vision was to see the complex interaction of technology with all aspects of our social and cultural reality.

At the heart of his thinking, of course, is communication technology— the medium that is the message. Why did this seemingly simple formula change my thinking? In great part, it was because McLuhan saw all of reality and the different levels of reality as one, unified system. For him, it was important to keep in view the whole system, with all of the interrelationships of its parts. This means that if the keystone of the structure is changed, the whole structure changes, as well as the meaning of every part of it. Thus, the introduction of electronic media has changed the meaning of all of our cultural institutions and every aspect of our structures of thought, including changes to both religious institutions and theological concepts.

Not surprisingly, I found several of McLuhan's convictions particularly disturbing, but they opened up aspects of his unified vision of reality. When I asked him whether the formula "the medium is the message" could be applied to Christ, he replied at once, "Of course. That is the only case in which the medium and the message are perfectly identical." And, in explaining the term *message*, he insisted that it was not the *words* spoken by Christ but *Christ himself* and all the ministries that extend him that produce an effect on us. "The message is conversion."[4]

Concise and raw affirmations of this kind call for a radical transformation of our ideas about religious communication. McLuhan's insight into the electronic forms of audiovisual media led him to emphasize that the message is not in the words but in the effect produced by the one who is speaking. I believe that modulation is the essence of audiovisual language, as words and their sequence are the essence of written language. The term *modulation* is deliberately used here because of its physical and technical meanings. Practically speaking, modulation indicates vibration frequencies, which vary in length, intensity, harmonics, and other nuances. These vibrations are perceived by our senses and induce emotions, images, even ideas (following some social codes), but first and foremost they are based on natural analogies and habitual effects on the mind.

For example, a violinist uses vibrato to lengthen and shorten a string's vibrations in order to add a trembling fragility to the sound. The ear picks up these hesitant and confused vibrations, the vagus nerve reacts, and the information is transmitted to the brain.[5] The listener feels emotions in which uncertainty, expectancy, and hesitation are mingled. A listener might perceive—hazily—an analogy with his or her own agitated and out-of-tune voice. Eventually, images form in the mind, vague memories, colors, shapes, or desires.[6] This is the language of modulation and the way it affects us. Of course, in audiovisuals there is more than just modulation, in the same way that in writing there is more than just the words. But from what I have seen and studied, the quality of the modulation is the determining factor in producing the specific effects by which the listener perceives the message.

From these insights, a new concept of the communication of faith gradually began to develop in my mind:

1. The message of faith is not first and foremost information affecting my understanding. It is the effect produced in me by the whole

complex known as the medium. In the communication of faith, the message is my conversion.

2. The message is not first and foremost the material vehicle of communication. The message is the whole complex of ministries and conditions that are required for an effect to be produced. In the communication of faith, it is the church, the places of communication, the face, the gestures, and even the clothes of the religious educator. The message is the interrelation of the print media, the electronic media, the use of live drama, and the preached word. It is also the forms of financing, both the marketing and the administration associated with the faith. All this is part of the medium that is communicating. All these conditions lead to faith development and conversion.

3. The content of the faith message is not primarily the ideas or the teaching, but rather the listeners themselves insofar as they are affected by the medium. In the communication of faith, the content is not first and foremost the teaching of Christ. Rather, it is those who are being taught, insofar as they are reached by Christ and his church; again, insofar as they are affected by the medium.

It should be clear from these examples that McLuhan changes the current meaning of words. That is the main reason why it is difficult to understand him. He has seen the world differently, has made different connections, and has revealed previously hidden aspects. But why has McLuhan done this? The reply to this question is always the same. Under the influence of electronics and new technologies, the functioning of the world has changed. If you want to understand the world, you must change your way of looking at it and the way you perceive its interconnections.

THE MEDIUM IS CHRIST

For McLuhan, the medium is not just a limited technical prop, but the totality of the infrastructures and conditions necessary for a medium to function. The significance of this began to transform my understanding of the Christian message. For example, reflecting one day on Jesus' statement that "unless you eat the flesh of the Son of man and drink his blood, you have no life in you" (John 6:53), I saw a new relationship between his physical body and blood and our new life in him. To understand the message of Christ is not simply to share in the content of the word-message but to partake also in the body-message: "Unless you eat my flesh (that is, if you don't take up the *medium*), you will not really understand the full message." No wonder Jesus' statement caused such scandal, then and today.

In McLuhan's vision, Jesus' stark pronouncement concerning his body and his blood has taken on two levels of meaning:

1. Jesus' message is a *body* in which we share: "This is my body; take and eat."
2. The Jesus-medium is not just the physical body, but all that the logic of his incarnate, bodily existence implies: his spirit-filled body, the clothes he wears, the group he gathers around him, his attitude toward wealth, all of the paradoxical values of the kingdom, the form of community that becomes his church. All this is the medium and all this is Christ.

I could see the enormous consequences of this vision for a new understanding of how faith is communicated. Chapter 1 explores how the incarnation of the Christian message in different cultural epochs, each characterized by different media, has introduced not just a new way of transmitting a message (print or electronic, for example), but a new form of Christian existence and a new form of church. Unless there is this continual total transformation, the Christian message and Christ himself are not communicated.

OTHER TRANSFORMING IDEAS
OF McLUHAN

Many of the central concepts of McLuhan were so different from my earlier background that it took a long time for them to penetrate my ideas of religious education and communication. One of the most important concepts is that of contrasting ground and figure, so fundamental to the audiovisual perception of the world. The "figure" refers to what is the direct focus of our attention: the printed matter on the paper, the persons or action portrayed in photos or on the television screen. The "ground" in print media is the paper of a magazine, the white spaces, the layout, the contrast in titles, the grain in the photos, and even the publishing house and distribution outlets, which quietly signal who is publishing the material. In film and television, the ground is the lighting, the camera angles, and the contrasts of silence, sound, and music. McLuhan suggests that the ground—what frames and contextualizes explicit figures—is the deter-

mining component of the mediated message. As I will explain later in
Chapter 3, "The Impact of Electronic Media on Faith," I came to see that
it is often not the explicit message or the rationalistic arguments that are
most important in communicating faith, but the deeper tones of feeling
and background, aspects that hardly enter into our awareness. In pilgrimages, young people's retreats, or the architecture of a church, this framing
ground of an almost indefinable emotional sense becomes more important than the ideas we talk about in these contexts.

McLuhan frequently returned to a statement that initially struck me as
odd: "In the world of electronic media, the impact is not best explained in
terms of *efficient causes* but rather as *formal cause.*" I recalled the distinction
between efficient and formal causality from my study of scholastic philosophy. The efficient cause is an external factor moving something to a new
state of existence, while a formal cause is the internal principle that gives
the change its shape and meaning. But it was difficult for me to understand this in connection with media, because I was so caught up in understanding media causality in terms of scientific models of effects. As I later
grasped more clearly, media studies had taken over from the physical
sciences concepts of causality in terms of external effects, and unconsciously I had absorbed this way of thinking. In what way, then, are the
media the internal principle of the shape of our existence?

One way of seeing this is in terms of the shaping influence of our
environment. If you surround yourself with limited models of acting and
thinking, you will unconsciously adopt the same sort of reflex actions and
thoughts. This is also the case in an environment of electronic media.
These media are not just technologies transporting content, but they form
a world, an enveloping environment like the countryside, which everywhere surrounds us with its rhythms of life and its mechanisms for coping
with problems. The electronic world is the programmable oven, the television which runs its daily routines of programs for seven to ten hours in
my living room, the radio in my car which accustoms me to a pattern of
news and distracting background music, the lamp which adjusts to different
levels of light according to my moods, and the thousands of other pleasant
gadgets that shape the pattern of my daily life-style. It is with this intent
that the Roman Catholic archbishop of Lusaka said, "We are all becoming
electronic beings."

The formal cause of our life is what many today call "systems law." If you
do not allow yourself to become part of the system, you are thrown to the
margins of today's life. The need for speed, the need to live in constant

resonance with a hundred electronic vibrations ranging from rock music to sirens, the need to have everything under control—all these establish the shape of the electronic world and the shape of our existence.

Another way of approaching the electronic medium as formal cause is to see the content of media not primarily as an object being moved externally from source to receiver, but as a mass of new configurations giving shape to cultural information that we are already aware of. Media sources are primarily pattern-makers. Advertisers, for example, are masters in taking soaps, automobiles, or other well-known products and fitting these to our contemporary aspirations and values, in this way producing an entirely new set of cultural connections. Much of television drama is a retelling of age-old story plots in a modern setting. Television and film are, above all, narrative media, which gather up disparate information and weave it together into the perspective of the storyteller. McLuhan was particularly attuned to this formal causality of the media because, being essentially a literary critic, he was accustomed to seeing the world of media as a kind of literary text, synthesizing and revealing the configurations of meaning in the larger culture. The media, for him, were metaphors to sum up the shape of the culture in which we live.

McLuhan's emphasis on formal causality helped me to see religious communication more as a giver of form and harmonious shape to our lives than as an efficient causality which overpowers people by the rationalistic power of argument. This insight clarified many of the intuitions gained through my association with young people and led to the approaches to religious communication that I explain more fully in Chapter 5, "The Way of Beauty."

It is difficult to explain all the ways in which McLuhan shook up and rearranged my thinking. For me and for many others, he offered an intellectually revolutionary explanation of our culture which is continually illuminating. At the same time, he had no intention of creating a new "perennial philosophy," and there are many aspects of our evolving technological environment that he did not, in my estimation, analyze sufficiently. McLuhan died too soon to throw light on the significance of the computer in strengthening linear and mathematical reasoning in our culture. In the early 1980s, I had a series of new encounters with information processing, which built upon many of McLuhan's principles but which have also distanced me somewhat from his thought. I discovered that McLuhan may have pronounced the death of the alphabetic, linear culture of Gutenberg too quickly.

THE AGE OF INFORMATION

I like going to big exhibitions and international fairs: they are the showplace for the spirit of the times. Walking among crowds of curious people and opening your eyes and ears wide, you can vibrate with the feelings and hopes of the age. It was at Expo '67 in Montreal that I experienced so strongly that the audiovisual medium is the new *language* of our contemporary culture. Similarly, it was at another exhibition, EPCOT (Economic Prototype Community of Tomorrow) near Disneyworld in Orlando, Florida, that I became aware of the significance of the information age. This instigated my conviction that the audiovisual medium is not just a new language, but also a new global culture. A better name for audiovisual media is *information*.

EPCOT popularizes the ideas of futurologists Alvin Toffler, John Naisbitt, and other well-known interpreters of the contemporary directions of our culture.[7] The entrance pavilion to EPCOT, Communicore, was unusually memorable. As you enter, great mobile structures which express the simultaneous movement of the communication media make you aware of the central theme of EPCOT. In addition to these structures, a slogan is repeated over and over in a song with a catchy, throbbing rhythm: "We are entering a new age, the age of information." The exhibition emphasizes that the tool of this age is the computer, which connects us with the whole terrestrial globe. And while we are being transported in capsules into the interior of the great globe of EPCOT, a voice describes to us, in solemn tones, the EPCOT interpretation of the meaning of our age.

Parts of the script of the Communicore Pavilion are particularly memorable:

> With the growth of knowledge and communication, we have changed our own lives and our worlds.

> From the confines of space to the depths of the sea, we have built a great electronic network.

> Our search for better understanding is unlimited.

> We have opened great storehouses of information.

Going through the pavilions which are crammed with creations of technology, I found myself reflecting on Naisbitt's statement regarding the "ten major transformations taking place right now in our society." It occurred to me that none of these transformations is more subtle yet more explosive than the first: "The megashift from an industrial to an information society."[8] Dawning in me was the conviction that this new society that is being born is one of invisible yet omnipresent electronic pathways, completely covering the world with a network of communication, knowledge, and power.

For many, exhibitions such as EPCOT are little more than the celebration of pop culture, reflecting uncritically many of the current cultural myths. Many would also be disturbed by the commercial undertones. But often, our first discernment of the "sign of the times" is precisely a confrontation with that pop culture. Indeed, EPCOT raised many disturbing questions for me.

In the following months, I found myself asking uneasily, "What do we really mean by information?" It was only after a number of meetings with economists with whom I was working at Lyon[9] that I reached this conclusion: The age of information is not essentially a matter of creating individual *pieces* of information or communicating information, in the sense of transmitting from sender to receiver. It is, above all, a matter of giving the existing information a new *form:* that is, putting this information into a new framework, which both reorganizes the internal relations of data and transforms their external display. Moreover, this process of newly organizing information and giving it external shape tends to transform the lives of the people involved in the process. The computer itself is an excellent metaphor of a new society with a central preoccupation for giving information a new form. The computer has enormous capacity for establishing simultaneous, multiple connections between existing data. More important, it instantaneously presents data in ways that make them easily used, harmoniously arranged, and pleasing to look at. In this process, we gain a deep, satisfying sense of harmonious, efficient arrangement.

The society of information, then, is a society in which giving a new form is more important than producing material goods or even data. It is also a society in which professions that create new forms are more numerous and important than any other trades. The emphasis on "giving a new form" often manifests itself in the seemingly insignificant connections of life. When I purchase a new sweater in a modern department store, the salesperson does not simply thrust the sweater into my hands. He or she puts it in a box and wraps it in attractive paper. It is all so pleasingly organized and displayed that I leave the store with a new sense of personal well-being and harmony. The values of the new society are concerned with creating more interconnections of information and giving to everything and everybody a more harmonious form.

The world today is full of data processing. But what is data processing?

Surely it is the most powerful, scientifically systematic way of giving every-thing a new form. This involves not only written texts, stocks, and invoices, but also secretaries, accountants, and even entire industries and states—putting all into a form.

I have also reflected on the economic and social implications of all this. We are not moving in the direction of a society of superbrains. We are moving toward a society of humble employees who are concerned pri-marily with giving things a new form. One observer notes:

> In the United States, the retail trade, hospitals and health centers, and the restaurant industry have created a great number of often badly paid jobs requiring little training. According to the forecasts for 1995, made by the Office for Labor Statistics, this situation will, broadly speaking, continue for the next decade. For example, it is predicted that, from 1979 to 1995, the number of property caretakers will increase by almost 900,000. This is appre-ciably more than the total number of jobs created for data processors, at all levels, during the same period.[10]

I cannot here enlarge upon all the different aspects of the age of infor-mation, but I would emphasize especially these three features:

1. The growing importance given to the quality of life and to cultural goods;
2. The increasing time given to education and leisure;
3. The new conflicts centering on issues and objectives of information flows, national and cultural identities, and different cultural values.

As I studied further what economists and sociologists are saying about contemporary society, I began to see an increasing number of interrela-tions between the evolution of the information society, the audiovisual media phenomenon, and the communication of faith. Increasingly, I became convinced that we are entering a time when putting on a show carries more weight than do values and underlying realities. Both the affective and the imaginative, strongly stimulated by audiovisual images, are becoming the central part of human and religious functioning. The computer and the audiovisual media, when brought together, unite the public relations and advertising functions with the distribution of goods. Whatever may be happening in schools and in churches, the computer and the audiovisual media are indissolubly associated in a society where giving things a form is the uppermost priority. Consequently, we can no longer speak of the efficaciousness of a liturgy, but rather we must speak of its beauty.

It was with a mixture of fascination and irritation that I read the following statement by Jacques Séguéla, the publicity agent who directed French
President François Mitterrand's election campaign: "The countries that
will dominate the world are those that know how to make people dream."[11]
He also commented about government, "Ruling is no longer seeing ahead;
it is being seen in a pleasing light."[12] Finally, Séguéla remarks, "It is not
those who reason, but those who tempt who will succeed now. The society
of communication will be the society of longing."[13]

On reading this, I thought of Jesus, who attracted, even tempted the
crowds, and I wondered how his approach could be transferred to religious educators of today. Young people do not want rational arguments.
They wish to be tempted. Training religious educators must be like training those who present information for television. The *manner* of presentation is what gives life and form to the material words of Christ. Therefore,
we should no longer speak of the content of the product. We should insist
instead that the religious educator make the product beautiful, attractive,
and tempting.

As I moved among young people with their taste for music videos, their
never-ending search for the new look, their preoccupation with peace,
their attempt to create identities through distinctive subcultures such as
the punk subculture, and their deep need for friendly relationships, what
came to me quite clearly was that they are more interested in the covenant
relationship than in dogmatic formulas. They are more interested in the
beauty of God than in the proofs of God's existence.

The society of information is one in which form takes precedence over
substantive matter and, metaphorically speaking, where relationships of
trade count more than the goods. In this society, the values of the spirit,
beauty, human relations, and harmonious presence are more important
than accumulating material goods.

Is it naive to speak of the society of information as one in which things
are transfigured by human relations and by the spirit? Obviously, forms
can also be diabolic. How can one avoid seeing the thousand deviations
that are possible? But we should also look to the hopes of young people,
which break through in their songs. Faith is there, and it leads me to see
not just the dangers, but the potential for transformation. Perhaps the
most important role of the audiovisual media and the computer is to open
the way for a civilization of "in-formation."

The communication of faith should recognize such development, but it
should also carry it to a more significant fulfillment. Being able to give life
a harmonious, pleasing form is not a sideline of religious education, but a

preparation for a "trans-formation" of the world. Communicators of faith should be specialists in "giving the world a divine form."

After reflecting on the society that is now coming into existence I could see more clearly the unity and relationship of clusters of experiences in our culture and the consistency of certain basic tendencies. It was like climbing to the summit of a mountain, looking out over the plain, and detecting more clearly the relationship of fields, forests, hills, and streams. I could now see the relationship of the audiovisual media and the computer, and the relationship of patterns of economic development and our civilization of mediated communication. In all this, I became conscious of "the entire creation groaning in one great act of giving birth" to a world in which the divine form is more clearly present.

ENCOUNTERING NEW CULTURES

Ideally, any in-depth encounter with a foreign country and its people should take place before a person reaches thirty, because at that age the walls of the personality may become like those of a fortress. I was lucky enough to be able to leave my childhood home several times from the age of twenty onwards. Those often painful experiences formed the substratum of my understanding of the possibilities dormant in electronics. How can anyone who has not crossed the geographical frontiers of their childhood, or who has never had the ecstatic experience of being abroad, ever understand what it is like to make an "electronic" journey?

When I first went to North America, my experience was shattering not only at the cultural level but also religious. With my background of religious communities which was strongly influenced by the spirit of Charles de Foucault, I found the American religious culture fascinating but disturbing. I wanted to penetrate as deeply as I could into that different religious spirit. I was warmly welcomed, but at the same time I did not immediately find close friends who could help me to understand and feel more completely at home in this different culture.

As time passed, however, I entered into communion with the spirit of the American people and discovered the sources of their great generosity and real holiness. As I began to accept the differences between the French and American religious cultures, I discovered that I was undergoing quite significant personal and psychological changes. The American experience had awakened aspects of myself that I had hitherto rejected or that had just remained dormant.

In the plane going back to France, the thought came to me again and again that God has sufficient breadth to be both American and French. I had opened myself to some of the qualities of Americans and, in so doing, I had discovered myself at the deepest level of my being and had enlarged my frontiers. That new awareness of myself had broken the barriers within which I had artificially confined God. In other words, the initial painful encounter with what was foreign had been a moment of growth and opened a door leading to a different knowledge of God. The contact with a different culture challenged the symbols that had motivated me up to that point, but challenge brought out new aspects of those symbols and expanded the richness of their meaning. The experience of the foreign may be the best way to grow in awareness of symbols in our lives and how those symbols unite us to God.

Later, I spent a considerable part of my life living, teaching, and working side by side with people in Africa, Latin America, and Asia. What has impressed me most in these people is not their wretched poverty or underdevelopment, but their richness. Treasure was to be found in their sense of life, their intuition of what is essential, their love of children, their capacity for suffering without becoming embittered, and their appreciation of beauty. Indeed, I was the underdeveloped one! In situations of poverty and persecution, I was conscious of the smallness of my words in comparison with the truth embodied by the living witness of the people themselves. How could I reveal something of God to them, aware as I was of my own spiritual poverty?

Then, I found in the words of the Chinese philosopher Mencius an illuminating insight into the experience of other cultures: "A person of another race is like a forgotten aspect of ourselves and a hidden mirror of God." I saw that it is only possible to understand a person of another culture when one begins to understand oneself. One can begin to understand God by rousing the dormant aspects of one's own personality and by eliminating the foreign aspects that keep one closed to other cultures and other peoples. Any deeper encounter with people of other cultures is a very special way of knowing God in the twentieth century, a century of travel and international exchange.

I hope the reader will interpret this outline of my spiritual odyssey with a certain amount of humor and indulgence. My intention is to provide the reader with keys to understanding the chapters that follow. I want to stress two things.

First, to understand the reality of our times more profoundly, we have to break out of circles confining our vision. It is impossible to enter into the electronic media's world without breaking the circle of the print-oriented universe. It is impossible to have real intercultural communication in the electronic age without leaving "your country and your kindred and your father's house" (Gen. 12:1). Becoming a full person in the electronic age is not playing with a camera; it is being born to new depths of humanity for which our previous education has not prepared us.

Second, today, technology is the privileged place of the incarnation. Formerly, when one spoke of incarnation, one referred to nation, country, and culture. Today, one must speak of technology, because the electronic technologies are shaping the new type of person and creating a world where national frontiers are disintegrating. I believe that technologies now constitute the greatest challenge and opportunity for the incarnation. But we shall have to enter this new universe with the same enormous sympathy that Christ has for his earth.

Let me conclude this introduction with a personal confession. I have firm convictions about the way in which faith should be communicated in our contemporary world. But, at the same time, I have become increasingly aware that the God of whom I speak, and Christ himself, are quite beyond my reach. My convictions are only a small part of the truth. They express the hesitant approach of a man who is trying to understand these times, holding in his hands before him the little book of the gospels. It is only by listening to God, day after day, and in accordance with the grace of each period of history and each culture that one can echo something of God's voice and reflect something of his presence.

1

RELIGIOUS EDUCATION FROM GUTENBERG TO THE ELECTRONIC AGE

When confronted with innovations in the technology of communication, the Christian churches evolved an entirely new way of communicating faith. What is remarkable is that only the Christian churches seem to have done this. Most of the other great religions have not matched this example. By and large, Buddhists and Muslims still communicate their faith in old ways that are essentially linked to their oral culture: symbolic actions, such as begging and going on pilgrimage; learning gestures and actions within the community; celebrating traditional feasts; and repeating prayers, texts, and stories.

In contrast to the other great religions, the Christians invented the catechism. What mysterious reason led them to accept the marvels of Gutenberg? When printing was invented, the church changed its way of functioning. It did not take the printed word into the heart of its oral culture but rather let that culture disappear and replaced it, in its pastoral program, with the catechism and the school system.

Whatever may happen in other religions, Christians should regard it, here and now, as a priority to apply that Christian law of adaptation to every communication medium. The Christian response to the print media could show us how present-day audiovisual media might well be used to point out the wrong path to follow—a way that is unworthy of our Christian ancestors, with their great zeal for innovation. Is the spirit of Christ's incarnation, becoming a flesh-and-blood reality in human history, calling on us to patch up our old church with electronic gadgets? Or are we not being called to make use of a totally different and all-embracing system?

COMMUNICATING FAITH IN AN
ORAL CULTURE

In some African countries, the culture remains predominantly oral. In the evening, when a young person comes home, a parent will ask, "Tell me what you have seen or done today," and will then graft onto the young person's facts of everyday life stories and parables about symbolic animals, which are eventually distilled in the form of proverbs. In this way, ancestral knowledge, traditional wisdom, and rules of life, intimately connected with the practice of communal living, are developed and passed on from age to age. "My child, learn the wisdom of the toad. . . ."

Our own ancestors were similarly taught from Old Testament times until the fifteenth century, the age of the invention of printing. "Fifty to sixty million men in the thirteenth century and forty million, that is ninety out of every hundred, in the fifteenth century, in the heart of a very ancient Latin Christian civilization, lived more or less completely outside the sphere of written expression and transmission of knowledge. . . . Only ten percent of the population could read and only two percent could read effectively."[1]

Feeling is combined with the intellect in the oral transmittal of knowledge. Based on a rigid framework of fundamental schemes and habits, the transmittal can include an enormous number of variations and deviations. It is also subject to changes caused by personalities and social disturbances. The transmittal depends essentially on the group remaining together. J. Fedry, working in Burkina Faso in West Africa, has described the dichotomy between the oral tradition and the written form, which impacts young Africans today (Figure 1):

ORAL	WRITTEN
Community Experience	*Collective Experience*
Wisdom is a vision of the world	Wisdom is amassing empirical knowledge or scientific details
Full-time education with more intensive moments	Selective education with specialization
A global approach and aim	Individual ideals and pluralism
A traditional, repetitive model	A cumulative model with processes of change
Direct, immediate, global, and communal communication	Indirect, individual, and fragmented communication[2]

Figure 1

It is within the oral framework that the catechesis came into being. Three principal activities emerge from a rapid survey of Christian history from the time of Christ until the fifteenth century: evangelization, catechumenate, and immersion. Whatever their mutual differences may be, all three are characterized by the preeminence of communal life, by liturgy and practice, by stories and images, and by the sacred part played by the person teaching. All of these are factors that those familiar with audiovisual language will recognize as important.

The first activity was *evangelization:* the proclamation of the liberating message of Jesus, accompanied by signs capable of disturbing the hearts of people and making them believe the messenger. The key words here are "proclamation" and "miracle." These characteristics soon occupied a place of secondary importance during the period of the catechism, but there is evidence—in the charismatic movement, for example—that they are being reborn now, in the audiovisual age.

The second of these activities was that of the *catechumenate.* This involved a long period of initiation, punctuated by symbolic and liturgical acts and instructions within the community.

The third activity, *immersion,* requires discussion for several reasons. First, because immersion's emphases are so close to the audiovisual language, one could claim that electronic audiovisual religious education is a return to the religious education of the Middle Ages. Second, catechesis by immersion, because of its excesses and defects, inspired a great church reaction when the catechism appeared in printed form. To assess the breadth and the originality of the revolution that it brought about, we have to examine the immersion process deeply.

FAITH BY IMMERSION

Immersion reached its peak in medieval Christianity, above all, in the Latin countries. J. Jungmann has described it as:

a strong community life entirely marked by religion. The members were initiated into the Christian faith in the same way that they learned their mother-tongue, without systematic teaching. It was not so much doctrine formulated in concepts as solidly established institutions that nourished religious thinking. And it was also . . . the liturgy. In addition to this, it is also essential to mention the extraordinarily rich religious practices, . . . the religious consecration of the emperor; the orders of knighthood; the guilds with their patron and their own feasts; the apothecaries bearing religious names; the inn signs, with their names which were almost always biblical in origin; the hospices dedicated to the Holy Spirit; and, finally, the life of the cathedrals with their stained-glass windows, their popular games, and their earthy sculptures depicting the battle between the sexes in marriage. There was no gap here between the sacred and the profane. The whole of life was bathed in a religious climate.[3]

What Jungmann says here applies also to the audiovisual world: to understand is to participate. What counts is belonging, forming a part of the community, being grafted onto the societal structure:

So what we have here is essentially a religion of participation. Membership in the church, which was identified in practice with Christianity, conferred a right—a possible access to salvation. . . . That religion of participation and of knowledge of the group conveyed means of grace. . . . It was a way of life and in no sense a favor. That religion practically granted an enormous amount of room to rites of passage and especially to that rite of passage that is the sign of membership par excellence—baptism.[4]

François Rapp, a historian of medieval times, emphasizes the importance of the many networks of influence:

Confraternities, convents, and parishes covered Christianity with a network of many different religious institutions. . . . Those souls who escaped completely from the net must have been very rare. No one, or almost no one, could avoid practicing in some way or other, whether that practice was episodic or regular.[5]

This influence was so sociological in its effects that the historian J. Delumeau, in his book *Le christianisme va-t-il mourir?* (Is Christianity going to die?), came to the audacious conclusion that "Christianity was more an authoritarian construction and a system of subjugating populations than a conscious clinging on the part of the masses to a revealed faith."[6]

In this context of being "bathed in religion," the momentous places and moments of catechesis were not in the school but during the feasts of the church. Following the time of the catechumenate, liturgical participation became central. A great deal of evidence indicates that the first great pressures concerning religious instruction began at the time of great church feasts. E. Germain quotes from medieval sources:

At least four times a year, [it is necessary to recall] at each important stage in the liturgical year the fourteen articles of the Creed.[7]

In conjunction with the Sunday Mass, parents must teach their children clearly and make them remember, both in French and in Latin, the angelic salutation, the Lord's Prayer, the articles of faith, and God's commandments.[8]

The practice of the sacraments must be closely combined with the communication of faith: the obligation to go to the parish church every Sunday to hear the Divine Office and the commandments, and to confess to one's own priest, who must question his penitent about his knowledge of the *Pater Noster,* the Creed, and the *Ave Maria.*[9]

How did catechesis by immersion work? It acted globally and imperceptibly. Above all, it gave direction to tendencies and form to the imagination. It expressed faith in habits and rites of participation. Catechesis by immersion did not encourage people to pray by thinking about what they were saying, but to function in a church expressing faith through song and under the control of the priests. It encouraged the people to go on pilgrimages and to be pious.

Although immersion undoubtedly led to marginal devotions and to doctrinal vagueness of the type in which Saint Anthony and Jesus were on the same level, it nevertheless produced sturdy Christian people.[10] It did not lead to a strict intellectual structure, but it created a doctrine of life.

Particularly interesting because of their similarity to the techniques of modern audiovisual publicity are two methods used in this catechesis by immersion:

1. memorization by means of symbolic procedures, in conjunction with bodily gestures and in association with acts of life, and
2. a dramatic presentation of images with the aim of producing a particular effect, such as using the color pink in a painting to imply health.

The symbolism of numbers and of bodily gestures was used excessively to assist memorization. The symbolism of the number 7, for example, goes back to Augustine *(De sermone Domini in monte).* This number formed the basis of a cult of numbers that included, among others, "the twelve articles of faith, the ten commandments and their transgression," the seven capital sins, and the seven works of mercy. In addition, there were also short pieces of verse, incantatory formulas, and cantilenas.

Monsignor Giustiniani's way of teaching the meaning of the sign of the cross provides an interesting example of Christian symbolism's importance: When they name the Father by touching the forehead with the right hand, they show that the Father is the principal of the Holy Trinity who has never come down to earth. When they name the Son and bring the hand down to the body, they show that the Son descended into the bosom of the Eternal Father, becoming man through his incarnation in the womb of the Blessed Virgin, then into the bosom of the earth when he died and descended into limbo to set free our fathers in the faith. Finally, when they take the hand from one shoulder to the other, saying the words "and of the Holy Spirit," they show that the Holy Spirit proceeds from the

Father and from the Son. By the whole sign of the cross on which Christ was crucified, they show the Passion of the Lord. The five fingers of the hand, used to outline the sign, proclaim the five wounds of the Lord, and the two fingers, the index and the middle fingers, with which they touch their forehead and the other parts of their body, point to the divine and the human natures united in the same divine person of the eternal Word.

Finally, let me give an amusing example of a young shepherd who could not memorize the Lord's Prayer, which illustrates the process of association frequently employed in catechesis by immersion and so favored by modern advertising:

> To help him to remember it, the parish priest asked him if he knew the names of his sheep in a given order. When he said yes, the priest suggested he should change their present names. So the young shepherd, when he was leading them, said the prayer by calling each sheep by its new name. The first was called *Pater noster*, the second *qui es in coelis*, and so on. When the time came for him to recite the prayer to the parish priest, he left out the word *sanctificetur*. This omission did not go without comment from the priest and received an immediate response from the shepherd, who said: "Sanctificetur? But she died last night, Father!"[11]

Even more important in modern audiovisual processes, however, is the part played by images. The historian François Rapp has written, "Below the élite [the aristocracy and the middle classes] there were the ordinary people who knew neither A nor B. They formed the mass of the flock and they had no other reading than that of images."[12] Images refer to pictures, statues, stained-glass windows, wayside crosses, altarpieces, and so on. Buildings and cemeteries were full of such images, as well as living pictures, scenes played by people both inside and outside churches, especially on the great liturgical feasts.

The historian Pierre Chaunu has correctly pointed out that a system of reproduction on paper, known as xylography or wood engraving, had been perfected at least seventy years before printed books appeared. This process was first used to produce a large number of pious images (the *vita Christi*, the Passion, and the "art of dying") and, as Chaunu adds, "the more closely one comes to modern times, the more the text gains in importance over the pictures."[13]

Three processes make use of images and were used in catechesis by immersion to stimulate the public's emotions. The first process was setting the scene, wherein explanations of faith concepts were given not merely by showing images, but also through dramatization, by making people weep or laugh. People were moved in faith when their emotions were aroused. Popular missions used this learning process as early as the fifteenth century. Vigorous and racy language was used in close combination with the image. The combination goaded people to think and to feel. We have only to think of how often "Vanity" was burned on a huge pile of rubbish, licentious images, and magical objects to realize the effectiveness with which this method was used.

The second process can be called learning by salvation. The studies made in connection with the images at Epinal in France throw a great deal of light on this process. The authors of these studies have selected three or four basic colors, one being the characteristic yellow-pink, for their ability to stir feelings of optimism, good health, and happiness. Pilgrims did not buy images to "make them think of" particular concepts but to bring them happiness and salvation. The same can be said of Lourdes water today. Children are made to drink this water when they have sore throats. The special purpose of images is to act on us through the emotion concealed in their forms and colors.[14]

The third process is that of learning by means of a conditioning environment. The stained-glass window does not have a primarily intellectual content. It is, above all, a vibration of light that unconsciously touches the emotions and resonates within the nervous system. What is a cathedral but a vast, global image that impresses people and gradually transforms them as they go forward? Studies have shown that many of the cathedrals on the way to Compostela and the Shrine of Saint James were built by architects who were alchemists. They wanted pilgrims to enter their cathedrals as if they were going into the alchemist's egg, to be transformed from their old selves into new ones.[15]

This predominantly oral learning tradition, which had been built up very slowly over at least ten centuries, nonetheless bore within itself the seed of its deterioration and many fatal deviations. The end of the Middle Ages was characterized by what one historian called "an immense appetite for the divine,"[16] but this existed amid such a huge number of spiritual deviations and doctrinal vagueness that one is tempted to liken the period to the apocalypse. It was at this time that printing was invented in Europe.

COMMUNICATING FAITH IN THE AGE
OF PRINT MEDIA

Printing from movable type was invented in Europe by Johannes Gutenberg between 1440 and 1456. It was an inspired act on the part of the church, the prophets, and the saints of that time to seize on this new medium to react against the degradation and the aberrations of faith at the end of the Middle Ages. Their tactic—and this has been said many times, but cannot be overemphasized—was not to sprinkle a few printed pieces into the oral culture of the period. On the contrary, they created a different way of communicating faith, which was based on the potential of the new print medium just then becoming available. Beyond the differences in the teachings of such theologians as Jean de Gerson, Martin Luther, Peter Canisius, Charles Borromeo, and Robert Bellarmine, and even of the Council of Trent, we can see in all these witnesses an agreement about the general direction of Christianity and also about methods of learning faith. This agreement can be summarized under three headings:

1. The need to impart one doctrine and firm moral teaching to the masses.
2. The need to train personnel, particularly by establishing schools and seminaries.
3. The need to "instruct and educate the humble people" in the most concrete and practical way, by producing "short and precise treatises."

The most important factor in the religious revival of the sixteenth century, both Catholic and Protestant, was the effort to ensure that the ordinary people learned the theological foundations of Christianity. Almost everywhere, both in Catholic and in Protestant countries, compulsory Sunday schools were set up so that children could be taught the basic truths of Christianity.

Lutherans, Calvinists, and Anglicans were not the only ones to restore the word of God to its place of honor. In the Roman Catholic church, the Council of Trent insisted that all priests should preach on Sundays and teach the faithful.[17]

What part did printing play in this revival? Richard Molard wrote in December 1975 when the magazine *Horizons protestants* ceased to appear:

Protestantism was born with printing and has been the religion in which printing—the printed Bible, the catechism, newspapers, and journals—has played a vital part. The present crisis in these publications is undoubtedly a sign of a very deep crisis of identity. How is it possible to be a Protestant in a world in which radio and television are the easiest forms of communication?[18]

Surely it is very significant that technology can be so closely linked to religious identity! And, in Catholicism, it is interesting to examine how closely the missionary movement linked printing to faith itself. It is not widely known, but is well worth noting, that the first printing press was imported into the Philippines in 1593 by Thomas Pinpin, in order to print the *Doctrina Christiana.*

The fulcrum of the new way of teaching faith was the little book called the Catechism. For four hundred years Christians learned their faith from it. It would not be an exaggeration to say that it was one of the greatest educational innovations of its period; it became a best-seller. Luther's *Kleiner Katechismus* appeared in 1529, and within forty years, one hundred thousand copies had been printed. Peter Canisius's Catechism appeared from 1554 onwards and, when he died in 1597, 233 editions had been published.

Catechisms were needed "to bar the way to anarchy," it has been suggested, "and to regulate doctrine and establish discipline firmly."[19] In his *Kleiner Katechismus,* intended for use by less well-educated pastors and preachers, Luther wrote:

> What has preoccupied me in reducing the catechism, that is, Christian doctrine, to such a simple and small form, is the desolate state of the church as revealed to me during my inspection of parishes. Good God! What miseries I have witnessed! The country people especially have no knowledge of Christian doctrine, and unfortunately a great number of pastors are themselves unable to teach. They all call themselves Christians. They are baptized and receive the sacrament. But they do not know the Our Father or the Creed or the Ten Commandments. They live like beasts and swine.

Scarcely twenty years later, the Catholic bishops met at Trent. They were troubled by the same evils and decided that "as far as the duty of teaching ignorant children and adults was concerned, educated men must write a catechism for them both in the vernacular and in the Latin language, based on Scripture and the orthodox Fathers."[20]

When he agreed to return to Geneva—urged by the city's leaders—Calvin modeled the government of the town literally on his "Ecclesiastical Ordinances" and his Genevan Catechism, the "Formula for Instructing Children in Christianity." This accounts for the forceful position that he took: "I refused to accept the ministry unless they gave me their word on these two points: the catechism and discipline."[21]

Bishop Alexander Sauli believed that the catechism was so essential that he had it printed at his own expense at Pavia in 1565, and himself distributed thousands of free copies. The catechism, in its many different forms, as a means of teaching and learning about faith, flourished in an extraordinary way in the sixteenth century, and above all between 1529 (Luther's Catechism) and 1597 (Bellarmine's Catechism).

THE CATECHETICAL WAY

I have often seen, in older presbyteries, pictures depicting a pastoral scene of a country priest, standing with a rod in his hand in front of children who sit on benches in the garden. He is making them recite the catechism. These pictures show that the catechist had become a kind of schoolteacher of that period. Moreover, the catechumens were not allowed to change one syllable and had to learn the catechism by heart, while the teacher's task was to explain what they learned. These were the main emphases in the catechism's teaching and learning process. This process is clearly and strikingly discussed in the preface to Luther's *Kleiner Katechismus* of 1529:

> It is necessary to make the pupils and the people learn by heart the formulas chosen to be included in the little catechism, without changing a single syllable. As for those who refuse to learn word by word, tell them that they are denying Christ and are not Christians. Do not accept them at the Lord's Supper. Do not let them present a child for baptism. Send them to the Pope, to the Official Principal and to the devil himself. . . . When the children know these texts well, they must also be taught their meaning, so that they will understand what the words mean. Take all the time that you need, because it is not a question of explaining all the points at the same time, but of taking them one after another. Take the great catechism therefore and give a more fully developed and extended explanation.

The most important results of this method were a strictness in doctrine and a uniformity of knowledge. In doctrine, the importance of a logical knowledge and of abstract notions was clearly stressed. Uniformity was achieved by everyone's repeating the same formulas. This overall uniformity was made possible by printing, which could produce thousands of identical examples with exactly the same words in the same order. Both Catholics and Protestants embraced the law of uniformity, brought about through this arrangement of questions and answers repeated over the course of several years.

Until the fifteenth century, the ordinary faithful were not given any systematic religious education. This is clear from these words of Guillaume Petit, the bishop of Senlis (d. 1536), taken from his *Via du Salut:*

> An expression of faith in correct theological formulas is a demand made by and a fundamental criterion for membership of the group in the great outlines promulgated during the Protestant Reformation. . . . This does not, however, apply to the simple people. . . . They are not obliged to believe [the article of faith] explicitly. They only have to believe their superiors.[22]

Solidarity with the community and in society at that time was much more important than a strong intellectual framework in the mind of each individual. Harmony in prayer and in performance of liturgical actions was more decisive for full community membership than a logical synthesis of the truths of faith—so much so, in fact, that Thomas Aquinas noted that believers should know and believe explicitly only those truths of faith that were the objects of church feasts.[23]

With the arrival of printing, however, the popular pastoral program based on moral and liturgical practice was completely changed, and what counted in Christian education was knowing the catechism by heart. This new pastoral program was taken all over the world without giving any consideration to the nature of local cultures, which were often oral cultures.

It is important to recognize that the catechism was not just a new technique or method followed with the aim of strengthening the teaching given in the Middle Ages. On the contrary, it was something quite different: a new way of teaching and learning, but also a change in the structure of communication. That whole system was gradually to change with the introduction of printing—not only the obligation to attend Sunday Mass to hear the catechism-sermon, but also, among many other things, the development of the school catechism and such institutions as solemn communion.

Thus, it was possible to write at the beginning of the sixteenth century that "another kind of Christian is in the process of being born." That new Christian was a Christian of uniform knowledge and practices, a replica of Christian teachers. He or she had been subjected to formulas and was not a creative and mystical Christian; but a person could also be a Christian forceful in thinking, generous, devoted, and faithful—an ideal Christian.

I do not want to praise the pastoral program of the catechism without reservation. It has been sharply criticized by several historians: Delumeau, for instance, has gone so far as to compare the catechism to Mao's Little Red Book, not only as a book but also as a method.[24] Alain Peyrefitte has spoken of the "Roman sickness" and has emphasized the cultural effect of the reform that resulted from the invention of printing: "One catechism, one translation of the Bible, the Vulgate, and one truth, that of Trent. The human mind is called to go to sleep. Everything that moves is shot at."[25]

Who could fail to recognize these mistakes and excesses? But what has always struck me forcibly in the revolution of catechetical education—and one certainly can say that a revolution took place—is the incredible courage of those prophets and saints who dared to give up a cultural system inherited from their ancestors and to create a completely different system based on a new technology.

COMMUNICATING FAITH IN THE
AGE OF ELECTRONIC
MEDIA

The initial days of reform have passed, however, and the mistakes made and the excesses committed at the introduction of written culture have burst upon us as those of the oral culture did in the past. What are we to think of attitudes such as that of the fifteen-year-old who told me, after the diocesan oral examination in religious instruction, "One question was: 'How many persons and natures are there in Jesus?' My reply was: 'Two persons and one nature.' My teacher was furious with me! But what difference does it make to me? He can have three natures and one person if that is what he wants!" This story points quite clearly to the risk involved in a purely intellectual instruction in religion, by means of a catechism or textbooks.

It would not be wrong to say that printing gradually led to the emphasis being placed, initially by church leaders and official teachers, on precise concepts and strict definitions, formulas of great uniformity, and logical systems and ideologies of vast dimensions, all of which were seen from a single vantage point.[26] Slowly but surely, rational analysis, the practice of making logical distinctions and connections, and the cult of obedience to formulas and to canon law became more important than feeling oneself at one with the church or taking an active part in the liturgy.

It is obvious, then, that we experienced a reversal of the faults inherent in the earlier oral culture. We may therefore say that, on the one hand, there was a confused Christian way of life, while, on the other hand, there was a life dominated by abstract correctness. The affective faith of Christians in the Middle Ages was vague, but it was a living reality—there was life. This was gradually replaced by a more cerebral form of faith; over the centuries, pipelines of rules and formulas were slowly and patiently constructed. But one day we woke up to the fact that, for the majority of people, the living reality of faith had fled. The beautiful buildings were still there, but the mystery had left them. There were nothing but empty pipes. In that case, what is the value of knowing that there are one person and two natures in Jesus Christ?

But now, audiovisual technology and electronic media have appeared on the scene, and once again the cards have been well and truly shuffled. We are, in fact, confronted with two types of crises and two types of new media.

What are these two types of crises? The first is the *Gutenberg crisis*. Attention was drawn to this in the 1950s by the catechetical movement, which reacted against a notional and cerebral faith that lacked any spiritual roots or any personal force. The second is the crisis brought about by the rapid penetration of the media and human studies into all areas of life, which has led to the equally rapid destructuring of faith's intellectual foundations and the growing power of gods dormant in our own blood. The second crisis has resulted, on the one hand, in a rejection of the dogmatic and cultic formulas which, it is claimed, are no longer in tune with our society and, on the other hand, in a search for religion that is fundamentally a search for meaning and for the absolute.

The churchgoing tradition bears less and less weight, and most young people who go to church now go because they are looking for something beyond—radicality, meaning and love, a sense of purity, and even enthusiasm and mystical experience. Their faith is nourished above all not by dogma, but by the fundamental forms and impulses of the imaginary. Saint Bernard declared, "You will learn more in the woods than you will in books. The trees and the stones will teach you what you will never learn at the school of the masters." What these young people are seeking is faith with natural and cosmic roots.

The images and the power of that nature are today amplified by the electronic media. What are the consequences of this? For many people, faith has acquired a Dionysiac foundation, reliant upon stimulation by drugs, powerful visual and auditory sensations, and video clips, all of which go beyond the restrictions of time and space and cross all frontiers in their search for "everything at the same time." It is interesting to compare these video clips with what theologians have said about our glorified bodies: in both cases, there is a "transfiguration" of the body. Its limits shatter: you are in one place and suddenly you are somewhere else, your body's dimensions change from one likeness to another, your face abruptly changes from sadness to illumination.

The primitive images of the collective unconscious and the fundamental impulses of the absolute and of paradise are thus making themselves felt. It would not be wrong to say that a person's soul is shaken. Whether you go to discos or to the great rock festivals, listen to pop songs, or look at the great posters advertising consumer goods or holidays abroad, you are bound to be conscious—even if irritated by and emotionally opposed to the experience—of the disturbing appeal of the old gods, making itself heard inside you. It is hardly surprising that young people at every level of society listen day and night to frenzied broadcast music: it excites them and provides them with a substitute for religion. The music reveals primitive heavens to them and gives them the illusion of paradise and a pseudo-experience of ecstasy. It is also symptomatic of a craving for the spiritual that a good deal of pop music is religious in its tonality and even in its expression. But it is predominantly a religion of earthly gods, and one that is closely in tune with the great forces of nature. It is a faith expressed in terms of sharing, vibration, fulfillment, and healing.

With its Dionysiac and cosmic overtones, the music of the young people forms part of their protest against nuclear armament, the despoiling of the natural environment, contemporary manifestations of fascism, and the imprisonment of political activists. They protest the inhuman treatment of humanity's world. This is an expression of the realistic and pragmatic aspect of the younger generation. But always it is the gods in their blood that call out in protest. Their revolutionary attitude, manifested in marches and demonstrations, is never expressed as a somber duty; it always has the festive air of a collective communion.

I said above that we are confronted not only with two types of crisis, but also with two types of media. These two media types are very different, and they correspond to the present situation of religion, which is largely influenced by recent technological innovations. The first type is the audiovisual media. These are more obviously associated with pleasure and entertainment. The second type is the data-processing media and the computer, which are closely linked to information and calculation.

What should our pastoral reaction be to these new media, to the dangers of the present situation and the opportunities it offers? That is, of course, the difficult question that confronts us. I cannot attempt to answer it as a historian, as we are only at the beginning of the process. Yet I am inclined to express my proposal regarding the communication of faith in the electronic age. That proposal will be elaborated and given more precise shades of meaning.

THE AUDIOVISUAL WAY

I do not think it is possible today to separate an audiovisual form of catechesis, one that appeals to the heart and to human feelings, from a purely notional form, one aimed more precisely at the intellect and reason. This new, combined type of religious education will hereafter be called *stereo catechesis*. It will be based in turn on each of the two types of media, those of entertainment and those of data processing, the latter in combination with the printed media.

The greatest danger threatening faith today, I am convinced, is not the absence of information and firm instruction, but the lack of interest in Jesus Christ and the failure of our hearts to be converted. We have knowledge, and sometimes we even practice. But our hearts remain untouched. Deep inside us the old pagan gods reign supreme. So I am convinced we must opt first of all for audiovisual and symbolic catechesis, appealing to the imagination and to our search for total fulfillment. We must turn unequivocally to the audiovisual media and the religious communication system they lead to.

But what is audiovisual catechesis? A few years ago, the authors of a catechism approached a number of audiovisual experts with the request, "Can you convert our book into an audiovisual instrument? We want to make it more contemporary and more alive." The audiovisual experts considered this, then came back to the authors with the reply, "Chapters in a catechism cannot be made into an audiovisual instrument, but we can do something quite different if you agree to it. We can produce stories, dramas, fantasies, and so on—bearing in mind what you have written in your catechism." The project went no further. The spirit of the catechism had to be expressed in books and, possibly, in educational talks. It is possible to make the system more interesting with the help of audiovisual materials, but to translate catechesis into audiovisual language—no, that is something quite different!

To express Christ's message audiovisually is to communicate the experience we have of Christ: his being and his words. That presupposes that we have discovered for ourselves the fundamental experience of Jesus and his disciples. The essence of audiovisual catechesis has in fact been expressed in the opening of 1 John: "That . . . which we have heard, which we have seen with our eyes, which we have looked upon and touched with our hands, concerning the word of life . . . that which we have seen and heard we proclaim also to you" (1 John 1:1–3). Audiovisual catechesis is the electronic extension of one's spiritual vibration as a believer. In a very real sense, it fulfills the claim made by the television producer Claude Santelli: "Speaking the language of television is making people accept ideas through their emotions."

How do teachers of religion who are just beginning to use audiovisual methods usually react to them? They wonder how they are going to be able to explain certain realities of faith, such as Christmas, by means of sounds and slides. But by responding this way to audiovisual technologies, they do not take into account that their point of departure is not their experience or that of their pupils on the reality of Christmas, but Christmas as explained in sermons and theology. It is, in other words, the doctrine of Christmas and not Christmas as felt by teachers or pupils. So they build a scenario on the basis of a theology of Christmas, even if they try very strenuously not to do so. The usual result is a hodgepodge of images and sounds that have nothing but the original underlying idea connecting them—"Gutenberg with illustrations!" Aesthetically satisfying it may be, but very tedious.

What, then, has to be done to communicate Christmas audiovisually? We have to go beyond the ideas, theories, and formulas that have previously made us intellectually conscious of Christmas and try to be more open to our personal experience of it as a reality. That experience offers itself to us in the form of feelings, emotions, tendencies, movements, images, and sounds. We "experience" Christmas; that is, we feel it, see it, and hear it. That must be the point of departure for all audiovisual catechesis. We must begin by disconnecting ourselves from doctrinal teaching, by emptying out. We have to go back into our mother's womb, so that our cerebral and very positive attitudes are not the first to be expressed.

The essential themes of the scenario we are attempting can develop from this fundamental experience of Christmas. They will not take shape in accordance with abstract logic. They will, on the contrary, come about following another logic, that of the imagination and of symbols. The atmosphere that we established initially will lead to images emerging, as it were, from the earth, and those images will lead to others. We shall work in an atmosphere of global experience and in a sequence of personal events that matches the movement of our own feelings. Vast spaces, a slow pace, dreams will be suddenly followed by the awakening of a vertical line supported by a change in rhythm. A successful scenario is a unified creation of time and space, which makes us relive an experience that awakens the feelings and imagination of viewers and listeners. At the level of faith, it is the audiovisual arrangement of a Christian experience, in tune with the intimate spiritual search of the viewers and listeners.

A RADICAL CHANGE IN THE
CHURCH'S POLICY

The Council of Trent did not simply introduce a catechism. Its program of reform set up a vast new pastoral structure. The same can be said of audiovisual catechesis. It cannot be reduced just to a great number of good films or scenarios about the Christian message. The whole of our system of communication is affected by it—the places, the times, those who are addressed by it, those who are in charge of it, the approaches, the methods, and indeed, the entire functioning of authority (see Figure 2). We shall look at each of these aspects in turn: first, *the places*. In oral cultures, the whole village was the central place of communication, both the market square and the family home. In the Gutenberg civilization, the school was the special place of catechesis, in the classroom or certain specialized locations in the parish. We should not be surprised, then, by the incredible pastoral attempts made by the church in recent centuries to establish and maintain schools. The school is the place par excellence of the written culture and of teaching by books.

But what will the special place of communication be in the audiovisual age? Considering the power of electronics, I would confidently say that faith will be communicated where there is community and, what is more, where affinity communities exist. These may include family homes, certain places of pilgrimage, religious or cultural centers, camps, and school centers. The issue is not so much one of concrete places but of places with a soul—places where a mixture of friendship and spiritual leadership exists.

What about *the times and those who are addressed?* In written culture, children and young people were the primary group catechized. This group is particularly closely associated with the school, with the result that the special times for catechetical instruction were inevitably the school hours. There was no instruction during the holidays.

What is particularly striking today is that this framework has been greatly enlarged. The catechesis of children and young people still takes place during school hours, but new forms are developing that are essentially linked to the affinity community and its needs and concerns. Age is becoming less important; other categories are considered more important in deciding times and groups: friendship, the leader, the framework, the atmosphere, and the intimate needs of the individuals and the group. The ages that are often turning points in life (the time of baptism, for example, and retirement), extreme situations (unemployment, illness, or the loss of a dear one), professional and family realities, social and psychological difficulties (alcoholism or mental depression): all these are becoming, more than ever before, the special times for a catechesis aimed at the heart. I am convinced this is a positive orientation, because Christianity can only enter the mind through contact with the great questions that confront us in everyday life. Here, too, it is possible to discern the influence of the new technological conditions. Electronics are changing our historical times into psychological times, and are changing those obliged to receive communication into those interested in receiving it.

And who are *the agents* in charge of communicating faith? At one time, they were primarily pastors, teachers, or catechists with a more-or-less rigidly institutionalized status; only secondarily were families responsible for such instruction. Nowadays, however, frequently the whole community becomes the agent for communicating faith. The community may be the parish or the family, members of spiritual movements, or young people who are finishing their studies and are concerned for those who are even younger than themselves.

The community is large indeed, and in it I would give a special place to certain religious leaders and to those I have called "awakeners." Young people do not want courses, lessons, and discussion groups so much as contact with spiritual persons. Talks and discussions must be intimately linked to the experience of prayer and Christian life. We should pay close attention, among the present agents of catechesis, to the increasing number of new agents who are making audiovisual documents which are aimed at an increasingly fragmented public. Examples of their work are videocassettes catering to families or groups and audiocassettes to be listened to in the car or the kitchen. I have surveyed those who have studied the gospel from cassettes produced by well-known biblical scholars. The cassettes, systematic and lively, have been used by thousands of people.

And what about approaches and methods? I shall later give increasing prominence to "the way of beauty" and "the symbolic way." These two approaches are completely in accord with both the genius of audiovisual language and the feelings of the younger generation. At the same time, however, I shall emphasize "the way of information." Involving both the commuter of today and the catechism of an earlier generation, this information way cannot be suppressed.

Finally, I must add a few words about *the functioning of authority* in this context. I do not intend to dispute the part played by the church hierarchy in such an important sphere as communicating faith. Church leaders have the task of preserving unity among Christ's disciples and communion between local churches, with respect for their differences. But there are obviously two changes in the practice of authority in the electronic age. Let us consider each of these in turn.

In the first place, that authority which has unity and communion in mind is, I believe, exercised more effectively by, for example, world travel by religious leaders than by official documents. In the age of Gutenberg,

THE FAITH COMMUNICATION SYSTEM

Print-Media Civilization   *Electronic/Audiovisual Civilization*

Privileged places

1. The school, home of the book

1. The home of the group: the family home; meeting rooms, friends' rooms or apartments; nature

2. The parish, church
   a. School-like catechetical classes
   b. Liturgical instruction (Sunday sermon)

2. Important spiritual places
   a. Places of witness and spiritual freedom (not to debate but "to be there")
   b. Certain monasteries; pilgrimages

3. Open cultural centers, or places of permanent training
   a. Places of dialogue and profound study, open to experts and to real experiences

Addressees and privileged times

1. Times of traditional schooling: children, adolescents, and young people

1. Times of leisure and learning: times when a person steps outside his or her normal life to reflect or to listen to something else

2. Church personnel: pastors and priests, church officials, catechists

2. Groups that have a religious dimension (prayer, study, and action groups; charismatics)

3. Demands of initial training: for example, ecclesiastical seminary

3. Worldly aspects of life and crisis situations: preparations for marriage; changes in age and situation; death of a dear one; forced rest; times when a person is confronted by great questions of existence

Figure 2(a)

The Faith Communication System (continued)

Print-Media Civilization	*Electronic/Audiovisual Civilization*
Agents of faith communication	
1. Priests and pastors (church)	1. Spiritual people (gurus, awakeners)
2. Teachers (school)	2. Animators and coordinators of learning, who ensure the creation of programs, publicity, and organization; communication between groups and leaders; and the training of leaders rather than direct catechesis
3. Catechists (under formal instruction)	3. Leaders in the field; parents; young people; church officials; various volunteers, distinguished not by scholarly training but by local involvement and training linked to action and life, associated with trainers and/or spiritual families
4. Family (secondarily)	4. Experts who ensure constant renewal and critical evaluation
Authority	
1. The church hierarchy, linked to the guardianship and power of books	1. A democratization of the word: information is given to all
2. The authority of teaching and pedagogy	2. Authority resides primarily in whoever has an intimate experience of truth and values. Greater importance is given to creativity, self-sufficiency, participation, commitment, and group relations.
3. Intent: instill in its pupils the main virtues of obedience, generosity, and faithfulness	3. Intent: assure the unity of the body while making the limbs communicate

Figure 2(b)

unity of faith was preserved by uniformity. In the electronic age, it is preserved by countless communications and relationships. The pope makes himself present everywhere by means of television. Ecclesial unity is established by his image and his voice rather than by the words he utters.

In the second place, young people today, deeply influenced by the subjective nature of the audiovisual system, are quite spontaneously replacing the earlier authority, which was based on function, with an authority based on value. Functional authority is certainly essential—I would not dispute that—but it will not be followed easily and happily if its value is not greatly increased.

What do I mean here by "value"? First, I mean spiritual value; second, friendship that is full of goodness; and third, that personal quality possessed by the human being who is living in close touch with the burning questions of his or her own times. Television programs must have this value. The viewer selects a program not because of its authority, but for the value that is attached to it. In an age when information is offered to everyone, the authority of value carries on above all through the media. It is not enough now for a catechist simply to have a mandate, as was the case in the past.

The future is already with us. We already see new forms appear among us, like bubbles of air bursting on the surface of water. I am sure there will be thousands of such bubbles bursting tomorrow. There will not even be an identifiable revolution. Inner forces are already slowly at work in the old church, making it appear new.

Shall we be able to do with the new electronic technologies of communication what Luther, Canisius, Bellarmine, and others did at the beginning of the Gutenberg age?

2

A NEW APPROACH TO
MORAL LIFE

There is no doubt that understanding a generation's moral development will help us to understand its spiritual shape. What, then, is the moral status of the present generation, influenced as it is by the increased use of audiovisual electronics? My answer is in the form of a drawing and parable (Figure 3):

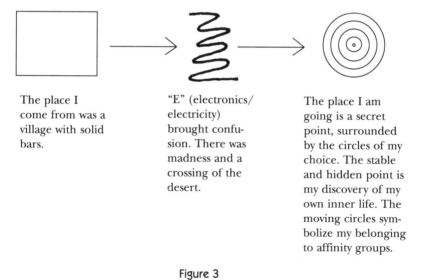

The place I come from was a village with solid bars.

"E" (electronics/electricity) brought confusion. There was madness and a crossing of the desert.

The place I am going is a secret point, surrounded by the circles of my choice. The stable and hidden point is my discovery of my own inner life. The moving circles symbolize my belonging to affinity groups.

Figure 3

In the beginning, there was the village. This does not mean we are all born in a village. The village is the symbol—the first extension—of our mother's womb, the place of tradition and solidarity. Morality is governed in the village by three forms of authority:

1. Authority of the leader, which appears in three types of leader: the pastor or priest (the church), the mayor (political power), and the teacher (school).
2. Authority of the elders (men and women), a fearful authority that follows you out into the street, where you know you are being watched constantly by unseen eyes from behind the windows of the houses.
3. Authority of Nature (N), the queen of wisdom, the source of regular yet varied rhythms.

Life was so simple in those days. Models were found first in tradition and then in the laws of the catechism: Follow the rules, my child, and you will live!

Then electricity (E) came to the village. Slowly and irresistibly, it worked like a worm in fruit. "E" killed "N," and people stopped going to bed at sunset and getting up at the cock's crow. They witnessed the birth of factories and the triumph of the town—the town that Gandhi defined as "the place where the electricity shines." Electricity was excitement. It destroyed the power of the elders. Sober dress was replaced by casual pullovers and jeans. Color burst upon us. Our models ceased to be our grandparents or other adults and became teenage or young adult television performers. Finally "E" dethroned the church and books. There was a new slogan: Seen on TV. What is shown in the media surreptitiously became an attraction and the model for behavior and truth.

The village times are fading from our memories. With "E," every little village has become a large town. Every isolated farm has its television set, cars, telephone, and soon its own computer. The generation of the 1960s, intoxicated by the coming of the new gods, experienced a wave of madness. The elders crossed the desert; the catechism and the neighborhood lost their power. The cathedral, which until then had dominated the whole city, became in New York the smaller church of Saint Patrick, crushed between huge skyscrapers. Who should we believe? Where should we go? We need more than an aspirin to calm our fever and a lightbulb to illuminate our darkness.

But the place we are going has already begun to appear. Among younger people and in many prayer, action, and renewal groups, the buds of a new spring can be seen. I shall use two terms to characterize them: interiority and affinity groups.

"E" IS THE FORMAL CAUSE

In this chapter, I refer to "E" or sometimes to the "E factor." This "E" can mean both electricity and electronics. It does not mean only the material reality of what is electronic but the electronic universe. This important point needs explaining.

I do not mean to imply by my parable that moral change comes directly from electricity, as rain comes from the clouds. That would not just be naive but wrong. Rather, it is important to understand the fundamental distinction between formal cause and efficient cause. Electronics are not the efficient cause of moral change but its formal cause.

What does "formal cause" mean? Electricity and everything that flows from it (light, television, computers, interconnected equipment) take the human being into a vast network which, by invading every part of the person, leads him or her inescapably to become part of that whole and to take its shape. The person who lives in the forest with wild animals becomes a "forest person." Not only their habits change but also life-style and moral behavior. "E," then, is not just a means: it is a forest, it is today's jungle.

"E" is the main formal cause of moral change. By this I mean that the electronic universe shapes another type of moral behavior that is distinguished by the characteristics of electronics. Vibration, speed, interconnections, dematerialization, globalism—all of which are properties of the electronic medium—give shape to new moral conditions. Here we have, at the ethical or spiritual level, what modern analysts call "systems logic."

THE BREAKUP OF STRUCTURES

The first or at least the most obvious effect of the mass media on human behavior is its destructuring, the breakup of its structures:

> What is the purpose of television? Once again, let us admit it: no one knows! In fact, television has no positive purpose at all. It is to society what an earthquake is to geology: When the tremors have ceased, everything is turned upside down. What, then, is the purpose of television? At present, television's purpose is to question us and everything, for it is one of the great causes of shaking.[1]

Television is undoubtedly a great bulldozer, but it also can be gentle. Speaking about the development that has taken place in the church under the influence of mass media, the late Fernand Seguin, who was in charge of Radio Canada's scientific broadcasts, said, "The entire operation is an operation of charm."[2] Let us take one example of his work. To remove scientific thinking from the framework of the omnipotence of divine providence, Seguin televised a number of scholars, all atheists to one degree or another, in "a library with a seventeenth-century ivory crucifix in the center . . . placed there in an obviously deliberate way. It could not always be seen, but it was always there. I wanted to draw attention in this way to the scientific data."[3]

The process of destructuring takes place irresistibly, just as water dripping steadily on a rock will, after many years, cause the solid stone to crumble. Primarily, of course, this happens because gradually but irresistibly the media bring everything—all acts of violence and all the opinions of the world—into the family or local circle. But it also happens because we become what sociologists call "fragmented" people. We crumble into fragments because everything we see on television, everything we hear on the radio, and everything we read in magazines come to us piece by piece, without any logical connections—an advertisement, a song, a catastrophe, a report, or the pope's blessing. A survey of children's television habits revealed:

> Watching a broadcast, the child is aware of a series of moments rather than logical development. The stories are very short. There is a juxtaposition of emotionally charged moments rather than a straight track where the events are placed in a causal and consequential chain.[4]

Our way of reading or participating has been tersely described as "flicking through and mixing." What do people become after flicking through and mixing for ten years? They become disjointed. They lose the solid bars that the linear logic of the book had given them. They forget the certainties of the earlier customs. What counts is not the rational structure of a good basic training, but being in the flow of information.

When I read my newspapers and magazines on the train, I am not consolidating my mind, but developing my membership of the world. I am not, therefore, still trying to live through the inner solidity of my joints, but am adapting myself correctly to this world. Humankind, which is now fragmented and dislocated, can feel at ease in an anonymous crowd of people in a great department store or on the beach. A person can stand upright there, not because of support by an inner ideological structure, but because of belonging to the group and reacting intuitively to the stimuli this world provides.

A regular churchgoer once told me, "In the past, when you went to Mass on Sunday, the parish priest's sermon took up the whole day and even the whole week. But now I receive fifty new pieces of news on the same day in addition to my parish priest's sermon." Beyond such information, there is emotion in what we are offered, which, even more than the lack of logic, keeps us in a permanent state of masked shock. Nothing disrupts our stability more than emotion. Television series are built on the pattern of a new drama every one and a half minutes; the rhythm of tension/drama/catharsis is what catches and holds our interest. But after so many of these pinpricks, which are like the drops of water on stone, we too shall crumble into fragments.

Not only the linear logic of our schoolbooks but also the organization of nature is disappearing. In July 1977, New York City suddenly found itself without electricity for almost a day, the unforeseen consequence of a storm. A London newspaper called the occurrence "the night of the beasts," as though humanity without electricity had become humanity without reason. Why was there this loss of control, this disorder in the human structure? Over the past fifty years or so, man has gradually been losing nature—and the law of nature—which previously surrounded and preserved him. In the cities especially, nature is almost totally supplanted by electricity. The night becomes as bright as the day, and businesses stay open all night. Heating, traffic control, city administration, work—everything is controlled by the "law of electricity."

What do we become when we are no longer protected by wood fires, the dark night, and the regularity of the sun? In George Lucas's parabolic film, *Star Wars*, what protects Luke Skywalker? What makes him moral? A little robot, a kind of mini-man, very humorous, wise, and intelligent, who warns him of every danger, provides all his information, and converses with his feeble conscience. What controls Luke Skywalker is a kind of modern image of the guardian angel, a substitute for natural law, an electronic product midway between the angelic spirit and the dog that follows its master.

Finally, in free-market economies, destructuring is brought about by a strange law of journalism and the media that dictates that the only interesting things are those that depart from the norm. "I am not interested in the trains that arrive on time at the station—only in those involved in an accident," the journalist insists.

So we hear, read, and see countless things that mean nothing to us, either at the level of usefulness or at the spiritual level. We are crazy about excitement and sensation. What, then, can become of us after a few years of this experience? We will think that it is normal. And what can a child think, spending life watching television? Surely that there are no more rules, that what is exciting is life itself, and that in such a life everything is possible and everything is permitted.

THE EMERGING AFFECTIVITY

Another effect of the media civilization on human behavior involves imagination and feelings. The term "affectivity" has been used in this context:

> The first and perhaps the most fundamental of all the phenomena is the disappearance of the hegemony of reason as a consequence of the appearance of the visual technologies. The first reaction of the human organism to the image, especially to the film image, is an affective reaction.[5]
>
> Film language tends to awaken archaic forces that man has applied to himself for centuries in order not to let himself freely develop. In it, certain primitive characteristics of syncretic thought, in which everything follows or alternates with everything else or is intermingled, are merged together or juxtaposed with other things.[6]

Influenced by psychoanalysis, psychosociologists have become very aware of the influence of the image. But what about sound as a factor that shakes us sensorily and reactivates our instincts? The sound of drumming on boosted amplifiers, a rhythmic beating punctuated by sparkling lights, a voice that gives color to the amplification, all hit us in the guts. Listening to music, and above all to music that is characterized and amplified by electronic equipment, is not an exercise in analysis or intellectual understanding. It is feeling, letting yourself be "grabbed." Who really understands this kind of music? Young people know that those who "become" this music understand it. Just watch a group vibrating with the sound of a band. They are not listening with their ears, but with the whole of their bodies.

Whether we like it or not, we must recognize that there is a new balance of human powers and that the imagination and the affections now form an essential part of us in modern times. Only a short time ago, Jean-Paul Sartre was pronouncing anathemas against the inherent dangers of the human imagination! Now, however, we fully accept that this is one of the paths followed in contemporary education and psychotherapy, a path that is quite different from past spirituality based on self-mortification and the power of reason.

THE SUBDUED INNER LIFE

The third important effect of the media civilization is externalization. The most serious sin of contemporary society is not that it destructures us or reactivates our affections, but that it alienates us by making us conform to that society. Advertising and brilliant images, unending references to achievements in sport, and appeals to youth have made us deaf to the voice speaking in our innermost depths. We live "outside" ourselves. Being "in" has replaced "being." In the language of Jesus, we have gained the world but have lost our soul. We have lost our intimate inner voices, and even when we revolt against the world, there is a risk that we will identify with that world.

The real danger for most young people today is an alienation so severe that it is a renunciation of the right to intimate possession of oneself, a renunciation of being oneself. I once asked the author Marcel Légaut what advice he would give to parents. He replied firmly, "Keep young people away from the world of adults!" That world has become much more unthinkingly oppressive than it was even a short time ago. It says again and again, If you want to be successful, develop your potential without restraint! Have relationships! Buy your clothes here! Have your hair done there! Take out insurance! Read this paper! Carry a briefcase! Go jogging! Go hang gliding!

I asked a group of young people between sixteen and eighteen years of age, "What really interests you? What do you want in the depths of your being?" After a long silence, one of the young women said, "That's a question you can't even ask yourself. You don't have the right to put it to yourself. It's our parents who want everything for us—clothes, exam passes, money. . . . You have to be like that, and that is all!" A young man told me, "On All Saints' Day I'm going to my grandfather's in the country. When I'm there, I'll have time to walk all day in the fields, alone. I'll think about your question then."

What do young people today need most? They need to be alone in the fields to think, to be called on to listen to the depths of their being, to feel their passions and the spirit of revolt rise up inside them, and, on their way, to hear more than the sound of transistors and to see more than the advertisements—to encounter a person whose foundation is in herself and who is living because she is and not because of her clothes.

Why do we experience this mortal temptation through externalization? It has always been with us, but now it is more powerfully orchestrated and more stealthily present. It is like an electronic vibration: not an enemy that we can unmask or attack openly, but the very air we breathe. In civilization after Gutenberg, social pressure could be felt in the weight of authority and the strength of the law. Nowadays, it is the huge worldly complex that addresses us, not dictating unambiguous rules to our consciences, but calling on us to take part in the system. To have the "look;" to shine; to appear one day on the television screen—that is what really counts. "Being seen" is being. In this context, it is worth quoting again the statement made by the publicity agent Jacques Séguéla: "Ruling is no longer seeing ahead. It is being well seen."[7] When we reach this point, our rules of behavior are quite outside us, alienating and fluctuating. Is this not the real mortal sin—the sin that kills?

EVERYTHING IS IN THE EYE

Being soaked in an audiovisual electronic culture confronts us with two fundamental questions:

1. How are we to remain steady in a world that has lost its traditional points of reference and the support of nature, a world now based on electronics? McLuhan used to say that man had become a superangel. How can a superangel be stable?
2. How are we to cling to what is true and good in a world swept by the winds of every idea and every passion?

An illustration of the dilemma exposed by these questions is revealed in a striking letter written by an American woman to her brother, a Jesuit priest. She explains the disorder and confusion she felt living in this age of the media:

> When we were very young, we were brought up with a very strict education. I had an uncle who became a parish priest at Waterbury, Connecticut—a very poor parish—and I spent several summers with him. My father used to read a lot of religious and classical books. He had a marvelous philosophy that embraced the whole of life and religion. He let his ideas penetrate deeply into our minds.
> Life was so simple then! There was only good and evil. There were no deviations. And we did not look for excuses when we were older and more often led astray. We knew when we were wrong.
> But now it is the same as in poetry and art and so forth. Things are not interpreted by everyone in the same way. From now on, everything is in the eye of the spectator. And maybe that is how it ought to be, but I do not like it.

> No one likes losing his fairy-tale illusions and finding himself exposed in front of the naked truth. What is the naked truth anyway? Maybe it is how the new generation interprets it. I do not know. Peter, pray for me!

What a symptomatic letter this is! There is clear evidence in it that the writer received a traditional education, in which the Gutenberg galaxy played a powerful part. This education was monolithic, even, full of the Freudian superego and resulting in that "marvelous philosophy" that was nothing but a wide-ranging ideological explanation making it possible to cover all the questions that were asked at the time. The deep roots, the lists of sins, the clear distinction between good and evil: you knew where you were going. You had a firm foundation and could hand on the training you had received to your children.

But notice how everything has been thrown into disorder by the "E" civilization. Nothing is solid anymore, and the old formulas—even if they are patched up—are breaking. Everything is said and done in the new generation. A deep disorder and confusion comes in the wake of the earlier training's clarity, and the writer of the letter is not the only one to feel exposed, naked, and defenseless. She is not the only member of her generation who lacks anything to help her to recover. And she uses this extraordinary formula: "From now on, everything is in the eye of the spectator." In other words, when you no longer have the objectivity of the lists and instructions, everything is brought back to an inner principle of evaluation, which is apparently without any objective criteria.

The writer's drama is the same as that experienced by countless Christians, and it is a harsh drama because none of them has had any eye training. Theirs was a head-and-book education. The eye was fully occupied in looking outside; it was closed to the inner world. The real solution for the person who has lost the solid bars is not to put up new ones, which will only collapse too, but to go forward relying on the inner point of balance provided by his or her own body. According to Harvey Cox:

> The sickness of our time is not the movement toward interiority, but the disappearance of it. . . . The contemporary Western . . . spiritual writers . . . correctly see us as a people so locked into the jangle of outer signals that we cannot hear our own inner voices. . . . The skills they teach us are indispensable. With their help we are learning . . . how to hear our own pulse and breath, how to reclaim our impulses, and how to feel ourselves once more from within.[8]

Confronted with this essential sickness, catechisms and laws are clearly inadequate. It is not possible to cure an internal illness by applying a remedy to the skin. Because everything is in the eye, what is required is stimulation of the eye, in other words, an awakening of our interiority.

THE AWAKENING OF INTERIORITY

Two parts can be distinguished in this concept of awakening our interiority:

1. An education, in the form of the awakening.
2. An aim, that of interiority.

Let us consider first the educational aspect. This can best be illustrated by an example. We can arouse a taste, for instance, a taste for wine.

Generally speaking, those who know how to taste wine do not get drunk.[9] Having recognized a certain quality in themselves, they have in fact discovered an intimate relationship between what they are and what wine is. Becoming intoxicated would therefore be a renunciation both of that human quality and of the pleasure of wine tasting. Connoisseurs of wine can distinguish the aroma or "bouquet" and the many other qualities that distinguish good wine from indifferent and bad wine. But it is possible to learn about these qualities from books? Can a professional cook prepare excellent meals simply from written recipes?

We can regard taste as an ability to distinguish subtle nuances, qualities, and shortcomings. This ability could not, however, exist if people did not have within their psychologies those subtle nuances and preferences, tendencies and feelings corresponding to what they expect to find in the object. Awakening taste, then, is essentially awakening people to certain aspects that are dormant in them. It is not possible to taste whether wine has body if you are not awake to the quality of having body yourself.

People who are not knowledgeable about wine often buy sweet and sparkling wines that connoisseurs regard as mediocre. What, then, do they do when they want good wine? They buy the most expensive bottle in the shop, or else one with the label of a vintage that someone has told them is famous. Their behavior is determined not by a sense of the value that might be conferred by an awakened taste for wine, but by the label on the bottle, which acts like a moral law telling them, "This is good." Or they might be swayed by the price, an external attribute, based on the judgment of other people and on economic laws which frequently have no connection with the quality of the wine itself.

In moral training, we have to move from an education by the label—the law, principles, habits, and so on—to an inner education of taste. The arousing of taste cannot be taught through the intellect. It is brought about above all by an awakener, thanks to repeated experiences over a sufficiently long period of time and in an atmosphere that corresponds to the reality to be discovered. We learn through masters and value groups, by living and by doing. This is followed by a period of communicating and intellectualizing, which in turn is followed by a third period of critical reflection. The traditional method of training young people through camps and shared activities bears witness to the excellence of this form of education. It has long been practiced, for example, in the scout movement.

This, then, is an education based essentially on experience and atmosphere. Experience is not enough, however. Awakening in this sense depends above all on an awakener, on a person who is himself awake, firmly established in the depths of his own being. A trainee cook learns to become a good cook in the company of a chef whose eyes sparkle when he or she tastes a sauce and who is angry if the right ingredients are not used. Freedom is likewise learned in contact with a liberated person. One awakens according to what one is!

There are many possible kinds of awakening and many kinds of awakeners. It is even possible to awaken oneself to the devil and to various forms of evil. There is, however, one kind of awakening that transcends everything: the awakening of interiority. Anyone whose interiority has been awakened is a firm rock in the midst of the changing tides and movements of this world. How are we to define interiority? In a child or an adolescent, it is merely an intuition: the intuition that you are someone unique and sacred, that you have intimate and absolute demands in yourself and more powerful than yourself. Such intuitions may be manifested during adolescence either in a revolt against the world of adults or in protest against injustice. Jesus was clearly manifesting his interiority when he was twelve years old and left his parents to go to the temple. Awakening interiority in children and young people is awakening them to listen to the voices of their hearts and to the absolute values and ideals that make themselves felt in their consciousness. Happy is the young person who becomes conscious of those ambiguous but imperious voices!

In adult terms, interiority is characterized by a more radical state. It is a recognition of the sacred and inviolable character of the human person: I am, and no one can lay a hand on that "I." At the same time, it is a recognition of the mystery that dwells underground in us, an intimate demand more imperious than any of our external pressures and an absolute reality that comes from us, but also impresses itself on us. Words fail us when we try to define interiority. It is the fruit of a direct and strictly personal experience. It is not reason, nor is it feeling or sensitivity, intelligence, or instinct; it is all of these and something more. It is the profound movement of one's being, proceeding from intimate necessities. The people who listen to their voices—who have the illumination of the treasure and of their own profound being—also possess the principle by which they can discern figures. Beyond all temptations and transitory deviations, they are spontaneously open to what is really good and true. They are that "good earth" of the gospel, that deep earth in which the seed of the word is able to germinate, grow, and bear fruit.

Interiority is stability and truth. Confronted with the "shock of the future," Orson Welles, interpreting Toffler in a short film, said at the outset, "To survive, I first bought a solid old house in the country. . . ." But that house of stone is ultimately no more than an image of the inner home inhabited by the light that never goes out. The Koran puts it thus (24:35): "Man's heart is like a glass lantern in the niche of his body and in that heart there is a lamp, that is, the most secret consciousness, illuminated by the light of the spirit. . . ."

Calming down the tumult caused by external stimuli, behaving with patience according to one's intimate demands, being able to listen to the voice that speaks in one's innermost depths, becoming translucent to the Holy Spirit who dwells in the depths of our being: all these themes form part of the educational process of awakening interiority. In this process, the techniques of zen and yoga should not be scorned, but they may not be suitable for everyone. Above all, we have to encounter those who make us long to be free and firmly founded in ourselves, because they are themselves free of all worldliness, external pressure, and concern for money; they are urged on by their deepest being. As Légaut observed, "Society must become a community of persons who are finally free and interiorized, or it will perish."[10]

Because of the emphasis I place on interiority as the first aim of education in our own time, I may be asked, What about active commitment to the great human causes of today? Are you not just a dreamer? I am aware of the possible danger of slipping from interiority into subjectivity and narcissism. Those engaged in education have to be alert to this. But it is also necessary to recognize that interiority is not in any sense opposed to commitment. Interiority is the source and it would be foolish to criticize the river for flowing from its source. Joan of Arc provides us with a good example. Surely the fifteenth century produced no one more committed in a revolutionary way than Joan. But everything she undertook she did in response to the voices that sounded in the most intimate depths of her being. She always said, "I follow the voice that I hear." I am not pleading for noncommitment—quite the opposite. We should move from ideology as a source, to interiority as a better source.

AFFINITY COMMUNITIES

At the beginning of this chapter, I said, "The place I am going is a secret point." That point is the source hidden in the most intimate depths of my being. It is also a fluid and sometimes multiple belonging to affinity groups.

The affinity community is the electronic version of the geographical community, whether this is a basic community or a parish community. It is a gathering of people who have chosen each other because of an affinity of character or interests or, in Christian terms, because of an inner bond of calling and mission. In these groups there are individual differences, but most have a mixture of friendship and spiritual reference to the same leader, memories and shared experiences, and certain overlapping interests and orientations.

What is distinctive to all these communities is that their members have chosen one another on the basis of intimate tastes and profound spiritual orientations. The members' social or professional situation, the demands made by objective apostolic motives, and geographical proximity to each other: none of these factors takes precedence in their decision to join or invite to membership. First and foremost are the intimate demands that rise up from the depths of the person.

It is, however, not only interiority that leads these people to form such communities. Subjectivity and affectivity also play an important part. What we have here comes directly from the human emotions that are stimulated by the media and, even more important, there is also a similarity to the functioning of the computers which calls on us to choose and make our own combinations.

Are these affinity communities different from parish communities? Not at all, at least insofar as an affinity community can also be a parish community. But what I have in mind is a group specifically adapted to electronic communications, a group that can form and maintain bonds beyond the restraints imposed by time and place. There can be no doubt that electronics is tending to eliminate bodily and direct personal contact from human communication. There is a secret link between electronics and the human spirit. Electronics will not destroy parish or church communities any more than it will local drugstores. But we are bound to recognize that other forms of community have come into existence because of electronics.

At the same time, questions inevitably arise: Why this insistence on community? Why make the affinity community, together with the awakening of interiority, the fundamental condition of moral life in the audio-visual age? First of all because the community—that of the *agape*—is the very essence of Christianity. It is not simply a mode of living, but the very meaning of Christian life. The *agape* community is the aim of our earthly and heavenly mode of being. However, the essential reason for my insistence on this kind of community is pastoral. Nothing is as pertinent and powerful as the community based on affinity in correcting the great dangers inherent in our electronic culture. The first of these dangers is that we may be imprisoned in subjectivism. The community can broaden our vision and objectivize it. There is also a danger of isolated individualism within the mass of people. The community calls for relationships with others. And there is a danger of paralysis and solitude. The community reassures and strengthens us. The media enjoy very great prestige in our society. The sounds and colors of the media make violent appeals to the heart, and the community acts as an exorcist. Finally, in my own observation, all life that is stable and exerts an influence always has an affinity with a community base.

In conclusion, however, I have to draw attention to one important factor. Group dynamics, growth groups, human communities, and Christian communities must be distinguished from one another. They are far too often confused. The psychological and the human elements form the substratum of the Christian impulse to faith; that is certainly so. But these elements should not be reduced to the same level. I have repeatedly observed that, if there is an obstruction by aspects that are too exclusively concerned with psychological elements, above all with affective and friendly relationships, the Christian community will stagnate and even fail. What really characterizes a Christian community is the ability of each member to go beyond the psychology and situation of each other member to discern each individual's profound calling on earth and to strengthen it. I gladly pass on these words that I have heard from members of an affinity community: "I know you where you are and where you are best. I know your faults and even your sins, and regard them as grace leading to your personal fulfillment and your mission on earth. By looking at you with faith, I strengthen your calling and understand you in your difference from me. By loving you, I increase your strength tenfold, so that the kingdom may come." In other words, the Christian community is always a community with a base consisting of viewing with faith and not simply viewing others psychologically. It is essential to preserve this ability to discern spiritually, because it is that which will evoke people's love for each other.

It is hardly possible to imagine that we shall enter an electronic civilization without an element of madness and without crossing the desert. It will take a long time. The moral system of a given period is not decided by what is written in books; those can only provide general principles. Morality is like health. You can fight infections for a while with medicine, but healing comes from the formation of antibodies in your own body. The contemporary moral reaction has not yet been codified in books. It is still at the stage of forming antibodies. It is still happily following certain special paths. The taste for interiority and the search for affinity communities are, I believe, the most pertinent signs of the moral growth and indispensable conditions that are required for moral education in the electronic age.

3

THE IMPACT OF ELECTRONIC
MEDIA ON FAITH

In the work of spreading the gospel, the outstanding feature of the decades between 1950 and 1970 was the part played by human studies and human psychological and social needs. Christ was presented as good news mainly by relying on the language of psychology and sociology. The years since 1970, however, have been remarkable for the explosive development of the media, including television and the computer. They cannot, of course, be responsible for everything that has happened in religious communication since 1970, but I am sure the most important element favoring a change in religious education is the language of the media. In other words, those aspects of the human personality that are developed by use of the media have inevitably been exploited in the work of evangelization.

It is important to begin our study of the age of developing electronic communication by considering the impact made by the media on culture and faith and how our approach to God and human realities has been changed by our use of electronic media or, rather, by our plunge into a world of electronics and media.

A LONG-TERM MARK

When sociologists begin to study media's role in society, they look first at its immediate effects on the population. When, for example, a president speaks on television, sociologists ask whether his popularity rating rises or falls—and why. This type of study has little interest in our particular sphere. Instead of considering the short-term effects of electronics and media on attitudes and opinions, we should examine the long-term effects on our understanding and feelings. In other words, we should examine the media approach to human realities. I speak not about effects but about the imprint, the mark left on a rock by an animal or a plant and, in our context, the trace left in the depths of our person, the functioning of our brain, and the orientation of our feelings.

In connection with this, Marshall McLuhan stressed repeatedly that programs were of secondary importance. What counted was the imprint which media technologies leave on our nervous system. It is not *what* we understand, but *how* we understand. Toward the end of his life, McLuhan spoke repeatedly about the theory of the two hemispheres of the human brain. This theory scientifically confirmed all his long-held intuitions. He believed that writing had caused the left hemisphere to predominate in man, whereas audiovisual electronic language has brought about a dominance of the functions of the right hemisphere (see Figure 4).

LEFT HEMISPHERE	RIGHT HEMISPHERE
(Right side of body)	*(Left side of body)*
Speech/Verbal	Spatial/Musical
Logical, Mathematical	Holistic
Linear, Detailed	Artistic, Symbolic
Sequential	Simultaneous
Controlled	Emotional
Intellectual	Intuitive, Creative
Dominant	Minor (Quiet)
Worldly	Spiritual
Active	Receptive
Analytic	Synthetic, Gestalt
Reading, Writing, Naming	Facial Recognition
Sequential Ordering	Simultaneous Comprehension
Perception of Significant Order	Perception of Abstract Patterns
Complex Motor Sequences	Recognition of Complex Figures

Figure 4

If this hypothesis is true, it has important consequences for us. Faith perceived by the left hemisphere cannot be the same as faith perceived by the right. The functions of the human brain are, however, very complex, and many aspects of those functions are still hypothetical. To understand

McLuhan's theory, it is helpful to examine his table showing the characteristics of the two hemispheres of the brain, as it was displayed in his Toronto center. The theory of the two brain hemispheres provides an ideal explanatory framework not only for our present cultural orientations, but also for our contemporary life of faith. The gulf between the two approaches to faith is briefly illustrated in Figure 4.[1]

According to this scheme, it is possible to say that under the audiovisual influence faith is perceived mainly by the right hemisphere, in a symbolic, emotional, intuitive, global, artistic, and creative manner. Under the influence of books, on the other hand, faith is perceived much more by the characteristics of the left hemisphere, in a logical, conceptual, analytical, sequential, temporal, active, and dominant manner.

A more exact study of audiovisual electronic conditioning would enable us to achieve a better understanding of the variations in a human approach to faith.

THE FRAMEWORK OF FAITH

"Realities seem to change when our senses change." This proverbial saying can be applied to faith. The message of the gospel and even the object of our faith seem to change when our sensory perceptions change. And I emphasize that they *seem to be changed*. We are not concerned here with the content of faith. What is involved is our approach to faith, our "new ways of understanding." Our eyes, ears, and hands are involved when we come into contact with the word of life.

In the last few centuries, we have slowly moved from the marks left by nature to the marks left by the alphabet, from dominant aural modulations to square, logical, and abstract alphabetical structures. Now, within only a few decades, the whole world is coming under the domination of electronic forces which combine an extreme form of aural and visual modulation with the severity of the computer. Our senses have never been so overdeveloped—I might even say "overmodulated"—as they are now, while at the same time they are so restricted. And because of the instruments that affect and amplify our senses, the functions of our brains have also never been so stimulated and modified.

And what about God? One is reminded of North American Indians who live in the Canadian wilderness. In some tribes, mothers plug their children's nostrils and close their eyes as soon as they are born, in the belief that this will help develop their sense of hearing so they will hear the movement of animals and survive in the forest. The Indian who has become "hyperauditory" is thus able to perceive direction and movement by hearing, and is sensitive to all the connections and anomalies within a given environment. They become aware of themselves forming an intimate part of a nonstructured whole. Everything is contained in everything. God's framework is that of the great spirit animating the universe, a universe of vibrations and interrelationships, expressed in Indian paintings by a tangle of roots and threads emerging from every object.

In contrast is the case of the eighteen-year-old American who, as a child, spent 20,000 hours in front of the television and only 10,000 hours at school. He could at any time choose between forty and one hundred television channels.[2] To this we could add such electronic influences as photography, computers, audiovisual instruments, pocket calculators, programmed tools, and so on.

This leads us to the question: How can the Indian living in the forest have the same frame of reference for God as the American living under the influence of electronics?

Instead of a camera, the photography teachers now often give a pupil a simple cardboard framework with a hole in the middle, the size of a slide. "Taking a photograph," the teacher says, "is above all centering in a frame. So you have to learn framing, and that means learning how to see everything through a little square in that frame and how to choose the best angle of attack." The same applies to our view of God. It is above all a question of framing God by the medium—the medium in the full sense of the word.

In television, the medium is a small screen in your home. It is a cathode-ray tube targeting your senses with imperceptible speed and determining form, color, and movement. The medium is also an amplifier transmitting an analogical sound. It is a strict program following a predetermined code. It is a special, illogical, familiar, and violent language. And the medium also includes the dealers, publicity agents, technicians, and all the trades and professions concerned with every aspect of the industry, as well as all the conditions without which the industry would not function. Finally, it is above all that "medium complex" that changes my dreams, previous knowledge, and feelings in all that I know about God.

What are the noticeable effects on faith of this framing by the medium? I would choose three signs of the many ways by which we are conditioned in receiving faith, not because these three are necessarily the most decisive, but because they seem to have had the most recent impact on the faith of the written-media generation:

1. The preponderance of the aural sense
2. A permeation of knowledge and activity by the imaginary and the affective
3. The importance of background and atmosphere in our approach to all realities.

Faith Framed by the Aural Sense

Many over the years have noted that we entered a civilization of the image. My hypothesis, though, is based on a claim that we are living not so much in a civilization of the image as in one of the vibration. Vibration conditions the ear much more than the eye. The dominant sense, therefore, is hearing, as is evident from the behavior of young people with their Walkmans, and from pop music, rock, and the predominance of rock concerts and clubs.

Such importance is given to aural reception not just because of the unprecedented degree of amplification, but also because of the improvement in the quality of sound. Listening to an orchestra with a good amplifier and headphones makes it present in a much more effective and fascinating way than does sitting in the auditorium where it is playing.

I also must point out, however, that the message received by the eye has gradually been changed by the media. In many cases the change has been imperceptible to us. Looking at a television image is quite different from looking at one in a magazine picture. In the case of the television image, a ray targets my eye and usually dominates me. In the case of the magazine picture, I am dominant; my eye scans the surface of the page. The impact is therefore quite different.

If hearing, however, predominates in the electronic age, it is less in a physical than a symbolic sense. The ear symbolizes our body. As I will explain in Chapter 4, the essence of electronic communication is modulation, vibration. The body organ most sensitive to the vibrating phenomena that surround us is the ear. The ear represents the archetype of perception through vibration. Consequently, because of the violence of auditory and visual vibrations which assail us, because of this electronic universe which supercharges all communication, the whole body, in a manner of speaking, becomes a giant ear.

Knowledge then tends to be transmitted effectively through vibrations. For many young people, if they are not shaken by the information, they are not interested in knowing. Like harps whose strings are stirred by thousands of electronic vibrations, young people are affected by the vibration alone. They can no longer understand, or pray, without being physically moved. Once again, we see the predominance of the ear and therefore a return to a type of oral culture.

The visual sense is also conditioned by aural reception. The two main characteristics of perception by means of the ear are vibration and totality. Today, little by little, our way of seeing is assuming these characteristics. We want to vibrate more and more with what we see, while we see it, and our vision is becoming increasingly global.

Just think of the incredible success of music videos among young people. Obviously many factors are involved, but it is impossible not to notice that music videos express exactly the mode of seeing and the perception described above:

1. The basis is a song = vibration of the ear.
2. There is a succession of rapid images from every angle, sent to us by the television's cathode-ray tube = maximal vibration of the eye.
3. There are image sequences which very rarely follow linear logic: they seem to reach us from everywhere, like a mosaic = seeing globally.

Slowly, the eye is freeing itself of the fragmented perception we have when reading a text, and is receiving a simultaneous, wide-angle perception of the component parts of the image.

Considering the configuration of our bodies, we find a symbolic understanding of the parts played by the eye and the ear. The eyes are in the front of the face and quite close to one another. This makes us look in a straight line. The ears, however, are lateral, on either side of the head, and slightly toward the back, thus balancing the forward emphasis of the eyes. The ears are also fairly remote from each other, on the circumference of the circle. Finally, whereas the eyes appear to project outward from the face, the ears, like shells, trace a winding path that leads inward.

This description provides us with a good image of the ways in which our perception is conditioned by the eye and the ear. The person whose eyes dominate and who is used to reading develops a perception that is dominant, active, linear, and capable of penetrating realities. Such a person moves from one point to the next, separating and reconnecting fragmented spaces. Above and outside the realities, she is able to approach them from a particular point of view.

The person whose ear is the dominant organ, on the other hand, who is attuned to global vibrations and views, will acquire a perception that is more receptive and exploratory with regard to realities. This person will not dominate realities, but let them penetrate himself or herself, and will not be above, but "in." People dominated by the auditory sense try neither to penetrate secrets nor to analyze or synthesize. They are sensitive to symbolic knowledge that forms connections between things rather than isolating them in order to describe them. They will be constantly in search of harmony and beauty. Unlike the person whose eye is dominant, their fundamental category is not intellectual knowledge or action but presence.

In addition to the category of presence, multidimensional space also should be emphasized in dominant aural perception, since it is above all through hearing that we feel an environment. Our two ears, which are wide open on each side of our face, do not direct our concentration in a straight line. On the contrary, they dispose us toward a global perception of our location. Understanding is participation and seeing is being present. Appreciating what is beautiful is well-being.

We should not think, however, that the hearing-dominated person goes no further than perceptions of external voices. Such people are particularly sensitive to inner voices—those that rise up from their own bodies or from their souls. We would not say of people who are concentrated, for example, on their health that they "see" themselves. We would say rather that they "listen" to themselves. Joan of Arc was a typically hearing-dominated person, vibrating with the environment of her times and to the intimate demands that she perceived in herself.

The Effect on Faith of
Aural Supremacy

If my hypothesis with regard to the influence of the medium is correct, it should also be applied to faith. But first, it is worth remembering that the majority of renewal groups in the churches, as well as the charismatic circles, depend to a great extent on the auditory mode of perception outlined above. The young people who go to these places or belong to these groups provide a very good image of this new faith-conditioning.

The values of transcendence and receptivity are always present wherever the ear predominates. By "transcendence," I mean a special sensitivity to what lies beyond things. When the Native American singer Buffy Sainte Marie chants "God is alive . . . magic never die," she is singing in praise not of Christ, but of the god of the wind that blows (we do not know where it comes from), and those present begin to shake with her to the "magic that is standing behind," a fascinating power that cannot be coerced. "That music," a young man told me, "leaves me as bitter as if I could do nothing." The feeling of transcendence that the auditory person perceives is the feeling of a presence behind the appearances and an intangible power echoing in the heart of realities. This experience is a psychological reality in its crude state where I discern the framing of God. It certainly remains to be evangelized.

Contemplatives also emphasize auditory stimulation. The anchorites of the East chose to live in caves which amplified and echoed their spoken prayers. This gave them a feeling of depth and timelessness. The same effect can be achieved today in old Cistercian churches in Europe. Saint Bernard, at whose instigation such churches were built, wrote, "In the things of faith and in order to know the truth, hearing is superior to seeing." He also wrote, "You should know that the Holy Spirit, in order to make a soul advance in spirituality, has recourse to the same method. He trains our hearing before delighting our seeing. Listen, my daughter, and see." Bernard, in fact, collaborated with an architect to whom he elaborated a number of learned ideas about the sound effects produced by church vaults, with the aim of developing the spiritual sense of the congregations and their ability to listen to the word of God.[3]

We should not be surprised, then, by a return to scripture in the form of a return to piety and listening to inner voices. We can make a spontaneous approach to God more easily through music than through catechetical instruction and more readily through our emotional experience than through rational or intellectual argument. Faith seems to be triggered by becoming conscious of the self and alert to one's own intimate and absolute needs.

Another major effect of auditory perception is our sense of our own presence within our environment. An example is the Chinese tradition of kung fu fighting, in which men can strike the enemy in front of them and the enemy behind them at the same time. How do they do it? They do not see. Like radar devices, they are able to perceive the currents that cross the air and to sense the harmony or the destabilization of an environment.

Once, in the mountains at dawn, I found myself in the company of a shepherd. Suddenly and without warning, he ran into a clearing in the forest and came back with a little sheep on his shoulders. "Did you not hear?" he asked. "It was a fox. I got there just in time." That day, I understood fully the parable of Jesus as an acoustic one, for the first time. I was not the good shepherd; I had heard nothing at all! My companion, on the other hand, had his sheep permanently in the range of his "radar."

An attitude dominated by aural perception develops our sense of presence with members of a group, the roles that we play, the places, costumes, and symbols inside the space in which we function. In matters of faith, the framework is that of the affective community and the spectacle. The auditory way is one of liturgical development rather than intellectual teaching. It is the atmosphere of the retreat house rather than the well-prepared sermon. We may suspect the evangelical value of celebrating the great feasts of Saint Peter in Rome, or of the travels of the pope. We may question the atmosphere of retreats and charismatic meetings. But we have to understand them through our ears. The ear is the framework. The ear is the way.

Faith Framed by the Imagination and the Affective

I believe that what determines the development of our sense of hearing most powerfully is technology: the electronic amplification of audible and visible vibrations. To do full justice to the resurgence of the imaginary and the affective elements, we must examine the programs and characters peculiar to audiovisual language. It cannot be denied that an accumulation of electronic effects overmodulates the nervous system. We are beginning to study the emotional shock, tension, suspense, and catharsis that result from this overmodulation. But being bombarded by images, stories, violent events, and highly colored personalities, we feel the images themselves to be most effective.

On several occasions in the past, I had the opportunity to watch Brazilian television. Although I could not understand a word of what was said, I was like a little child watching an ad or cartoon. Essentially, I think they affected me that way because they dramatized emotional situations, and because the mimicry was violent. I was fascinated: my body was led by a kind of pleasure to reproduce the gestures of the actors in an imperceptible way, while my feelings became excited. What a terrible power audiovisual language has! It is able to drive one to love vibration just for the sake of vibration itself, to the point where it is separated from the human need to understand! Advertisers are well aware of this:

> The entire object of a communication is to obtain a reaction, a feeling from the targeted persons. . . . Creative people have to reason much more with their feeling than with their intelligence. . . . In the media, one tonality is particularly widespread. This is a powerful emotion with all its variations, from horror (accidents, murder, and war) to terror (the shark or the criminal monster) . . . , the sexual dimension, and so on.[4]

In the 1950s pessimistic moralists said that television would destroy children's imagination by its prefiguration of images. Experience has, however, shown that the very opposite is true: with greater availability of television comes a greater dependence on imaginary creativity. It would seem that an accumulation of feelings and emotions rouses and excites our affective life.

Would it be true to say that our imaginary and affective framework is determined by audiovisual language? First, faith is soaked in the archaic forms and impulses of primitive religion. There can be no resurgence of faith, only a resurgence of religious feeling. The specific forms of a committed, historical Christianity tend to be replaced by a Christianity that fulfills our archetypes in dream and spectacle. We have moved from the Christ of the artist Pasolini to the Christ of Franco Zeffirelli, a director inspired by a visionary's descriptions. I have seen children weep watching Zeffirelli's film, and during the film *Jesus Christ Superstar*. The imagination is fully satisfied, even as far as the cross. The God of Jesus Christ asks to be grafted onto the gods of the blood.

It is also important to speak about the framework of human affectivity. A Christian communicator cannot put forward a message nowadays if he or she does not engage the affective life of the group. And if faith is not made affectively desirable, it is very difficult to manifest faith. In that respect, it is easier to speak of Jesus than of the Trinity, and biblical stories are more acceptable than systematic, dogmatic statements. It may seem that has always been the case, but why hasn't the importance of this tendency been recognized? Our approach to faith calls not only for a witness, but also for an actor; not only a teacher, but also a friend.

The emotional and imaginary framework has to arouse in us an acute sense of certain aspects of Christianity which are grafted onto archetypal forms. These include the cult of leading symbols (the heroes of our own history, the prophets, the founders of orders, and the saints), an interest in sacred texts, the veneration of great living leaders (Pope John Paul II and Mother Teresa, for example), and those great popular movements that are, to some extent, mythical (pilgrimages, demonstrations, and festivals).

There can be no doubt that groups of people of differing temperaments and varying spirits have given the church a balance and helped it retain its universal character. But the framework described above points clearly to a present and a future more mystical than dogmatic, more generous than realistic, and more concerned with the quality of life and with health than with intellectual justification.

It is, however, not easy to forecast the future with the possible intervention of so many variables. I have already spoken of one of these: the computer. Because of its mathematical, reductive, and separatist language,

the mental framework of the computer is clearly opposed to other electronic media. It takes us back to the alphabet and stifles the affective and
imaginary powers.

Faith Framed by the "Ground"

The idea of "ground" is an extremely important subjective notion in
audiovisual language. It defines what does not appear in the foreground
of the consciousness either in a program or in an image, but that which
nonetheless determines its impact. By contrast, the "figure" is what is
clearly perceived intellectually and holds the viewer's attention. The ground
of a photo is usually the organization of the lines and masses. It also
includes the light, the framing, the color, the texture, and even the spatial
and temporal environment within which the photo is presented. The figure is the subject itself. It is usually possible to say that, contrary to appearances, the ground is the most important aspect in audiovisual language. In
fact, it delivers the real message by creating the effect in the viewer. In
literary language, on the other hand, the figure—that is, the words and
not the paper or the graphics—is the most decisive element.

In this context, it is interesting to note a comment from the director of
the magazine *Geo*, which has a consciously audiovisual style: "The text is of
secondary importance. What I want above all is good glossy paper and
first-class photos. I want my readers to go on a journey as they are reading." According to A. Behravian, "What is said counts for seven percent on
television, the tone and the output of what is said count for thirty-eight
percent, and the gestures and facial expressions count for fifty-five percent." If this is true, then the ground adds up to ninety-three percent of
the message!

In contrasting two languages in this way, we are in fact contrasting two
ideas of the message and two modes of understanding. That is, moreover,
the basic problem raised by the notion of framing. Framework is not
simply an external filter leaving the recipient and the message untouched.
On the contrary, it converts the realities with which it comes into contact.
In audiovisual language, the message is the global effect produced on the
recipient. In written language, it is the information transmitted.

But what does the message of Jesus become if we see it in the perspective of the electronic media, within the framework of the ground? What
are the phenomena that affect the listeners? If we are to believe the
gospel, I would say these phenomena are first the miracles and then the

way of speaking: "He taught them as one who had authority, and not as their scribes" (Matt. 7:29).

I would not go so far as to say that the words are nothing. There is no ground without a figure. But what gives the words their impact are the gestures, the environment, the relationships, and the extraordinary power of the man Jesus. And even more, in the absence of words, this ground can be called word of God, an intentional sign, the revelation of the personality of Jesus. When Jesus is asleep in the boat during the storm and then rises up to command the wind and the waves, what he may have said is of little importance. What speaks is his calmness and power. The proof of this is in Peter's reaction.

There is a certain similarity between Jesus' way of speaking through the ground and audiovisual language. Here we have the same kind of functioning. In psychological terms, there is continuity in the mode of communication from the miraculous actions of Jesus to the fascinating power of the small screen. There is a similar way of approaching the message demonstrated by both the woman who said, "If I only touch his garment, I shall be made well" (Matt. 9:21), and by the girl watching television who says, "Watching *Family Ties* makes me happy."

I would like to stress that the ground leads us to give, in faith, special importance to the values of vitality rather than to those of truth, and to values of beauty rather than those of strictness and validity. No one can, after all, have failed to notice how important miracles and healings have become in recent years in Christian life—especially, of course, in charismatic groups. Similarly, the warmth of the liturgical atmosphere has clearly become more important than the sermon or the validity of the sacramental signs, at least for young people.

The same applies to television news. Most viewers are concerned less with the truth of the news than with the quality of the newscaster's expressions. It is also clear that more attention is given to form than to matter. It is through the beauty and the atmosphere of the temple that we reach the god of the temple. A Japanese Shinto high priest said, "The worshiper is more impressed by the trees surrounding the temple or by the little lake than by some theory or other." This can certainly be applied to the audiovisual generation! What is absolutely essential is to put information in a form, and this is as true of religion as it is of everything else. We come to faith more through the ground than through the figure. The door by which we enter is not reason but longing, not the strictness of concepts but the "look."

TESTING TWO APPROACHES
TO FAITH

I have devised a test of religious feelings with the purpose not only of understanding the two approaches to faith, but also of explaining the gap that may exist between two generations of believers. Categories are based entirely on my discussions with young people and their parents. There are no right or wrong statements, simply the expression of points of view and various feelings about approaches to faith. Some are cerebral and catechetically oriented in their form, while others are global and audiovisual in form.

The statements are in groups of two. Identify those that best suit you and that best describe the way you more typically see or do things. If you cannot decide, do not make a choice.

1a. When I go into a church for a service, I look for a place where I feel most at ease in order to pray.
1b. When I go into a church for a service, I look for a place where I shall best be able to see and hear.

2a. What is needed above all for a good retreat is a very good preacher.
2b. What counts most of all in a retreat is the atmosphere of the house.

3a. I love talking about religion. I make up my mind about all these theories: the miracles, reincarnation, heaven and hell, liberation theology. It is marvelous to know what one believes in.
3b. It irritates me to hear Christians talking about theories and religion. It is just not important. They would do better if they were more concerned with the Third World.

4a. If we do not fight day and night for the truth and the church's doctrine, religion will soon collapse. The most important task of the church is to preserve the doctrine of faith.
4b. Doctrine is not the most important thing. What counts most of all in true religion is being humble, praying, and participating together in worship activities.

5a. Having faith is not believing in formulas. It is loving Jesus and following him as the disciples did in the gospels. Jesus told his disciples, "Come and follow me"—"Come and see." That is not religious instruction.

5b. Having faith is not believing in Christ in the clouds. It is being baptized and keeping to the truths taught by the church. Jesus said, "You are my disciples if you continue in my word and keep my commandments."

6a. I prefer a small church, somewhat intimate, a bit dark in places, with old statues. I like services with atmosphere.
6b. I like a church that is rather bare: a fine altar, the Bible clearly visible, a bright, sober place of silence and truth, with few statues.

If your choices are largely 1b, 2a, 3a, 4a, 5b, and 6b, you are more cerebral and catechetical. You have the "Gutenberg attitude." If you have chosen 1a, 2b, 3b, 4b, 5a, and 6a, you are audiovisually oriented and associate closely with electronic culture.

If you have been unable to choose in at least three instances, you may not be interested in religion, you may have a hesitant nature, or your response may be the mark of your intellectual training.

BELIEVING IS BEING "IN"

Since Saint Augustine, three aspects have been distinguished in the act of faith: *credere Deum*, "believing God," holding as true what is said about God; *credere Deo*, "believing in God," because God speaks to the individual; and *credere in Deum*, which in English is also "believing in God," having that impulse mixed with love that drives me to and makes me always seek God.

Theologians have pointed not only to the indispensable bond that exists between these three aspects of faith but also to the decisive part played by the third. Augustine spoke of belief as "touching through the heart." For the past five centuries, because of our written culture and the demand made by teachers of religion for precise knowledge of doctrine, the emphasis moved to the importance of "believing God."

Today, however, we are witnessing another change of emphasis. What dominates now is "believing in God," in the sense of both *credere Deo* and *credere in Deum*. What we have is really "clinging to the voice of God," since that voice echoes in the most intimate depths of a person's being, both stimulating and filling the person to overflow. This attitude can be described as an insistence on the inner experience of seeking and on global openness to the voice that speaks.

This new approach was well expressed in the broadcasts made by Jim McLaren of the Catholic Communication Center in Sydney. In 1968,

McLaren began his radio work with a series of programs, each lasting only seven minutes. Eventually, he expanded to thirty minutes and established a direct telephone link with listeners. His programs had become so successful that he was eventually given three hours of air time. I was in the studio during some of the broadcasts and tried to analyze what took place. Most of the listeners with whom McLaren talks in a broadcast are young people. One caller may ask about drugs or leisure activities, while another may question McLaren about records, religion, or relationships. A broadcast might include listener responses, short conversations, religious news, songs, and a little music.

But the secret of the broadcasts' success is not the content, but McLaren's voice. His voice is the warm, welcoming voice of friendship; it is the very opposite of dramatic. It breaks through loneliness and recognizes the individual behind the anonymous appeal. It calms people and helps them enter into communication with all the other voices. To telephone McLaren is to become a member of the family. His replies are almost always general and are often commonplace, but what counts is the appeal in the voice asking and the tone of voice replying. "If I reply in a hoarse voice," McLaren assured me, "my broadcast is a failure."

As a result of his approach, a huge church of interconnecting currents has been built in the air around McLaren. The connections are based not on formulas or acts of worship but on shared enthusiasms and mutual bonds that help and strengthen everyone.

Some listeners want to go even further. They see McLaren, take part in collective events, and read various books. They listen to "Sounds of Silence."[5] We should not say they have formed a new church, rather that this may be the door by which they enter faith.

Jesus spoke of sheep listening to his voice and of the shoot grafted onto the vine. These images can be applied to describe faith marked by audiovisual sensitivity. Believing is "being in tune with," "being grafted onto," or being "in." It is being in close and secret contact with an individual or a group. In the recent past, we had pupils in catechism classes. Now we have disciples.

The ecumenical community of Taizé is a good example of faith lived by the audiovisual generation. Take, for instance, a service in the Church of Reconciliation in Taizé on an evening of Pentecost. The church is filled, mostly with young people. Some are sitting on the ground. Some have guitars. They all have lighted candles. In the choir, the brothers are dressed in white habits. In the middle of the group are Brother Roger Schutz and two children. The organ plays and there is singing. Then Schutz begins to speak in a slow, deep voice into a cluster of microphones. His voice, full of intimacy and conviction, is heard over the many loudspeakers in the church. The microphones and amplifiers are the framework for the desired effect. Is it a form of manipulation? No more than with a good book. But it is a kind of communication that brings about both an entry into oneself and a vibration in all those present.

Faith is a "taking part together" in the amplified voice, the shifting light of the candles, the singing, and the silence. It is a seeking together in the same direction. Is it an orthodox faith? If orthodoxy means conformity to the definitions and formulas of the church, it is not. But if it means being in intimate contact with a group and an experience of being moved inside oneself, then it is. It is a living faith because it leads to a sincere and often very committed search. It is a confirmed faith in the permanent members of the community, and may become such through conversion of those listening to the voice.

This framework of faith is not something that happens unquestioningly, but through it we become once again aware of certain essential aspects of Christianity. It takes us back to Jesus, the one who tempts and heals us, to the stirring post-Pentecostal communities, to the outstanding spiritual and charitable movements in the history of the church, and to the beautiful and profound liturgies of the Christian past. There is no doubt that this new framework is risky, but I hope the future will show that it is a risk worth taking.

4

A CHRISTIAN APPROACH
TO COMMUNICATION

In the media age, it is not just the functioning of religious education itself that is called on to change. Even the presentation of the message must be modified. By presentation, I mean not only the wrapping affecting the external form but also the lines of force determining Christian calling and the focal point that is at their center and point of summation. Through the development of this presentation, the "thoughts of the heart [of God] are passed on from generation to generation." Presentation means, in other words, making present. In light of this, I would say that the center of the Christian message is communication. As educators in faith, what we have to transmit in words and deeds is, above all, communication.

COMMUNICATION IS THE CORE

For Christians, communication is not just a simple psychological movement inherent in human nature. It is a gift. It is not discovered or invented, but received. It is certainly possible to learn about communication in books and in sessions involving group dynamics, but this does not take us beyond the level of human functioning. Christian communication may be based on observable psychological and social phenomena, but it ultimately goes back to an "elsewhere," which colors everything and constitutes a fundamental apriority underlying everything. To try to conceal this apriority is to describe a house without referring to its foundations. It is from God that the Christian receives a certain gift of communication, and that gift is both a revelation and an original impulse.

What strikes us at once in people who have received that gift is that they do not communicate as everyone else does. On the one hand, they conform to the Hollywood style, but, on the other hand, they soon challenge it. This behavior is almost impossible to explain. It is clearly determined by some higher reason beyond common human reason. Jesus himself provides us with the best example of this behavior. Virginia Stem Owens asked, "Was Christ the perfect communicator?"[1] According to the laws of the media, the reply would undoubtedly have been No. When he spoke, Jesus was not always clear. Sometimes he was quite incomprehensible, even to those who were always with him. He was not accepted by the rich and powerful, although he did not take part in partisan politics. Above all, he was unpredictable, attractive, but reluctant to be swept along by success. Sometimes he was violently angry; at other times, he was gentle.

We may summarize this by saying that he cannot be pre-packaged by the system. He is not marketable and can only be sold in fits and starts. His image is made by Someone quite different from advertisers, but his book has sold better than any other! For centuries he has had an extraordinarily high audience rating and a remarkably global audience. A high quota of enthusiasm has greeted him, to the point of martyrdom. Then we consider the publicity of Jesus, always done by a group that is both "in" and "out"—the church, which is both old and out of date while remaining curiously new. The church's marketing continues imperturbably on its paradoxical way. We are bound to recognize that this phenomenon cannot be simply explained in human terms. Jesus has a revelation that does not come from this world.

Revealing the Reality of Communication

The revelation of Jesus' communication does not consist of an intellectual idea; it discloses a way of being. It makes us understand ourselves differently. A new reality makes its presence felt in us and we are authentically and radically bound to each other in a great ocean of love, its source and its currents known to us as God, the Son of God made man, and the Holy Spirit. This revelation is one of the fundamental unity of the human race, crossed by the love of God.

Many people ask themselves whether they are "in" or "not in." But for those who have this revelation, becoming part of the movements in this world is of secondary importance. The Christian knows. Even more, he or she knows from experience that being "plugged in" this way is no more than a fleeting vanity overlaying the true state of being plugged in. Revelation is when we see that all human beings are radically "in"—plugged into the merciful love of God. John describes the mystery of communication in words both peaceful and far-reaching:

> That which we have seen and heard we proclaim also to you, so that you may have fellowship with us, and our fellowship is with the Father and with his Son Jesus Christ. And we are writing this that your joy may be complete. (1 John 1:3–4)

The first Christians used the term *agape* to describe the reality of communication in God's love. They referred to an exchange of love rebuilding the fundamental unity of humanity from which we come and toward which we go.[2] We can understand this revelation and *agape* more easily if we imagine a great room plunged in darkness. When I enter, I touch chairs, tables, bodies. I am aware of movements and of hands seeking mine and taking them. I hear voices: from one side, cries, whispers, and muffled groans and, from the other, powerful and dominant voices. I am conscious of objects being moved and of people moving. I hear different kinds of music, some of it cacophonous. But I can see nothing. I grope my way forward with nothing to lead me. Like the protagonists in Ingmar Bergman's film *The Seventh Seal,* I cry out "O God, have mercy on us, who are without knowledge." Suddenly a great lamp is lighted. This is the "revelation." The details take their place within the whole. Everything is made coherent; I become at once aware of the meaning. I find I am in a great banquet hall.

Even more important is that I have a clearer view of myself and of the beings surrounding me. I see everything as having a double face: an apparent face and a more real, hidden face. On the one hand, I can see we are beings defending our territory, calling out for more room, making use of everything for our own pleasure, grimacing, and making imperious gestures. On the other hand, however, I become aware that we are also beings of light, who belong to the great central light, and that we hide within ourselves certain other lights, each one receiving and giving. The chairs, benches, and tables may have been obstacles, but they have now become ways for movement and well-being. The music that was cacophonous in the darkness becomes whimsical. If I take a photo, I have a picture of aggressive or unhappy beings. But, if I look with eyes that have become enlightened—if I go deeper than the surface of things—I can see forms that are growing, open and pierced by light.

This, then, is the revelation offered to us by Christianity: that, beyond appearances, everything is fundamentally one, the body of Christ, loved and saved by God. And these hidden faces, these incomplete beings uncovered by faith, are more consistent and definitive than the faces presented by the world. What I have is the revelation of love, charity, and unity realized by the first Christians.

A discovery of this kind unleashes fears and inconsistencies but it also sets free in me new energies and impulses. It makes me sympathetic and compassionate toward all the beings at the banquet. They attract me powerfully. I am aware of the tempter who divides me and the powers of darkness calling to me, but above all I am conscious of the revelation of unity which works in me like leaven, more powerfully than anything else.

Can the traditional categories of communication—such as transmitter, receiver, and feedback—be applied to this revelation? I think they can, as long as we recognize that transmitters and receivers are basically one, that, although they may be different drops of water, they are still of one ocean which transcends the individual elements. Likewise, at the level of appearances, the beings are universes without any connection other than the negative association of different inclinations or forces. At the deeper level, the beings are crossed by a priori mutual knowledge and fundamental unity. In the eyes of a Christian, what is at the origin is communion with God in the body of Christ. In the eyes of the nonbeliever, what is at the origin is a number of scattered and wandering beings in search of encounter or of some cosmic unity without God or Christ.

Christian Feedback

The term "feedback" has been used in the media to describe the reaction to a signal sent by a transmitter. It is the audience rating, a type of reaction. Let us apply this concept to the signal sent out by Jesus. Is there a specific feedback on the part of those who have accepted the revelation of communication?

A specific example of feedback is indicated simply in the Book of Acts. After Peter's address on the morning of Pentecost, the crowd asked, "What shall we do?" Peter's reply was simply, "Repent and be baptized" (Acts 2:37–38). For a long time, I was troubled by these abrupt words, but there is, logically speaking, no other possible feedback than an act of awareness. Repentance and conversion, in other words, call for a change in one's way of seeing and living.

In terms of communication, repentance and conversion mean that an individual's heart has changed and he or she is converted to the universal sodality as the ethos of existence. I recognize Christ as leaven working in the human dough and making us all into one single body. I recognize God as the absolute transmitter and receiver. This is very remote from feedback in the form of a debate full of unnecessary words. The feedback in this context is a disturbance of a person's psyche, a renunciation of the ambiguous, threatening, or imperialistic attitudes, and an act of trust in the power of Christ to do what is impossible.

But Peter also adds, "Be baptized." This means if you have had the revelation of people's new status, you must from that point be a member of a community who, among themselves, form a single body by uniting within the body of Christ. The baptized Christian tries to experience seriously, in a special place and at a special time, the gathering of all people in the body of Christ. He recalls the last supper, when Jesus said, "This is my body," while sharing the bread and looking upon his disciples. So, with a limited group, the baptized Christian too shares what is most precious, in other words, the reasons for which he or she lives. In this way the Christian looks forward to the universal communion, when all people will be in communication with the Holy Spirit, with all the doors open.

There are two other concepts which typify the Christian feedback in a truly original way: turning the other cheek, and that of abba.

Christian feedback differs from every social form of feedback, and even from many other religious systems, in forgiving others not "seven times, but seventy times seven" (Matt. 18:21–22), and in offering the other cheek: "If any one strikes you on the right cheek, turn to him the other also" (Matt. 5:39). No society seems able to live by such feedback. Confronted with those who threaten and strike, all states punish, exclude, and even murder. But the divine system revealed by Christ is quite different. It is a system in which everyone is given a chance: God "makes his sun rise on the evil and on the good" (Matt. 5:45). The Christian feedback when applied to human communication is both realistic and improbable. It is realistic because the wheat and the weeds grow together in the same field like brothers; to try to root out evil is simply idealistic. The feedback also has improbable consequences. Who says that the good seed will not be destroyed by the weeds?

We must realize, however, that it was never Jesus' intention to manage society or its institutions. The kinds of feedback that he describes are not laws but ideals of behavior. In politics, the feedback aims to be as perfect as God himself. But the scriptural feedback of forgiveness is by its depth beyond the reach of human beings. For people, the feedback is the riposte to the parry; for God, it is a feedback of mercy. Only the one who is divine can make good come from evil.

The second feedback that characterizes Christians is that of abba. Early in the church's history a conciliar prohibition ruled against praying on one's knees on Sunday.[3] It is a pity that this meaningful law has been forgotten for the Christian feedback here is very democratic. Christians do not speak to God either prostrate as slaves or on their knees as suppliants. They speak to God standing as sons and daughters. They are members of God's household, belonging to the body. They address God as "Abba," which is a bit like "dad."

What are Christians' prayers if not feedback of the highest kind, assuring God of our attention as children and the "trembling" of our reactions? Prayer is not a duty; it is a necessity inherent in our beings.

Without going so far as the level at which communication with God is that of a free child, we still must recognize the failure of the usual schemes of communication to consider that experience. In social communication schemes, not only do we neither listen nor speak to God, we do not even take into account the profound voices and the imperious demands that rise from our conscious minds. Everything that may savor of transcendence is systematically overlooked; there is no hint of either intimate growth or of the idea that communication may have a transcendent, or absolute, source. This is undoubtedly the most serious shortcoming in all the usual schemes of communication. There are many people who are not Christians, but who are conscious of people's spiritual dignity. These people can only reject patterns of close functioning between transmitters and receivers. If we are truly human, communicating is receiving and transmitting a message of which we are not completely in control, because it comes from our inner depths, where the necessity and the mystery dwell.

The Aim of Religious Communication

The Christian purpose is to be the salt of the earth; today, the Christian aims to be the salt of a civilization of information and communication. This does not mean that Christians aim to be superior to others, rather that they aim to be "in" in two ways: in the world and in the love of God. The Christian wants sometimes to be a star and at others crucified, sometimes present and at others elsewhere, but is always anxious to rebuild the broken unity of the human race.

The revelation of communication is not borne like glory. It is more like a fire which burns us. At certain times of special grace, it gives us fullness and intimate reassurance. But most of the time, we bear this treasure in the twilight and often the complete darkness of doubt. So, what we usually experience is not affective enthusiasm, but a deep dynamic urge: We are conscious of being called in a way that cannot be forced. Do we not, after all, have the certainty that, beyond even the worst difficulties, love will win? A struggle to the death, yes, but death is always a seed that germinates. I am conscious of the evil that devastates the world, of the signs of the times unleashing the powers both of God and Satan. Electronics have broken through the frontiers that separate us, but this breakthrough coincides almost exactly with an increase in racist attitudes. We live in the time between Babel and Pentecost, but I believe that the Holy Spirit is already present and that the spirit of Pentecost will triumph.

Christians living today and conscious of what is at stake in this world know that their greatest mission on earth is to build up the covenant between people and God. Disclosing and building that covenant may well be the ultimate aim of religious education. It is an aim that will be achieved through the building up of the Christian community and the unity of the churches.

What, then, is the revelation of communication? It is the revelation of the communion of all people with God in Christ. The test of that revelation is our burning desire to achieve the fundamental unity of the human race and to straighten out all that is twisted in that communion. In our hearts there is the old dream of the holy covenant, but it is not the same as the medieval vision.

A Christian Look at Schemes
of Communication

The term "catechism" was used, as we have seen, to represent catechesis or religious education in the age of printing. The term "communication of faith" could well be used to denote the same in the electronic age. With this and the sociological image in mind, I try to reflect on the church's various schemes of communication. Also, with both this world and the gospel in mind, I seek models to explain how God's word functions in people, both in the world and in the church. I am preoccupied by such questions as: How do people receive it? Do they receive it at all? How do they enter into *agape*? Do they enter into it at all? Are there any special systems of communication or attitudes by which people can hear and respond to God? Are there any great schemes of communication that characterize our churches and explain its successes and failures?

It is impossible for a single scheme to provide an answer to such questions. Therefore, I offer several complementary schemes, which correspond to various different points of view. To begin with, I feel the need to set up spotlights at certain points in the enormous field of communication. Then, as various factors seem to predominate and others to lead to separation, some elements attract while others repel; certain habits and convergences emerge, and several schemes become apparent to me. I ask myself whether these schemes are operational and if they could be fed into a computer. I conclude that they could not but that they could help us understand and evaluate our catechesis or religious teaching. Perhaps they could reveal to us the paths we followed in the past and could, from that point of departure, show prophetically how to find the paths that we should follow today and in the future.

THE SCHEMES OF LANGUAGE

The first two schemes are fundamentally language schemes. They show how communication changes radically according to the alphabets and the media that are used. Human relationships, the teaching and learning processes, understanding, and even policy are always changing according to whether we belong more or less to a certain language code or to a certain kind of media. In the case of the churches, communicating in accordance with a dominant oral or literary factor seems to me to have an importance that is as great as it is unconscious.

I have become very conscious of the importance of the media in other cultures. Communicating with percussion instruments, the transistor, and books produces three quite different modes of being. I was struck, for example, by the complaints and the reticence of young catechists in Indonesia, who told me, "You cannot get in here with the catechism, but you can with music or audiovisuals. Audiovisual—that is us!"

Scheme 1: Communication of Modulation

In the communication of modulation, the following are important factors:

1. Listening precedes speaking. Attention and receptivity are inherent to expression.
2. Being together takes precedence over differences in points of view. Communication is participating, not saying.
3. We communicate above all through our blood (the power of instinct), our body (our hold on the world), our breath (the first fruit of the spirit), our traditions (the souls of our ancestors), and our ground (what gives realities their place and value). We communicate music more than words. That is what I call "modulation."
4. The feedback is a global reaction from person to person or from person to group, a reaction of belonging, indifference, or rejection.

It is generally expressed with respect and sympathy in order to maintain good relationships and the unity of the whole. What unites the individuals or the group is more important than what distinguishes or separates them (see Figure 5).

SCHEME 1: COMMUNICATION OF MODULATION

"Jerusalem—where everyone remains together." The marketplace is a mother's womb extended. The child is a telephone receiver. Communication is participation.

Figure 5

The Call of the First Sounds

Communication begins before birth. Naturally, it continues in the first years of infancy, when the parents and the environment are omnipresent and omnipotent—not only the communication of the mother rocking her baby but communication in the village square; not only communication within the family but communication inside the local pub. In other words, this communication is one of global participation, in which to understand is to participate. This stage, with its own scheme, can last for the whole of a person's life.

The first communication is the womb of all communication. Freud's ideas have harmed us by making us suspicious of this. We are no less mature because we are childlike. The people of the East, Native Americans, and the people of Africa have never had this negative suspicion concerning the paradise of communication, the state where everything is in everything, where the circle is in the square, and where roots are also radar.

It is an enormously important task to make our contemporaries, especially those in education, aware of the permanent value of these first modes of expression and communication. If we fail to do this, we shall continue to undervalue non-Western cultures, audiovisual language, and the mystical approach to faith. Could we ever understand the way the orthodox express themselves theologically if we had never responded to their music? Could we ever understand their flow of images if we do not take modulation as our starting point? That is the fundamental reason why our churches became divided. The same senses do not predominate in us, nor do we plug in to the same linguistic points; and our understanding of the unconscious life is unacceptable to the orthodox.

The Relationship with Audiovisual Language

Our early exposure to communication is not only the necessary basis of all later forms of communication but also bears a close relationship to audiovisual language. Our basic ways of communicating and the sources of our language are not of the written but of the audiovisual type. The great producers of audiovisual material have preserved not only the myths and the whims of childhood but also the resonances of our first language.

Some elements of this first language of modulation and audiovisual expression need discussion. The first is hearing, which is, in this case, the dominant sense, the one that sorts out the first perceptions and gives us a global perception of the environment and interconnections, a sense of space and of the whole. Understanding by means of hearing is, in fact, being inside the reality, whereas understanding by means of reading is being above it.

An emphasis upon sound effects and noises in communication obviously correlates to a communication dominated by hearing. In the case of audiovisual elements, sound effects are fundamental to communication and establish a place, an event, or an atmosphere. For instance, the sound of grasshoppers is a device used repeatedly in films to indicate a rural environment. It is interesting to note that the first sounds that conditioned our ears—blood in our veins, breathing, the echo of voices—produce the effect of waves in the sea. That was our first place.

Closely associated with the use of such sound effects, but at a much higher intellectual level, is the concept of *modulation:* a whole complex of vibrations varying in intensity and pitch, with special rhythms and tones of their own. This is the kind of modulation that would register on an oscilloscope. We have to give a broad meaning to modulation so that it includes everything presented to the senses as vibrations which can be seen, heard, or felt and which have a rhythm, intensity, or scope that nowadays can be increased electronically.

Electronic games, rock clubs, Walkmans, and programmed timers on domestic cooking devices all modulate. Even the wind in the trees and leaders of nations modulate. When the crowds are no longer plugged in to their own modulation, their power disintegrates. Pope John Paul II also modulates: his gestures, voice projection, and body language are all actor's modulations, which electronics exaggerate. Electronic media heighten modulation to the extent that people listen to the tune more than to the words and follow the image more than the speech. The pope certainly speaks, but his address has to be understood above all as an image or as music, so that the meaning he conveys is "I am standing upright like a rock. I am fighting for people in the name of Christ." On his 1984 visit to Thailand, citizens of that country remarked, "It is impossible to understand how he can be so natural and smiling after so little rest and after enduring the heat in our country." It was not Pope John Paul II's words, but his modulation that led to so many conversions on that visit. The same can obviously be said of Christ's miracles: it was the modulation that was effective. The modulation is itself word.

I have noted the difference between words (as in addresses or speeches) and modulation, not between *the word* and modulation. "Word" represents the maximum precision and intelligibility for a strict definition of a reality. In that sense, it is the opposite of modulation, which represents a maximum appeal to the senses and the imagination. The words are a framework. The modulation is a temptation. But *the word* goes further. It expresses an intention, a truth, a presence that reveals itself. Unfortunately, many addresses or speeches are not word, but only a confusion of words. In our audiovisual culture, there is a need for word, and we should give priority to modulation to express that word. If you want your public to follow you, your words should be word and modulation, expressing in some way that warm, personal loving-kindness that children expect from us.

A final characteristic common to both audiovisual language and modulation is the environment or ground, which was discussed previously. The ground plays a much more important part in these language forms than does the figure that appears clearly to our consciousness. It is not words, or figure, that count above all in communication, but what surrounds them: the whole environment, the atmosphere, the material conditions, the media employed, and everything that usually passes unnoticed. Audio-visual language is like the earliest type of communication, and your search should focus on what surrounds the words. It is not the words that count for the child, but the tone of voice used. The language of modulation is a language of ground. Listen to the music more than to the words!

What Kind of Feedback?

I vividly remember a religious feast abroad in which I took part, a solemn Mass where an archbishop presided, surrounded by more than a hundred priests. The acoustics were poor and the language was unknown to me, so I could not understand a word, apart from the name of Jesus. But I followed the modulation: the dress, the gestures, the lighting, the movements of the crowd, the singing, and the mimicry of the preacher. What was my feedback? I walked behind. I followed, humming and singing wordlessly.

Beyond these general reactions, one moment for feedback stood out: the act of communion. At that moment, I really understood Jesus' discourse on the bread of life. He told those who were listening to his words, the crowds following with only half their minds, "Eat my flesh and drink my blood." In this, he was advocating a response that was both symbolic and physical. Far too often, feedback means no more than speaking, engaging in dialogue, pressing a button, writing, or telephoning. We should never forget that the first and most important feedback is eating and drinking, as it was in our mothers' wombs.

Rehabilitating the Feedback

The time has come to rehabilitate modulation as fundamental communication and to rehabilitate audiovisual language together with every form of culture that lies outside literary or scientific canons. The time has come also to reemphasize the value of modulation in the communication of faith. In Psalm 103:20 we read, "His angels [are] hearkening to the voice of his word." The "voice of his word" is, of course, God's voice, not the literal sense of the words. The first clinging of faith is oriented not to explanatory statements but to the modulation, the intensity, the quality, and the beauty of the person expressing that faith. It was modulation that made the disciples follow Jesus in the first place. They clung to him: "Lord, where do you live?"

A religious from Burundi in Africa once told me, "My mother, who is sixty-five and illiterate, came to see me one day and took part in a Mass celebrated by a foreign priest. I noticed how attentively she watched him and asked afterwards if she had understood him. "Yes," she said at once. I laughed and replied, "You couldn't have understood—it was not in your own language!" She looked at me and said: "You are religious and you don't know. But I understood. Jesus was speaking to me in him."

What a splendid answer! It explains the gift of tongues. Inwardly illuminated by the Holy Spirit, that African woman had penetrated the meaning of the sermon through modulation rather than the unintelligible words. She had gone beyond the priest's "cinema" and had been attentive to the inner word, which she followed as a disciple. Her feedback was not critical reflection based on an analysis of the sermon, but consisted of following. Feedback of this kind is global, while also being human and personal.

We must also rehabilitate the act of receiving in communication. We do not communicate because we speak, because we listen, or because we express ourselves, but because we are receptive. We shall never love if we are not loved first: "We love, because he first loved us" (1 John 4:19). In the same way, we shall never communicate if we do not first receive the breath and the message. We have to become receivers before we can become transmitters. Being shaken and upset by everything we receive is the secret of youth and creativity. If we merely repeat the catechism, we shall not be communicating. So many television and radio communicators have failed because they no longer received that breath and that personal agitation. They were no longer inspired, but rather had become mere technical experts. Those who receive the word in good soil, on the other hand, have the power to communicate (Luke 8:8). They may not produce immediate, explicit feedback, but their inner reflection lasts and their attitudes and behavior change.

If we do not rehabilitate these fundamental aspects of communicating, we shall fail to understand the special language of our own times and remain closed to great contemporary religious movements: charismatic renewal, the spirituality of Taizé, the pilgrimages, and the many spiritual groups. Even worse, we shall close the kingdom of God to the poor, insisting that they should enter by a critical door through which most people can never pass. Further, we risk losing young people, the whole of Africa, and the East.

A Necessary, Critical Attitude

There are dangers associated with an emphasis upon modulatory communication. Many people today are afraid of sects and political groups that mediate through loud music. The mother's womb is certainly more conservative than these factions. We still shudder when we think of Hitler's modulation.

I intend to show later that an indispensable role is played by certain intellectual groups, which act as "guard dogs" helping people to avoid either a misleading overmodulation or a conservative rigidity. But the response of these groups is not enough. It is in the realm of modulation itself that we have to criticize modulation. It is wrong to criticize it by an external application of critical instruments.

Over a long period, I have observed how people react critically to modulation. There appear to be five main paths for criticizing modulation, and they need to be deepened, widened, and given a more consciously permanent and popular critical shape. The first of these is a *change of environment.* A young person once said to me, "This is too much for me! I need to breathe and look elsewhere." By changing our environment and our state of saturation, we can relativize our subjective imprisonment in a given modulation. A sense of humor is needed here.

The second path is *an exchange with others.* I have often heard it said that "when I see an advertisement, I want to buy the thing at once. But before I do, I talk about it with other people." An exchange of views with others moderates a first impression and weighs it in relation to other emotions and points of view.

The third way is a *sense of history.* Africans speak of "proverbs," or "the wisdom of the old people"; in other words, a criticism of modulations and patterns of behavior in the context of people's history. A mere knowledge of the steam engine's history is of no use in overcoming resistance or overenthusiasm for electronics. A device must be examined as it relates to people and their behavior.

The fourth path, perhaps the most frequently followed in our society, is *reflection of relevance.* A young person told me, "I wonder whether the people and things presented to me really correspond with what I am looking for. More and more I get the impression that I am faced with decoys." The key here is to enter into oneself and measure the degree of relevance and discern the extent to which the modulation corresponds to oneself or to the group with which one is associated. Meditation forms an essential part of this process, because it compares the word of God with the modulations of this world.

Finally, there is a fifth path, recommended by Jesus in the gospel: an *evaluation of the fruits.* A person must question whether following a particular group or a certain modulation will cause him or her to bear more fruit. Will that fruit be the source of life or of death? Will it bring freedom or division? Perhaps following other modulations might make one happier and more fertile.

Jesus was condemned to death because he attracted people. Audiovisually oriented people must, like Jesus, preserve a balance in their training of disciples and avoid either excessive enthusiasm or simplicity. In this basic training, they have the example of the apostles, which shows clearly that a scholarly education is not needed. The prophets and the leaders of the people in the Bible were all people of modulation. They were formed by action, exchange, and reflection.

Scheme 2: Alphabetical Communication

Alphabetical communication has four characteristics:

1. Speaking is more important than listening.
2. The dominant language is words, which lead to oral or written discourse. This discourse, which is determined by the Phoenician alphabetical code, imposes on communication a certain strictness, reason, abstractness, and choice of special points of view.
3. It is above all systematized ideas and doctrines, laws, formulas, codes, and emblems that are communicated. The separate and abstract nature of the Phoenician alphabet makes ideologies flourish— ideologies with clearly differentiated territories, definitions of aims, and interest groups.
4. Feedback is expressed above all by an exchange of words and ideas about precise points. The need to react and to establish distinctions takes precedence over the need to achieve unity. The key words that characterize the feedback of alphabetical communication are defense, combativity, speech-making, and competitiveness (see Figure 6).

From Modulation to the Written Word

In Figure 6, vibrations are shaded off in the background and the arrows predominate. They separate, give clear direction, and are even aggressive. By "alphabetical communication," I mean a mode of communication characterized by conditions of abstraction, strictness, and logic, the archetypes for the Phoenician alphabet.

Professor de Kherkove of Toronto University, who undoubtedly has been the leader in communications theory since McLuhan, summarized the process by which we reach alphabetical communication: "At birth we receive our first programming: the cell program. This biological program is followed by another universal program, the modulation program. Finally, we are programmed by our alphabet, relayed by the printing press."

SCHEME 2: ALPHABETICAL COMMUNICATION

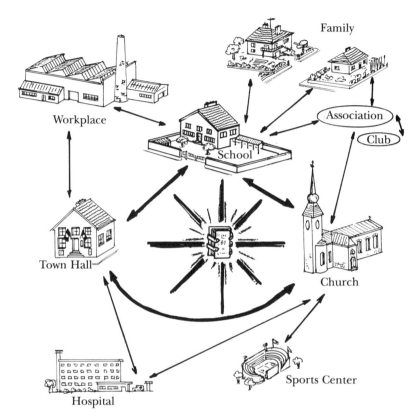

The book in the center imposes its model on everything. It illuminates the three special places of communication: the school, the town hall, and the church. The newspaper replaces the public square. The arrows follow the vibrations.

Figure 6

The Phoenician alphabet has always been one of humanity's greatest mysteries. It appeared once in a precise place on our earth and has never reappeared. It was not adopted by the Chinese, who understood quite clearly that they would lose their identity if they adopted it. But it is obvious that the people of the West, including, above all, the French Cartesians, were to become, through the medium of this alphabet, the most gifted in the task of communicating clear ideas and arguments—to such an extent that they made it their principal form of communication.

In the communication of modulation, the dominant medium is a physical vibration rooted in the primitive movements of the body. The African child learns how to dance first in his mother's womb and then on her back. Alphabetical communication is the opposite medium, the one most opposed to vibration, a medium of words conditioned by the form of the alphabet. These are words tortured by conventional graphic signs and made abstract twice over because, unlike Eastern ideograms, they represent sounds.

The dominant organ in the communication of modulation was the ear; in alphabetical communication it is the eye. The eye cannot see behind the head or see everything at the same time but looks at a particular object. The eye reads words one after the other in an isolating and coordinating process in order to construct a sentence that makes sense. This lengthy operation has become automatic and widespread with the development of the printing industry, and the resulting literary and scientific communication has led to a process of reasoning and abstraction.

Because of alphabetical communication, the church gradually and unwittingly came to undervalue the original forms of communication and to give priority to the catechism to communicate faith. This form of communication influenced life-styles and life processes: Learn the catechism—strict, abstract, systematized, and stereotyped—and you will be able to make your first communion. You will become a member of the group. Marriage as a family sharing is followed by marriage as an individual contract. The seminary, religious life, and the whole functioning of the church have been regulated by the separating and clarifying power of ideologies and canon laws. What are shared in this environment are ideals, aims in life, doctrines and aspects of knowledge, rules and methods, and struggles and conflicts. Administration, with its reports, statistics, and accounts, is our substitute for parenthood and friendship.

Am I justified in moving so abruptly from modulation to alphabetical communication? African people would remind me of their oral culture, that way of communicating from the mouth to the ear, in which words are mixed with gestures, images, and music and not channeled through the printing press. There are certainly many different intermediary schemes. But I have wanted to describe those modes of communication that have been the most contrasting and the most significant in the history of the Western church. I am also convinced that oral communication is fundamentally connected with the communication of modulation. Gestures always accompany the spoken word, an interactive relationship develops through speech or discourse, and rhythms underlie the talking. Other cultures also have differed significantly from the West in written communication. Most Asiatic people use a mixed alphabet that is partially based on images and partially abstract. They have a special ability to mix the abstract with the concrete, the ground with the figure, and modulation with strictness. In other words, they can combine the right and left brain hemispheres. They are less divided than we are between modulation and the alphabet or between television and writing.

The Value of Alphabetical Communication

We have seen how necessary it is to rehabilitate modulation, but we must also recognize the value and necessity of words and ideologies. The development of science and knowledge is closely connected with our ability to separate, analyze, and abstract on the basis of our alphabetical writing. There can be no doubt that the Roman Catholic church rediscovered and developed its unity after the Middle Ages because it obliged people to define and to memorize texts. This experience cannot be eradicated. There is no doubt either that the printing press, which has led to the spread of our alphabet, has also enabled us—and still enables us—to go beyond the restrictions of modulation. If alphabetical communication's danger lies in its formalism and pharisaical pride, then its positive virtues are openness and boldness. The language of radio and television is essentially that of modulation and therefore also of pleasure and tradition. Journalism, which is more firmly marked by the alphabet, is characterized by strictness and distance, force and novelty. A good journalist looks for facts, exposes secret relationships, and reveals the approximations of those who often lead us astray.

The language of ideological communication is learned at school, and this learning process is continued at a higher level at university. It would be a tragedy if these traditional institutions were to lose their original status and become places of approximation, modulation, or group animation. On the other hand, we should not surrender to Cartesian temptations and claim that communicating through modulation is unhealthful and only communicating ideologically is sound. In the confusing period of transition between Gutenberg and audiovisual culture, we should remember that our use of these two types of communication, one after the other, makes us all the more human. At the same time, we should also recognize, without claiming any superiority, that because of our culture and our temperament we are still more enriched by one or the other. The fact that one language is dominant is not disastrous. It can be a disaster only if one language drives the other out.

Alphabetical Communication and the Church

Realizing the importance of different communication modes in impart-
ing and sharing faith must cause Christians to ask, "Why, Lord, did you let
yourself be alphabetized first by the Jewish and then by the Christian
church? Was that just a historical accident, or was it a mysterious plan—a
connection with the West for the first stage of development, an affinity
with centralism and uniformity to maintain unity, the chance to have a
developing church?"

Whatever the replies to these questions may be, the alphabetization
question does not really apply to Christ, because his dominant form of
communication was that of modulation. At the same time he was able to
use the other mode; he exhibited both ways of speaking: "My sheep listen
to my voice" and "Those who come to me listen to my words." Jesus spoke
to the first disciples as an Indian guru speaks in his ashram: "Come and
see." But he also said what no guru would ever say: "Not an iota, not a dot,
will pass from the law" (Matt. 5:18). The church, then, began from mixed
communication origins with modulation predominating. But later on, and
especially in recent centuries, it became almost exclusively concerned
with the alphabetical and ideological way of communicating faith, as evi-
denced by papal encyclicals, the catechism, canon law, and seminary
training. Orthodox Christians have never embraced alphabetical culture
as dominant, but have remained far more closely affiliated with modulatory
methods.

Should the church now take advantage of the audiovisual wave and
return to communication that gives more authority to modulation? I think
it should, for one very important reason: we shall never have real dialogue
with the other religions if we do not take this step. We shall never make
progress in ecumenism or in intercultural exchanges as long as we remain
firmly embedded in the precondition of words and formulas. Before
opening any discussion at the level of dogmas, we have to modulate—to
celebrate—together. It is farcical and a disservice to dialogue to speak of
the process while we continue to obscure the program underlying our
interaction. Finally, if audiovisual language is one of the great languages
of our times, we shall no longer communicate with young people if we
do not modulate more effectively. Charismatics and members of prayer
groups inspired by Eastern examples have long used this device almost
exclusively.

Bearing in mind the need to enlarge the vision and practice of the
church, we must hope that theologians become increasingly open to the
language of modulation and discover its instruments of analysis. Is this

really possible? To be a theologian of modulation, one has to be able to speak, to some extent, the language of modulation. One must be able to move from one language to the other. In a church whose tradition has been literary and analytical, we may look to young people—the television and computer generation—to take up this challenge. They will study the essential problems that have been obscured by centuries of Cartesianism, including such questions as the importance of dreams in faith and revelation, the part played by music and the ground in communication, the forms of government and church structure connected with modulation, the new modes of presence determined by electronics, the strength of charismatic experience, and the spiritual influence of the saints and holy places.

This does not mean that we have to abandon our alphabetical programming. Can we not simply overcome such insidious effects of the Gutenberg inheritance as hardness, proud security, cultural domination, and extreme compartmentalization?

Two Churches

Pastors often complain, "People don't pray. They are afraid of silence. They always expect others to animate them." I have come to the conclusion that there are modulation churches and alphabet churches. Each has its own particular type of architecture and its own specific manner of animation.

The Modulation Church	The Alphabet Church
The church is like a cellar. The general darkness, reduced visibility, areas of light and shade, nooks, and small chapels give the impression of a forest. There are few straight or geometrical lines (e.g., Romanesque churches). The few lights are warm, predominantly orange and red, often candles and votive lights. Intensely colored stained-glass windows.	The church is like a public hall or theater. A large bare altar faces the people and is situated quite apart from the congregation. Desks and microphones face the pastor's assistants, giving prominence to the one presiding. Everyone and everything surrounds and helps him or her at a lower level. Good visibility is essential. Pews or chairs are arranged in ordered rows. The church is arranged on straight lines, without dark nooks, corners, or intimate little chapels. The light is predominantly white, and shadows are suppressed. Often there is fluorescent strip lighting.

(continued)

The Modulation Church (continued)	*The Alphabet Church (continued)*
Sound effects are very important, particularly rich low notes and harmonics. Sounds issue from all parts of the church, not just from the altar area. Microphones are placed in various parts of the church. There is a deep resonance, giving a vibrant foundation to the silence. People are reluctant to cough or blow their noses.	Little attention is given to sound effects; there is almost no resonance. Everything is presented in the dominant key, without bass or harmonics.
Christ is in the center, a mysterious presence. The pastor is not central. The sermon is short and sober, without explanation and with little or no teaching. Silence is essential—each spoken word is punctuated by it.	The pastor is in the center. The sermon is essential, lengthy, and everything has an explanation or commentary. What is said is affective and democratic. It has authority. It is addressed to people who belong, to convince and mobilize them.
Worship is marked by sacred attitudes and slow, hieratic gestures.	The choir leader uses generous conducting movements and holds everyone's attention.
The music is often repetitious. No one leads the singing. Organ music may accompany, but it is never dominant.	Modern hymns with frequently complex rhythms and difficult part-singing are emphasized. The mood is not sacred. Voices are lost in a vacuum.
A church of contemplation and meditation. Atmosphere takes the place of explanation.	A church of explanation and teaching, stimulating a verbal response and acts of belonging.
Participation is taking part in the vibration.	Participation is understanding and responding.

THE SCHEMES OF AFFINITY

Granted, media techniques determine the development of our cultures and civilizations. At the same time, however, I have come to the conclusion that in the communication of faith the quality of relationships, friendship, and spiritual intensity have played a more important part than the languages described above. Although they are of an order that is totally different from the linguistic frameworks, it is important to emphasize in this context both schemes: affective affinity and spiritual affinity, leading to a communication of friendship and of spirit. These two forms should not be sharply divided; they overlap and become intermingled like the waves of the sea. And they have this in common: No outside force can make them effective. The communication of both friendship and the spirit goes back to personal impulses and attractions that cannot be scientifically analyzed or controlled by an authority.

Scheme 3: The Communication of Friendship

In the communication of friendship, four factors play a part:

1. The movement to communicate originates in a personal inclination that is not dependent on any necessity, but is based on complementary and shared interests.
2. The exchange takes place between equal partners, one usually more active. The roles of transmitter and receiver and the part played by feedback are merged within a climate of shared interest and loving-kindness.
3. What is communicated is essentially a stimulus to be and to live, owed to an exchange of qualities concerned with being or having. Different languages are used, varying from words to actions or gifts. They generally take on an affective, even a sentimental aspect.
4. The deeper the inclination, the more relative individual positive possessions and clearly defined territories become. This can include the sharing of bodies. The communication of friendship can transcend the usual categories of time and space (see Figure 7).

The Religious Importance of the
Communication of Friendship

It is difficult to speak about friendship or love.[4] They are realities that resist definition, mainly because loving goes back to an inclination that is beyond our understanding. In one mythological representation, love is a child blindfolded and pierced by an arrow. So, loving is being held captive, being the victim of an elsewhere, and, in a sense, becoming blind. The mythological representation is right: To know love you must have the heart of a child; age does not matter. This is why communication on the basis of a loving inclination can be recognized as a special way to reach God. Anyone who enters into a true communication of friendship experiences transcendence. He or she goes beyond various forms of expression and has the feeling of being transcended, of not being able to express the inexpressible.

When we love, whom do we love? Blaise Pascal noted, "We never love

SCHEME 3: THE COMMUNICATION OF FRIENDSHIP

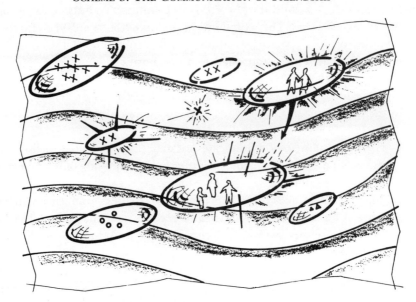

Going beyond the waves of time.
going beyond situations and events,
in the current and in the countercurrent,
beings are drawn to each other and come together,
stable or fleeting constellations,
their only need being their grace.

"Blessed is the one whose longing for God
is like the passion of a lover for his beloved."
—St. John Climacus

Figure 7

anyone; we only love qualities" (*Pensée*, 582). This may seem a pessimistic statement, but basically what it says is that loving consists of being sensitive to qualities and giving them priority. In other words, loving is being sensitive to the divine aspect of the being who is loved, and giving priority to the divine in that being. This is a formidable power. Being loved is responding to the call to make ourselves holy for one another, owing to complementary qualities and the gift that each one of us has to stimulate those qualities in others.

For all these reasons, and however ambiguous each communication of love may be, that communication must be given a special place. If we treat it as a gift and a surprise, this communication of friendship brings us to God's level. If we let it become a possession, a rule, or a routine, it ceases to be a divine way. Such wrong ways are often followed, and, to avoid them, attempts have been made to provide rules. Saint Augustine rejected all such rules, however, in a well-known statement: "Love and do what you will." There just is no rule—except, possibly, this one: When you love, amplify the transcendent character of your love by exposing yourself to the love of God. But this is not really a rule. It is an amplifier.

The Communication of Friendship and the Society of Information

Whatever our aspirations may be, our friendships do not contain any promise that they are lifelong. How long they do last depends on whether the partners can continue to stimulate each other, even though some of their complementary physical and psychological characteristics may change. In fact, apart from the conditions imposed by time and place, the duration of the partners' love will depend on their spiritual depth and their level of communication. The experience of their first affective inclinations may well be followed by an awareness that they are complementary in spirit: they have a call to friendship that is lasting. According to Marcel Légaut, "It may happen to one who has gone further than the first steps in the spiritual life that events will be in accord and that life will be mysteriously arranged, in such a way that apparently impossible encounters will be made possible."

It may seem that communication based in friendship is not part of a media society, but this is not so. The modern communication technology has not, as it was thought it would do in the fifties, sixties, and seventies, reached down to all people; it is, on the contrary, moving more toward individualization and group structures. In this environment of cultural change, which is upsetting even the traditional family bases of society, relationships based on personal inclination and friendship are becoming the most secure reality—in any case the least challenged. The relationships of the future will be those of friendship and small groups.

At a deeper level, the communication of friendship is the necessary counterbalance to a civilization of computers. It transforms what can never be reduced or foreseen into necessity. It inaugurates a different order, in which "what is important is the rose." According to John Naisbitt, the civilization of information can only succeed if there is a high level of human investment. Naisbitt has invented a powerful formula to express this idea. His striking phrase, expressing the need for a great human response to high technology, is "high tech/high touch." He writes, "What happens is that whenever new technology is introduced into society, there must be a counterbalancing human response—that is, high touch—or the technology is rejected. The more high tech, the more high touch."[5]

Naisbitt explains that high touch consists of the odd jobs, the techniques of human development, and, above all, the restoration of deep affective communications based on natural inclinations. It has even been suggested that relationships of friendship may from now on be the basis for our society.

The communication of friendship will be the source of and model for all forms of communication, and also the fundamental dimension of our knowledge of God. Augustine sounded surprisingly modern when, in a villa near what is now Milan, he reflected in the company of family and friends about living together in a community in a common search for God. In this text he expresses the basic intention of his religious rule through a dialogue with Wisdom, who asks, "Augustine, why do you want to live with friends?" He replies, "In order to seek together with common purpose to know God and our souls." Wisdom insists, "But Augustine, what if your friends do not want or cannot do this?" And he replies, "Oh, I shall convince them. I shall win them over!" "Very good, Augustine," Wisdom continues, "but if your friends really do not want to or if they put obstacles in your way in this search, what will you do?" Augustine's answer is, "Then I shall leave them!"[6]

Friendship forms the basis of every great spiritual life. Freedom almost always withers in a life in which friendship is no longer surprising. I think the church of our times will become more and more characterized by the communication of friendship, not only for theological reasons but for cultural reasons, and, above all, to ward off the risks of a bureaucratic technology in which computers increasingly dominate the church's administration. We talk more and more with machines between the speakers; but how dangerous it will be for the church if friendship ceases to cause some disorder in the souls of the church's administrative leaders! In this permanent process of reactivating our instincts by means of the media, what better security, together with prayer, can we have than the communication of deep friendship?

Scheme 4: The Communication of Spirit

In the communication of spirit, the following factors play a part:

1. The point of departure is a revelation in the depth of being of all the partners. It is the intention of each one of them to understand him-

self or herself as well as the others, and to share in a unique way the same reasons for living and the same fundamental options.

2. Generally speaking, the communication of spirit is rooted in affinities and even in complementarity between individuals, but it goes beyond these, as a river goes beyond the bed in which it flows.

3. What is communicated is not, primarily, information or psychological assistance, but the spirit that makes us live, the vision we have of ourselves, our unanswerable questions and insoluble problems, our fears and attitudes, and our hopes and essential motivations. This human spirit is closely connected with the Holy Spirit. It is a communication from being to being. It presupposes, on the part of the partners, an acceptance of their deep poverty.

4. In terms of quantifiable reactions, the feedback is often minimal, and it is possible for silence to dominate. The feedback is maximal, however, in terms of mutual stimulation and an increase in being and profound services.

5. Communication of spirit leads to the appearance of special networks or families of spirit, which act as leaven in society. Because of its newness and freedom, this communication arouses strong reactions of attraction or repulsion (see Figure 8).

It is not easy to distinguish between the communication of friendship and that of spirit; they usually overlap. After all, surely the best gift is communication of spirit on the basis of friendship! But the need to distinguish between them makes itself felt. Very intimate communications of spirit exist, for example, between the spiritual awakener and the disciple, the teacher and the pupil, the grandparents and the grandchildren, and these forms of communication do not necessarily cause an affective and reciprocal inclination of friendship to intervene. They may arouse admiration, compassion, or some other human feelings. On the other hand, a lively friendship and, even more, a passionate love, can communicate more affective pleasure than spirit. But it is not a question of communicating just any spirit. What, then, is at stake?

In all languages, the word "spirit" points to the essential element that cannot be grasped, the element that animates beings. In the Pauline epistles, "spirit" is written sometimes with a lowercase initial letter and sometimes with a capital. With a lowercase *s* it refers to the spirit of things and of humanity and signifies a vital but ambiguous principle. For example, presidents transmit their spirits to their nation and parents transmit their spirits to their children. Spirit with a capital *S* is the Spirit of God, the Holy

SCHEME 4: THE COMMUNICATION OF SPIRIT

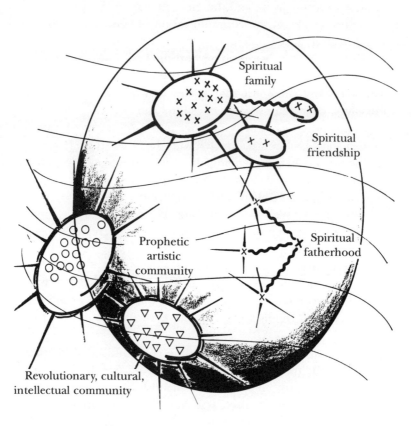

No one knows why
Some human beings throw light on each other
When they encounter each other.
The Spirit passes between them
For a day or for ever.
Then they become fruitful and confident.
They take fire into the world.

Figure 8

Spirit who was manifested to the world in fullness when Jesus entered into his glory.

So, when we speak here of a communication of spirit, we mean "Spirit," with a capital *S*. If it were only a question of communicating the spirit of the family, for example, we would have no need of a special and different scheme than communication of friendship. But although the communication of spirit may often be closely connected with that of friendship, it is still of a different kind. Communicating the spirit definitely presupposes an agreement with God and, ultimately, obedience to the will of God.

It is true that spirit may appear when our bodies are exalted or when we are successful as human beings, but that is only a beginning, a way, and a promise. The Spirit came in fullness at Jesus' death: "If I do not go away, the Counselor [the Spirit] will not come to you" (John 16:7). What we have here is not some heavenly coincidence for the establishment of Pentecost, but a law. There is an intimate connection between death, the diminution of purely physical or affective powers, and the communication of spirit. Spirit only occurs deeply in the wisdom of the body, the integration of the senses and the heart, and the total decision of love.

The best gift of which Saint Paul speaks is the one that Jesus made when he communicated both his breath of life and his spirit. Death and Pentecost are one. That is the highest point of communication. And it is from that point that all communication should be judged, both in aim and in form.

The aims of communication should be judged first. The most human aim is not profit, success, audience ratings, or the transmission of knowledge. These elements are of secondary importance only. The ultimate aim of communication is the spiritual fruitfulness of the partners. The question is sometimes asked whether the aim of spiritual love is not the achievement of some shared work. There are countless examples of this in the history of the church: Francis of Assisi, Teresa of Avila, and John of the Cross. But apart from the fact that these and similar examples have to be demythologized, the communal achievement of a plan, however evangelical it may be, cannot be the aim of this kind of communion. If it becomes an aim, a plan can only limit and falsify such a communion. The communication of spirit has only one aim and that is the communication of spirit. Thereby the aim is Pentecost, not the church, fruitfulness, or work. Of course, giving life to each other bears fruit in itself. But experience has shown that people communicating at this deep level are not always harnessed to exactly the same task and do not always produce the same fruit.

The Communication of Spirit Relativizes
All Other Communication

How is it possible to remain young and life-giving for the whole of one's life if one does not know the gift of communicating love and spirit? How is it possible to remain a child of God without going back sometimes to one's mother's womb, in order to receive some revelation there? It is certainly not possible to stay all the time on the heights, but a person who has never known those special moments when talking ceases and wordless communion takes over will soon die.

I do not think a Christian communicator can be an active worker for the covenant between God and humanity if he or she does not experience that kind of communication that goes far beyond the noise of the media. Nothing is so effective in relativizing cocktail party conversation as an experience of the deep forms of communication that occur for a few moments when beings become translucent to the spirit that animates them. It may happen that one day it will become very difficult to endure the kind of chatter we usually indulge. All the same, testing the validity of communication of spirit will always include making ourselves more receptive and increasing our loving-kindness toward others.

What happens to the feedback in silent communication? Because it can take so many different forms, it becomes elusive. It goes beyond the power of psychology or sociology to define the feedback in these instances. The reaction may be expressed not in a flow of words but in a trembling of the whole being. It is up to the partners who are communicating in spirit to decide on the gestures, silences, gifts, and sacrifices which are most suited to them.

A Condition for Lasting Communication

However intense our wishes may be, communications of friendship do not contain in themselves any guarantee that the communication will last. Certain communications, however, pass the test of time, not because of routine or material convenience, as is unfortunately the case in some marriages, but because they have a kind of intimate necessity.

What gives a communication a guarantee that it will last is the recognition of a shared spirit which the partners have to obey. The guiding principle here is not affectivity, but the dominant necessity of that spirit: the spirit recognized in each partner's own history and past commitments, the spirit seen as leading each partner to offer his or her life for the other. At this level, there is no need to be afraid of words. An eternity of deep communication can be traced back to obedience of the spirit and even to adoration by each partner of the other's mystery.

Légaut has distinguished between two major forms of spiritual communication. One, he believes, flows from relationships of spiritual childhood and parenthood, and the other from a spiritual communion at the level of existence. He also acknowledges that, after a period of maturing, these two forms merge. He wrote:

> There will not be a situation of leader and disciple in the long run . . . but a communion of mutual respect. In the long run too, not only parents but also sons and daughters and the unity of all will be too intimately connected to be clearly distinguished. Bound together like a sheaf in each other's silence, they will expand in charity.[7]

A deepening of spiritual communication, then, overcomes the distance caused by age and bodies. The other person is seen from within, as another self, in a communion of dizziness and hope. This breaks spiritual isolation, and one being merges gently into the other, due to a revelation of each's deepest and most intimate self. This is certainly one of the greatest experiences of eternity that is possible on earth. It is easy to understand how this may be the best way of communicating faith.

Families of Spirit as the Leaven of Society

The communication of spirit is expressed at its highest level in those special friendships that have just been described, but it is also expressed in groups. We have noted the existence of spiritual families or affinity communities and have seen how these demonstrate deep, affective bonds and intimate knowledge. These groups cannot exist unless they have a foundation of friendship and unless there are times for encounter and conviviality. On the other hand, we have noted that they also need a common breath. What is this breath?

This breath might encompass prayer, a common ideal, a sharing of money and of tasks, the same spiritual education and orientation, and a recognized bond with spiritual leaders. But however true and sincere these may be, there is a risk that emphasizing them may produce a hardening of what lies at the heart of these groups: the soul, a common way of experiencing life, feeling fear, and fighting, and a common way of knowing God. A family of spirit is animated not by rules, but by a breath upon which the communication of spirit is also dependent.

These groups are of the greatest importance in a high-tech society or in a church that has, of necessity, an administrative way of functioning. They maintain life. They are criticized by some and praised by others, but they leave no one indifferent. For young and old alike, they are the most important place for growth in faith. As Légaut observed:

> Those who have recognized each other at the level of their being in the present or through the past are linked in a genuine tradition. They do not

constitute a school of spirituality or a society in the strict sense of those terms, but a family according to the spirit. This family is invisible. It cannot be defined. It develops unit by unit, from generation to generation, without any sound and without any sociological importance other than that of each of its individual members. These members are scattered in space and time. They are all different both in behavior and attitude. They are also hidden in the mass of humanity. At the same time, however, they are closely united to each other in the most authentic reality. They are the heirs of those who went before them. Because they are faithful to their mission, they secretly prepare the way for those who follow them. These spiritual families are as diverse as individuals themselves. Because of their paradoxical conditions of existence, they seem to be at the mercy of every hostile event. They are, in fact, more vital, and they live longer than whole societies. Far more than all societies and civilizations, which pass, these spiritual dynasties are the first fruits of humanity of the future.[8]

THE SCHEMES OF CHRISTIAN FAITH

The final two schemes are directly determined by Christian faith. First, there is the communication of the poor. This derives from the biblical constant, which insists on the higher quality of the prayer and attitude of the poor. Second, there is the communication of faith. This territory touches the church in its very heart, and it will never cease to be discussed in Christian circles.

Scheme 5: The Communication of the Poor

In the communication of the poor, five factors must be considered:

1. The terms used in this communication—"God," "the poor," and "the rich"—do not apply primarily to persons or sociological entities, but to fundamental complementarities or conflicts. These attitudes significantly explain how the communication or noncommunication of the gospel functions. God has explained through Jesus what it means to be poor in spirit. According to the gospel, it is detachment from material goods, a love of truth and justice, and a mixture of weakness, confident strength, gentleness, and humility in human relationships. The rich are characterized by sufficiency, insensitivity of heart, and attachment to material goods and to the laws governing their possession.
2. Attentive loving-kindness and receptivity are closely connected to expression of poverty in spirit.

3. What is communicated is, above all, what one is; hence the importance of the values of the heart and of solidarity in the exchange process. An exchange of what one *has* naturally follows an exchange of what one *is*. Words count less than actions.
4. The feedback assumes different forms. It includes a demand for justice, a rejection of violence, and a demonstration of patience and mercy.
5. Confident communication with God permeates all human communications by the poor in spirit (see Figure 9).

SCHEME 5: THE COMMUNICATION OF THE POOR

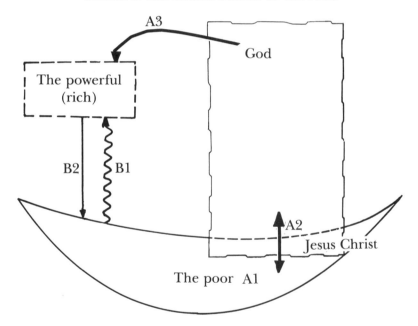

"For your sake he [Jesus Christ] became poor, so that by his poverty you might become rich." (2 Cor. 8:9)

God is a poor man in Jesus Christ.

In this scheme, the poor are an open circle touching God (A1–A2). The poor modulate toward the rich (B1). Most certainly, they pass through God (A3). The powerful (the rich) are in control and make their domination felt (B2) (see Matt. 20:25).

Figure 9

Speaking about the communication of the poor is not giving way to fashion or sentimental pity. If we are really born of God, a voice within us always asks, Do you communicate as the poor do? When you speak on television or from the pulpit, with all your knowledge, do you speak as one of the rich or as one of the poor, as one in control or as one who receives? Do you look for the ideal way of communicating among leading businesspersons or among children? In the office or at home, do you let the language of the heart dominate the language of reason? When you speak of God, do you communicate ideas or your own personal contact with God?

The communication of the poor is the conscience of the church, an absolute norm in its heart. As soon as Christians cease to be influenced, even judged by this norm, they cease to be Christian according to the spirit of Christ. Some people look to the poor out of pity or guilt, but that is the wrong way. God does not listen to the poor out of a guilty conscience, but out of faithfulness and truth. The communication of the poor is the true attitude, not only for humanity but also for God.

To describe this attitude, communication between the poor and the rich must first be examined. At the human and sociological level, the poor person is the one who is materially deprived and, because of this, excluded from the conditions that give value to life in society. The communication that the poor have with the rich is dominated by revolt or by request, complaint, or resignation, and, finally, by gratitude. The rich person's communication with the poor, on the other hand, is dominated by self-assurance, a mastery of the possibilities, the theme of giving, and, sometimes, by a guilty conscience.

Dominating the communication in both directions is money, the highest symbol of the services that the poor and the rich exchange. The money is the message. The roles, territories, and attributes of each of the partners are carefully determined and very distant, leading to mutual distrust, paternalism, and dependent attitudes, which destroy the integrity of the communication. The feedback may take many different forms, from gifts to warfare, words to forced silences, organized claims to acts of suicide.

Although there is undoubtedly a bridge between the communication of the sociologically poor and the poor in spirit, there is also a great gulf. The distance between them calls for a conversion, marked first by a change in attitude, from trust in man to trust in God. Second, there must be a change from resignation to fire, since the Lord came to light the fire for justice and truth. Third, a change from purely human political methods to the evangelical norms of mercy must occur. We are, after all, children of the One who "makes his sun rise on the evil and on the good" (Matt. 5:45).

The condition of radical poverty provides the best path to the communication revealed by the gospel. All of us become, to some extent, alert to it every time we feel a sense of loss or are made conscious of our own fragility by failure, illness, or some special deprivation. But radical poverty is, above all, a situation that lasts a long time and for which there is apparently no remedy or solution. Purely temporary states of poverty, which can be solved in some human way, are much less conducive to communication of the poor—a communication that opens the doors of the kingdom.

For example, a community of nuns going to live in a shanty town in Latin America is told by the inhabitants, "You have come here because you wanted to and you can leave when you want to. We live here. We don't want to and we can't leave. That is the difference between us." No doubt the physical and experiential closeness between the poor living in the shanty town and the community of nuns would lead the latter to poverty in spirit. But the great difference between them would remain. For the nuns poverty is a choice that can be revoked. For the inhabitants of the shanty town, it is a necessity without a remedy. So the connection between God and the realities of this world is a difference between freedom and necessity.

The communication by the poor has two essential characteristics: (1) an appreciation of true values, and (2) a trusting and happy dependence on God. I remember an old film in which an airplane crashed in the desert. After finishing their food and water, the two crew members, who had become radically poor, were called upon to relativize everything of secondary importance and to confront what was essential. One of them humorously opened his wallet and used the bank notes to make paper airplanes that he let fly away in the desert wind. Gradually, however, the two unfortunate men became closer to each other and began to communicate about what was left of importance in their lives. Their masks were removed, and God appeared at the same level as their consciousness. They were no longer self-sufficient. The reality, that God was standing at the door, became clear to them.

This is, of course, a well-known psychological mechanism, but the revelation of poverty according to the gospel goes infinitely further than any mechanism. The poor in heart are led by their situation to possess what is essential: knowledge of God. In a sense, they become like God. There is total communion between them and God.

As long as we fail to understand that poverty is the fundamental quality that characterizes divine communication, we bypass the beatitudes. Our minds have been led astray by a mistaken interpretation of scripture. A rich, omnipotent God who is the absolute Lord—this is a correct description if interpreted in the light of the cross, but it is totally incorrect interpreted in the light of chiefs of state. God does not rule because he has economic and legal power and control over the media. The revelation of Jesus means that God is poor, listens while speaking, looks not at a person's face, but into the heart, is rejected, and forgives. It means that Jesus' death is his glory. It means, too, that his way of communicating manifested itself most clearly at the end of his life, when he washed the feet of his scandalized disciples.

It is therefore possible to recognize that the scheme of communicating with the poor, however remote it may be from our everyday practices, is both absolutely essential to Christianity and the norm for the church. Several conclusions can be drawn from this:

1. If we set conditions, such as monetary requirements, all human communication is distorted. The important thing to communicate is our hearts. Communication is first and foremost an exchange of love.

2. It is impossible to maintain Christ's level of communication if we are not regenerated by an association with the poor, the experience of deprivation, and frequent meditation on evangelical poverty.

3. The quality of our communication depends primarily not on learning techniques, but on converting the heart. Group methods and communication techniques are useful in helping us to express our intentions correctly and to perfect our attitudes, but these techniques are harmful if they suppress our poverty.

4. Reason, analysis, strictness, and marketing are necessary, but only if they depend on the heart. The greatest catastrophe that can happen to communication today is for it to be governed by reason alone. When this happens, a secret desire for power prevails under the pretext of efficiency. People are then treated as objects.

5. The categories of caste, race, reserved territories, rich and poor, master and servant, employer and employee, and others can be traced back to historical necessities, but they poison our human communications. The revelation of Christ's communication sets us free from these antagonisms and separations. By right, there are no rich or poor and no masters or servants. But we are actually very far from

that paradise. It is the task of each successive generation to evolve these historical necessities.

Communication and Poverty

If God is poor, the ideal for communication is to be poor—a poor person among the poor. But how many books and publications urge us in the opposite direction: if we want to succeed in communication, we must have diplomas and qualifications; we must dress in the right way; we must become known; and we must master the processes. In other words, we must have the outward signs of riches—to be dominant and invulnerable. But Jesus is a revolutionary in this matter. The highest point of communication is reached when God deliberately becomes most vulnerable. The truth is revealed on the cross. When the heart is pierced, God at last ceases to speak in parables.

The earliest ways of representing God were in essentially perfect forms, with the circle occupying the place of pride. But God in Jesus Christ challenges this archetypal presentation. The Lord is not spherical; the Lord is pierced with holes. God is not self-sufficient; God lets his face be wiped and a prostitute kiss his feet. God has needs. The schemes of communication inspired by Christianity, then, are not schemes of spheres that attract or repel, but schemes of complementarity and reciprocal desires. Communication takes place via wounds, not via perfect forms.

It is in the dialogue between the rich countries and those of the Third World that our mortal sin exposes itself. We present ourselves as successful and as models. How false this is! Those who have real value and the truth and who have some chance of being real models for humanity are the poorest people of the Third World. If we serve them, we shall receive the grace of coming close to God. We can only communicate with them if we are aware of being poorer than they are.

In deep communication between one being and another, each of us must live genuinely convinced of our own radical incompleteness and intimate and insoluble weaknesses. Communicating is accepting both one's light and one's shade. It is letting others touch us and giving them the power to heal us. All communication from teacher to pupil, from doctor to patient, and from senior to junior should be affected by this twin attitude: each of us is a rock in authority and faith, and a reed in the trembling of the being.

According to the evangelical revelation, the relationships of communication are as follows: God is poor and Satan is rich. Satan is our lasting temptation spread out in this world. God is the secret call to communicate in a different way.

Scheme 6: Communicating the Christian Faith

Parenthood in some circles constitutes the highest level of human achievement. But begetting faith is a special achievement at an even higher level. Paul's words to the Corinthians are audacious: "For though you have countless guides in Christ, you do not have many fathers. For I became your father in Christ Jesus through the gospel" (1 Cor. 4:15). It is significant that so many parents should work in so many different ways for their children to receive this vision of life and the world—the vision that comes from faith. And they are right to do this. But what is communicating faith?

There is only one real difference between the communication of the poor, as I described it (scheme 5), and the communication of faith in the church. Radically and ideally, faith should only be communicated between two poverties. The first poverty is that of the communicator of faith (the transmitter). What is said comes not from the communicator but from the Lord. The communicator's soul waits for the Lord and she trembles with what must be transmitted. The second poverty is that of the receiver, who can only hear if her heart is made ready by God.

A shared poverty that is open to God is not, however, enough. Faith in Christ will only be communicated via the church, through a witness to Christ. There is the need for evidence: God can be invented through reason, but Christ cannot. "How are they to hear [of our Lord] without a preacher?" (Rom. 10:14). It now becomes important to place the church in the process of communicating faith (see Figure 10).

Here the medium is the word, in the broadest sense of the term: the expression of a being who deliberately discloses himself to others.

The Communication of Faith Calls for Saints

A clear distinction must be made between the communication of faith and the communication of the catechism. Many people have given up the struggle because they have not made this distinction, having believed that faith was the aim and result of sound doctrine and good teaching. But, as Paul has said, there may be countless teachers in Christ, but begetting faith is something quite different. We can communicate doctrines, beliefs, and even Christian enthusiasm, but we cannot communicate the spark of faith, either at the beginning or during the course of a person's formation.

Christian formulas, laws, and habits have to be communicated, and this

SCHEME 6: THE COMMUNICATION OF FAITH

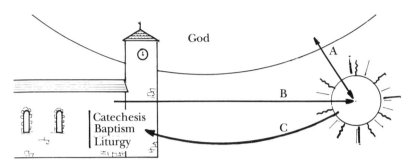

In this sixth scheme:
A being is open to God (A). A witness to Christ touches him (B) and triggers illumination. The person joins the community of Jesus' disciples (C). The feedback is conversion, catechesis, baptism, and liturgy.

Figure 10

communication depends on good teaching methods, including oratory and audiovisual techniques. No serious communicator can dispense with these studies. But what about faith itself? It is difficult for us to admit that we are both the necessary channels through which the word of God comes to others and, at the same time, radically inadequate transmitters. We cannot under any circumstances give faith through our media; all that we can do is to desire that faith and to hope for it. If faith comes at all, it will come in its own time and place, through its own channels and in forms that may be predictable, but are never predetermined. Yet, paradoxically, we are still its necessary instruments.

There certainly is an absolute need and it is material: the word of God needs channels and media in order to be expressed. But there is also another great need in the communication of faith: a need for saints. That is often forgotten in countries where there is a powerful religious feeling or where there is a long-established Christian tradition and the environment can put personal faith on the wrong track. But that is not the case in Western societies, where secularization has been imposed upon so many aspects of our lives and the demands made by audiovisual language upset us even more. If "what has been touched by the word of Life" is only expressed well in audiovisual language, then only a saint can speak well of Christ. What, then, is this holiness?

Considering this question specifically within the framework of the language of the media, I have concluded that there are, above all, three characteristics that give power to the communication of faith and also define the essence of holiness. The first is that the communicator "speaks under the influence" of a higher power. He or she seems to speak taking something other than the self as a point of departure. Communicators do not, in this case, emphasize their arguments or their knowledge, but a power greater than their own which makes itself felt in them. They speak "subject to necessity." They are certainly theologians, but what is seen in their eyes, their hesitations, and their flashes of irritation is that they are preoccupied with and led by Another, who transcends all theological knowledge. I have often noticed that speakers with a perfect mastery of theological language can excite admiration on the television, yet *arouse* nothing and nobody. Only someone who listens to God can make others listen to God.

Second, the communicator displays a permanent paradox of power and weakness. If communicators were merely weak or even inconsistent, no one would listen to them, so those who communicate faith have that mixture which cannot be defined and which made Paul exclaim, "When I am weak, then I am strong" (2 Cor. 12:10). An example of this quality is Cardinal Decourtray, the archbishop of Lyons, who gave the impression of being quite disarmed during a television interview given by several very sharp journalists. Few of his replies to their questions were immediate. He spoke reflectively and the camera revealed his hesitations. Then suddenly, upon a particularly sensitive issue, he replied vigorously, "No, never!" One journalist admitted later, "He took my breath away when he just replied, 'No!' to one of my questions. Almost everybody would have made excuses or would have given lengthy explanations at that point!" The journalists were unusually hesitant in their questions, as if the archbishop's behavior made them go back to themselves and not just to their papers. The archbishop's attitude during the interview was totally different from that of a political or even a religious leader whose aim was to encourage his members. He spoke instead to people's hearts. A mixture of weakness and strength will always be the test of spiritual communication.

Finally, the communicator of faith has to surrender his or her interiority: not only passions and intellectual convictions, but also the mystery that animates the individual. Such communicators do not disclose that mystery because they want to, but simply because it makes them who they are. It is an intimate secret that is revealed by their remarks, their eyes, and their gestures. Modulation is more revealing in this process than words.

Reading between the lines, it is not difficult to see in a description of these characteristics an outline of Jesus the communicator. Repeatedly he pointed out that his power and his words came from above, as in John 14:10: "The words that I say to you I do not speak on my own authority." It is the indwelling of a love or an inner necessity that makes the person omnipotent. And it is this kind of holiness that is called for in the communication of faith: not moral perfection but a trusting openness to God.

With the exception of the first two schemes in this chapter—the more material schemes of language—these outlines may seem vague. A person who favors precise thinking may therefore find them disappointing. But profound communication cannot be programmed on a computer. It is inexpressible, as God is. The person who wants to communicate faith must plug into these schemes in which, in the words of Pascal, "The heart has its reasons of which reason knows nothing." And whoever wants to communicate faith audiovisually must give priority to the schemes of modulation and influence, which always go beyond words and clear outlines.

5

THE WAY OF BEAUTY

I would like to suggest two special ways of developing religious education in the audiovisual age: the way of beauty and the symbolic way. Let us look first at the way of beauty.

Orthodox theologian Olivier Clément told me in an interview, "Instead of beginning with what is known as the purgative way, the way of penitence, in order to cleanse oneself of devious and illusory attachments, let's begin with the way of illumination. This way is characterized by a euphoric sense of freedom and human fullness by the grace of God."[1] Triggering divine illumination by means of photos and paintings, music and song, liturgical actions, and audiovisual devices can lead to a rediscovery of the great tradition continued in Eastern Orthodox religious education. It can also deepen our roots in the category of pleasure that is basic to modern people living in a media civilization. What can we say to a generation that is crazy about music and video clips if we are not in tune with their fundamental feelings? One of the most important tasks in education today is to develop religious sensitivity to beauty.

Beauty and Pleasure

I call the "way of beauty" a process that raises us from a passion for human fullness and a recognition of earthly beauties to a search for absolute beauty and fullness. Following it, we move from sensitivity to earthly wonders to fascination with the absolute.

Understanding the concept of beauty is important because the word "beauty" often has an abstract and elitist flavor. The Greeks coined a more suitable word, combining the good and the beautiful: *kalokagothia*. And Plato declared, "Beauty makes truth splendid." Beauty is what gives fullness to people. People are beautiful when their appearances emphasize the depths of their being.

Three successive discoveries have disclosed my sense of beauty. I owe the first two, above all, to my association with people living in southern Europe, the East, and the Third World. For the third discovery, I am indebted to young people.

In Corsica I first discovered that beauty was not so much an affair of the eye as one concerning the whole person. I saw a number of old people sitting quite motionless under a tree, facing a mountain range. At first I thought they were contemplating the beauty of the landscape. But when I questioned them, they did not say, "Oh yes, it is beautiful," but "We feel good here." This was quite an important difference! I said to them, "Your village is beautiful!" and they replied, "Do you feel good in our village?"

Because of these people, I was able to see how narrow, exclusively visual, and cerebral my idea of beauty was. From a notion of beauty as aesthetic satisfaction in looking, I moved to one of a harmonious fulfillment from people. This evolution took a long time, but it has led me to regard beauty as a secret correspondence between people and the environment. What is beautiful is that which gives being and fullness to a person. In that sense, there is no beauty like that of an Indian village.

Associating with the most deprived people in the Third World led me to make another discovery. In many villages, the poorest in Asia or Africa, and on the beaches of Madras, there is a kind of perfect beauty, a harmony, a balance, a whole orientation that is in contact with the absolute. How astonishing it is to find, then, that, in remote corners of Iran, there are old people who are more concerned with roses than with loaves of bread! In the Third World I discovered an idea of beauty that was also radically human and social. In Zaire, for example, a person is only called beautiful if he or she is loved and lovable, and the word "beauty" is not used to describe children. People speak only of "spirit." "Beauty" is used of young people of marriageable age "because their real identity gradually begins to emerge at that age."[2]

By imposing Western models of development, especially industrial development, on the poor, have we not despoiled them of their beauty? For them, the most important values have been the feast, the harmony of the group, and the beauty in the pleasure of simply being. For us, they are comfort, usefulness, function, and yield. In exporting our values, have we not overthrown a process of human development, the signs of which have been beauty and wisdom? What I have learned from the countries of Asia and Africa is that material development was of secondary importance, that beauty was not aestheticism but a kind of human fullness, and that this was the first and most important value.

Finally, young people have taught me that beauty was music rather than image. Two young people from Vermont playing folk music in a restaurant fascinated me by their deep personal involvement in their songs. When I asked them what they thought of doing later, they said, to my enormous surprise, "Expressing God with music. After all, music has been the way for us." These young people subsequently committed themselves to pastoral ministries of animation and liturgy. They were adding their own signature to the words of the Indian musician, Ravi Shankar: "Music is my way to God."

I have had extraordinary experiences of what lies beyond, experiences such as the call of paradise and the glorious body, at rock concerts and, more recently, in viewing some video clips. Music has given me the most ecstatic experience that it is possible to have. With Walkman headphones over my ears, I have become music. Is this the way of foolishness or the way of human fullness? Is it the way of God or the way of Satan? All I know is this: It is a way of the greatest intensity.

Going beyond all that I have learned from these experiences, I would suggest the following definition: Beauty is what accords with the human being's deepest aspirations. It is the life-giving and harmonious arrangement that rouses, restores to peace, and heals. At the deepest level, beauty reveals itself when beings and things follow their path to the distant horizon, in faithfulness to what has given birth to them. Beauty of this kind does not exclude the slums or those who are condemned to death. It is vibrant. It is present in the poetic music of Pablo Neruda and in the eyes of children. It is what Paul called creation groaning in the labor of giving birth. Beauty is an emergence from chaos and an orientation toward a summit. Becoming aware of beauty is accepting that which is orientated toward fullness.

We cannot define beauty without expressing God in one way or another: a source that cannot be grasped, or a way and a homeland for everything that persists and goes forward. Revealing beauty, then, is revealing what underlies beings and things, the essential bonds that bind them together. It is revealing how all things subsist in fruitfulness and in dynamic unity, thanks to the mysterious presence of God the Creator and Savior. The Eastern leaders of the church claimed that in each being, each thing, and every situation there is a "logos of God," in other words, a word, a reason, or a wisdom that God gives us. Discovering beauty is deciphering the word of God that is already there, the word that wants to be realized. The discovery is a kind of contemplation that is really a deciphering of the deepest level of things and a kind of surprised wonderment. Beyond all appearances lies the source, the resurrection, the fullness of the cross that joins earth to heaven and east to west.

The Call of Pleasure

Beauty creates an intimate link between knowledge, emotion, and pleasure. An Italian proverb says that beauty is not what is beautiful but what gives us pleasure. But is it possible to make pleasure a way to God? This sounds "bad" to many people. I think it is impossible, however, to speak of the way of beauty without at the same time speaking of the way of pleasure.

There can be no doubt that Augustine gave his assent to the way of pleasure. His youthful experience convinced him of its dangers, but also of the possibilities of spiritual pleasure:

> I would state firmly: You are only partly drawn by your will. You are more drawn by total pleasure. But what does that mean, being drawn by total pleasure? . . . There is a pleasure of the heart for the one who tastes the sweetness of this bread of heaven. If the poet was able to say, "Each man is drawn by his pleasure, not by necessity, but by pleasure, not by obligation, but by delectation," how much more emphatically ought we to say that—we who are drawn toward Christ, the man who finds his delights in truth, who finds his delights in blessedness, who finds his delights in justice, who finds his delights in eternal life, because Christ is all that! Or ought we to say that our bodily senses have their pleasures and that the soul is deprived of its pleasures?
>
> Give me someone who loves and he will sense the truth of what I am saying. Give me a man tortured by desire. Give me a man tormented by his passions. Give me a man walking in the desert and troubled by thirst, sighing for the source of the eternal homeland. Give me such a man and he will know what I mean![3]

We need not reject pleasure, the total pleasure which Augustine says is a source of revelation. Rather one must pursue the true pleasures. What is meant by pleasure here is the feeling of fullness and satisfaction connected with the fulfillment of a desire that rises up from the depths of our being. The deeper that desire, the greater the pleasure will be. When a pleasure is only the consequence of a physical impulse, it may be violent and it will not fulfill a person's being. It will be a blow, not a revelation.

True pleasure consists in releasing that desire and fulfilling it. Modern artists such as Marc Chagall have, like the great mystics, been drawn by the marvelous fullness of pleasure of the kind described in the Song of Songs.

Christian life is itself pleasure in fullness. Even Jesus' crucifixion bears the pleasure of the cross, which is that "there is more joy in giving than in receiving."

Because we are entering the audiovisual age and because we are tired of scientific rationalism and are saturated by "high tech," emotion and pleasure have become the special ways of gaining access to faith. Doctrine and, even more so, ideology can no longer offer that way. Only experiencing the pleasure of being Christian can accomplish faith. The key to religious education is, first and foremost, offering people places and times where they can have a spiritual experience with a taste of paradise. Christianity has to begin with a leap into paradise, for its beauty is a pleasure that is paradisiacal and absolute.

Sensing the pleasure of beauty is becoming aware of the mysterious relationship that exists between beings, things, and the aspirations that God's image has placed within them. I have provided below a number of analyses of how a revelation of this kind can take place. Acknowledging their inadequacies, I have provided them simply for the purpose of justification and explanation. But revelation usually follows different paths and, in particular, that of the "awakener." In this matter more than in any other, the religious educator cannot simply be a teacher, but must awaken beauty. The religious educator must be a "seer of the flesh," one who is passionate about quality and who appreciates nuances, not because of an acquaintance with the different schools of painting but because of a deep personal sensitivity to the harmony of lines, the tension between objects, the delicate light and shade of colors, the placing and the movement of forms, the trembling of life, and the wick that is still smoking. The only one who can arouse others to beauty is the one who is beautiful and maintains this beauty, not with the beauty of salons but with the beauty that shines on the wrinkled skin of some older people when they are faithful to life and their eyes are looking elsewhere.

SOUNDS AND IMAGES REVEALING GOD

The Line of Research

How can this fundamental beauty that will open the doors and give us a glimpse of the absolute be perceived in sounds and images? What is it that gives sounds and images their ability to reveal the divine and, possibly, even to express Christ? Music, sounds, and images have invaded the world through the fearful power of electronics. What should we choose in our search for God's face?

My thoughts in this matter are based on a very general study of religious art and, even more so, on critical pastoral practice. For more than twenty years, I have worked with educators and, in particular, with Photolangage, a group associated with the collection of illustrations,[4] examining the factors that give a sound or image its ability to arouse or to stimulate faith. I began with a simple intuition that was confirmed by events. In 1967, J. Letartre, a producer working on programs for Radio Canada, asked a camera operator to select ten photos of modern children expressing childhood according to the gospel. Our choice of photos was the same as the camera operator's! There was clearly something in this "coincidence," but what it was exactly, we could not say.

My next step was to take part in sessions in different countries where we distributed questionnaires and then evaluated the replies. I would show a group of people twenty photos preselected on the basis of my intuition and my experience as a religious educator. The people were invited to look closely at each photo and then to list the photos that pleased them most and least. They then had to write captions for these photos. Their responses were studied and contrasted with the reactions of artists or audiovisual specialists. A number of principles were formulated from the conclusions drawn. Initially we felt that these principles would be given a certain light and shade by the culture of each country and their local differences. The conclusions, however, revealed a genuine consensus with regard to general principles.

FUNDAMENTAL DISTINCTIONS

Denotation and Connotation, the Religious and the Christian

At the beginning of our research, it became obvious that we had to maintain a clear distinction between the objectively religious document and that document which, while perhaps profane, was filled with religious connotations or could stimulate faith. The cross and the crib, for example, are religious images. The "Salve Regina" or Bach's chorale, "Jesu Joy of Man's Desiring," are religious music in themselves. These images and this music are linked objectively to an event, a person, a story, or an object that refers to religion as a known social or historical fact.[5]

The image of the sun setting over the mountains is quite different. It has no definite and objective link with Christian revelation. What, then, are we to make of the fifteen-year-old who covered the bedroom walls with sunset wallpaper, saying, "It gives me a good feeling"? "It makes me feel warm. It makes me dream of infinity, and sometimes it makes me think of God." Another, who danced several times a day to rock music, told me, "Life is soon over. I want something that lasts."

There are religious connotations in both of these cases.[6] The subjects, seeing or hearing these images or sounds, are led in the direction of a religious experience of what lies beyond. According to our research criteria, when a profane document has a religious connotation to at least fifty percent of a population sample, we consider that document capable of awakening or stimulating religion or faith in that population group.

But behind the distinction between the religious document and the document with a religious connotation there is a fundamental question: What is meant by "religious"? And is it enough that an image has a religious connotation for it to be called Christian? From these questions a further distinction emerges, which ought to illuminate the whole of our thought about this matter: There is religion and there is faith, and they are not identical. There is the document with a religious connotation, such as the sunset wallpaper, and there is the document that is able to awaken or stimulate faith and that leads us in some way to Jesus and his attitude.

The religious connotation has been defined in terms of Jungian symbolism. In that sense, it is the transcendent dimension of which the user is aware beyond the material and pragmatic denotation of a reality or a document.[7]

A man is praying in the square in Madras. He is facing the ocean. His hands are raised in an attitude of adoration. "I love this place because of its peace and its immensity," he says. "I am not praying to the ocean, but to the great God. I am almost blind and I am praying: 'Take me, Lord, take me.' " This man is moved by the enormous mass of the waves to look forward to the calmness of death. Behind and beyond the ocean, he has an intuition of God, a sense of absolute peace and rebirth. What he sees and experiences takes on a religious dimension, not because God is objectively in the ocean waves but because his soul bears the imprint of God and he experiences everything in accordance with that imprint. Reading between the lines of pure text, his soul sees God in the ocean.

THE INGREDIENTS OF
WHAT IS "RELIGIOUS"

According to people's feelings and the time and culture in which they are living, their awareness of the religious dimension can take many different forms:

1. An awareness or an intuition of a mystery that gives a fundamental impetus to realities, a mystery that impresses itself on humanity, even though we are unable to grasp it or make it our own by knowing it—a mystery beautifully expressed in Rembrandt's paintings or in Carl Dreyer's or Ingmar Bergman's films.
2. An awareness or an intuition of a source inherent in the whole of life and in every expression of mortality; there are eyes that go beyond eyes.
3. A feeling of a "supernatural" power of salvation, healing, forgiveness, and being put back on course. Some forms of African music, some tones of voice, and some vibrant colors have this power of healing.
4. An intuition of a perfect, stable, and absolute order, which is the foundation of and the model for all our fleeting earthly orders.
5. An awareness of a moral necessity that impresses itself on us as an absolute and is linked to human dignity, a necessity without which nothing can last, a necessity that goes far beyond the law and is expressed in such concepts as uprightness, faithfulness to oneself, justice, peace, and self-sacrificing love.

In the context that we are considering here, the religious dimension cannot be limited to the traditional concept of God. Whenever a person is led by listening to music or seeing a film to ask questions about the meaning of life or the basis of morality, the words "religious dimension" are brought to mind. Where is my love going? Why should I tire myself by sitting at the bedside of a sick or dying person? How can we tolerate the injustices or the material disorder of the Western world? Questions like these have a religious dimension that goes beyond the pragmatism of here and now.

One of the most successful photos in the Photolangage collection was a rather poor one of interweaving rails (see page 118). The reaction of at least eighty percent of those who viewed this photo testified to an interest in the meaning of life. Because of this reaction, I overcame my hesitations about the aesthetic quality of this document and decided to include it in this book. No one reacted to it by speaking about the functioning of the railway network or trains. Everyone spoke about the directions taken by life, the mystery of human destiny, the difficulties experienced in committing oneself, or fear of the future.

But Jesus Christ is of an entirely different order. He is the salt of the earth, and first and foremost the salt of religion. He is the sharp point that stimulates religion, gives it a precise definition, and challenges it. Religion

The rails. Photolangage collection. Used by permission of Société Nationale des Chemins de fer Français.

is the ocean, whereas faith is Christ crucified. Religion is the circle of stars turning around the pole star. Faith is Jesus washing his disciples' feet.

An image that arouses and stimulates faith will be religious, and it has been shown again and again that, without that fundamental dimension, every Christian image would be pale, neutral, or powerless. But the Christian image has to be more than just religious. If we are really educators for whom Jesus is everything, then we have to try to define this "more" as precisely as we can.

THE RELIGIOUS DIMENSION

According to Saint Basil, if we are able to admire the order and the harmony of the heavens, we shall come to the gospel as listeners prepared to hear the word. Christian faith cannot be built without that openness of heart that creates a refined religious sense. That is undoubtedly the essential virtue of music or an image with a religious connotation—not that it corresponds to the word, but that it disposes us to hear the word.

The most important effect of the sacred is its creation of an inner silence. When everything has come to an end, we are taken to the essential. The fragility of our being turns toward the burning bush: Take off your shoes—"I am" is there and all the rest is unimportant. All the great saints and masters of the spiritual life stressed the need for silence.[8] But what silence? And how is this silence expressed in sound, music, and images?

Beginners in audiovisual work usually do not know how to keep quiet or how to place silence. They are obsessed with the need to introduce music everywhere. A good audiovisual religious program allows the peak moments to be reinforced by silence. That silence is not a void or a lack, but an intense moment in which the word penetrates into the most intimate depths of our being, a moment in which "the word is made flesh." It is not accidental that the Roman Catholic church should celebrate the moment of Jesus' incarnation in the silence of midnight. When the Credo used to be sung in Latin in the preconciliar liturgy, the solemn moment of the "Et incarnatus est" was marked by a slowing down, a lowering of the voice, and a genuflection.

The meaning of silence is the union it creates of the word and the depths of a person's being. It is, therefore, a form of language: "Every word is born of silence and returns to that silence. Language is the union of words and silence."[9] There is no silence without the word. Silence is opening oneself to someone who is speaking. Like the word, silence can be deep or shallow. What characterizes the religious document is that it silences in man everything that is superficial and worldly, creating a radical silence that opens the way to the essential word. The reverse of silence is the modern sin of being completely "outside."

The images of statues of the Buddha, especially those found in Thailand or Burma, are a marvelous example of a religious image effecting a radical, meditative silence in the attentive viewer. They do this by means of totally harmonious forms, depiction of a gaze that seems to be directed nowhere, the predominance of circular lines ending in an invisible point, and a deeply stable basis. The regular striking of the gong by the Buddhist monk standing close to the statue is a highly developed technique to enable humanity to penetrate the religious universe. The regularity and the reverberation of the same sound permits a penetration of one's inner depths. The effect is like that of a road becoming lost on the horizon, moving from width to an apex, and from breadth to sharpness.

It is significant that Jesus never used the marketplace as the setting of a parable. He chose a banquet but he did not choose a market center, because that is a place where communications are superficial, a place of appearances and not of being. It is in the marketplace that the Pharisees would draw attention to themselves. The banquet could be the parable of the kingdom because of the mutual service, the recognition of God's gifts, the mutual appreciation of the guests for each other, the shared joy that creates an appetite for another joy. The word of the meal is rooted in the silence of welcome, whereas the word of the marketplace is chatter.

In his work *The Sacred*,[10] R. Otto concluded that Western art has essentially two "negative" ways of expressing the sacred: darkness and silence. We are now on the threshold of a civilization of multiple media and are bound to denounce the terrible misunderstanding in which a multitude of sounds, words, and images are confused with communication. Never before have we suffered as we do today from a pollution of information. Our atmosphere is contaminated with such a surfeit that people are no longer capable of receiving information. Introducing the religious into our modern world is, above all, reintroducing silence into communication. In audiovisual terms, this means finding religious documents that will help a person to enter into his or her innermost depths when someone is speaking.

What is the first effect of the sacred? It is, in a sense, to cut off our breath. An image that produces this effect would be the temptation of Saint Antony in the desert, as depicted by Salvador Dali: On one side is a bombastic procession of threatening animals, half horses and half camels with spider's feet, ridden by temptation figures of silver and flesh; on the other side is a small, naked, prostrate Antony, raising a ridiculous crucifix, and the first animal, horribly overcome. Fascinated by this picture, I enter into silence. This image is my story: power overcome by weakness. Whether or not one finds Dali and his work agreeable, one cannot deny that his painting expresses that transcendental power of the spiritual, confronted with which one is left without words.

Expressions of the Religious:
Transparence

After studying documents concerned with various religions and discovering the constant landmarks of contemporary religious audiovisual language, I noted five significant shared characteristics: (1) transparence, (2) the effect of eternity, (3) the effect of inaccessibility, (4) order and beauty, and (5) the effect of breakdown and death.

The first characteristic of the religious document that makes us open to silence is transparence—a transparence that is revealed above all in the effects of vibration and reverberation. In fact, the term "transparence" is inadequate. One might speak instead of "transvibration" or "transspirit." Here, *transparence* means *the ability of a body to let the reality that is behind it appear clearly and intensely.* Such transparence can be seen in the eyes of a saint who reveals the ineffable; in Michelangelo's *Moses*, which reveals the spiritual genius of the prophet; or in oriental icons that stir the soul.

Religious transparence depends on two qualities:

1. The quality of the reality of the document, that which lies behind it—God or Satan.
2. The quality of the object and/or the being that makes the essence show through—the artist and his work, the preacher and his word.

When Jesus said, "Blessed are the pure in heart, for they shall see God" (Matt. 5:8), he was speaking of the transparence of simple beings, without compromise or deviation. In them, God presents his image without a veil.

Marcel Brisebois, a religious broadcaster in Canada, told me, "Before any interview in depth, I stand at a distance and am silent for at least ten minutes . . . to be completely available to the grace of the other person. This is, for me, a condition of the validity of the interview. Otherwise, the interview may be artificial, full of padding." Jim McLaren of the Australian radio service said the same thing: "I pray before each of my programs. If I have God's grace, the listeners will hear it in my voice."

Of course, this transparence may result in comedy, which is, after all, vibrating in tune with oneself. Television strips the personality and radio strips the voice so bare that it is not possible to lie or deceive for very long. What is there physically and in human experience in the voice of Brisebois or McLaren that makes it possible for us to detect there a state of grace? The state of grace or transparence in their voices is marked, above all, by a kind of vibration.

In the human voice, this vibration of the vocal chords comes not so much from the head as from the pit of the stomach. The "religious" voice is not one that is trying to convince, but one that is inhabited. It is not one that is calling out for followers, but one that is vibrant with powerlessness in the presence of the inexpressible that is urging it on.

In his book on the anthropology of the gesture,[11] Marcel Jousse has stressed the importance of the voice and its connection with the throat: "The throat is the most expressive center of all the expressive mechanisms of *anthropos.*" He also points out that, in the beginning, man received into his nostrils the breath that "irradiated and aroused his *naphsha*-throat and made it a living, speaking, and melodious throat." The people of Palestine, Jousse says, believed that "human life is centered and concentrated in this *naphsha*-throat, which is a term that cannot be translated and is badly translated by our word 'soul.' For the Jews, the 'soul' is the voice, the vibration of the vocal chords."

An interviewer on Radio Canada was asked by a bishop who were the most difficult people to interview. The interviewer replied, "Politicians and church leaders. They always say what they are expected to say, not what they really think." Do you speak in your voice, or does a political party? Is it you, or is it the spirit of Christ in you? Is it you, or is it formulas of the church that speak? You are religious when the spirit of God makes you vibrate. You are only an ecclesiastic if you are repeating formulas.

The religious document is the one that makes the depths of a person's soul shine through, the breath that comes from God, and does not simply try to convince rationally or influence a person's will. Professional teachers and intellectuals for the most part make a bad impression on television or radio, not because they are bad speakers but because they speak from the head. They do not give themselves to the people listening and watching but remain behind the barricades of their own perfect construction. The same can be said of many politicians, because they have the type of vibration that comes from the will to power. They claim to speak in the name of the people, but in fact they usually speak in the name of party policy. Vibrating in the breath of the spirit is having a quality of vibration, characterized by its discretion (affective control), its interiority (the breath coming from the depths of the body), its rhythm (a revelation of peace, harmony, and freedom), and its amplitude (fullness).

The objection is frequently raised that we have no control over our voices, because each one of us has the voice that nature has given. Experience of training sessions has taught me that the problem is not primarily concerned with the quality of our vocal organ; it has to do above all with the technical and spiritual training of the human voice. We can be taught how to recognize the "breath" (the spirit) that animates us and we can learn how to be physically faithful to that breath. It is not so much a question of changing one's voice as of releasing it, so that it is free to vibrate authentically. There is also a problem of knowing how to record and amplify one's voice correctly.[12]

Reverberation

Certain musical instruments have been traditionally associated with religion. Organs, bells, and gongs are among the best known of these. The harp and the cithern are also mentioned in the Bible. But why has the organ always been preferred to the piano? There are many reasons for this. The organ has greater fullness and depth and a greater range than the piano; but, above all, it is able to create a profound effect of vibration and reverberation. Like the gong, the organ has an undefined resonance that can be compared to the concentric circles produced by a stone thrown onto the surface of a calm lake. "If you want to create a religious effect," a sound-effects expert told me, "use reverberation. It gives the impression of being in a cathedral." Why, then, were reverberating acoustics cultivated in so many cathedrals and monastic churches? Why is God given a re-sounding, echoing voice on so many discs and in so many films? Before examining reverberation, we should remember that, in audiovisual language, the message is in the effect produced.

By "reverberation" I mean a prolonging of the sound, created through reflection or repercussion. Pushed beyond its limits, reverberation becomes echo. The effect produced by this prolonged vibration has some kind of link with the religious or the transcendent. The listener has a strange feeling of being surrounded by sound, without knowing clearly where it comes from; a feeling of an indefinite continuity of the sound, which leads toward an elsewhere. The effect is one of a voice sent back to us to lead us to our innermost selves.

Behind the vibration of sound in the pipes of an organ, there is a column of air. Jesus is being extremely audiovisual when he says of the spirit, "You hear the sound of it, but you do not know whence it comes or whither it goes" (John 3:8). The "religious" is precisely what cannot be grasped, whether behind, in front, or beyond. Anyone carried along by the echo of a gong or a bell will go on a journey from one vibration to the next and toward the infinite. Many traditional Indian songs are based on techniques of reverberation that awaken the spiritual element. The singer's voice vibrates with increasing fineness, goes deeper and deeper into a tunnel, and then travels beyond it toward an inaccessible point.

In the Christian tradition, Saint Bernard had the most profound intuitions regarding the importance of sound. With the help of his architect, he discovered the most suitable kind of reverberation for training the human ear to listen to God's voice. The result is that the churches he built resound extraordinarily well to Gregorian chant. In fact, winding crevices whose function was for years impossible to explain were built to correct the acoustics in these churches. Bernard himself declared that the singing of his monks had to resound in three vaults: the vault or roof of the mouth, the vault of heaven, and the vault of the church. This reverberation gives the human voice a depth, a seriousness, and a mark of eternity which make it the voice of Christ.[13]

The Image and the Stained-Glass Window

What I have just said about sound also applies to the image. The stained-glass window belongs essentially to the religious tradition, and above all it demonstrates translucence. It vibrates with the sun's rays. There can be no better example than "The Veronica" at Rouault, embedded in thick glass (see page 126). It is full of striking contrasts: the deep blue; the point of red surrounded by the coarse lead; the lengthened face from which two immense eyes shine, black and white and vibrating in the light, reflecting a deep mystery of compassion that the viewer can never fully fathom.

Filmmaker Carl Dreyer's statement is very relevant in this context: "Mimicry and contrast are the two fundamental ways of expressing the soul." Mimicry is the spirit vibrating in the body. The "religious" photographer looks for this mimicry above all. It is the luminous point in the darkness of the eye, the intensity of gesture when the person is suddenly without a mask and mundanity. It can also be found in the eyes of little children and the poor, expressing the beatitude of those who are pure in heart (see page 127).

All great religious images can be traced from an art form dependent upon the vibration of light or a "reverberation" of what cannot be expressed beneath the surface of matter. This can be seen in works by Rembrandt and even more, perhaps, in the icons of the Middle East, in which the inner light that is unique to each being emerges from the painting. But the principles of the great works of art in the past can also be found today, even though the techniques employed may be different. "What I look for in my films and what I try to obtain from my actors," Dreyer declared, "is the penetration of their thoughts by means of their most subtle expressions."[14]

Dreyer used the term "abstraction" to account for his art, which described "the interior rather than the exterior aspect of life." By abstraction he meant a removal of everything from the reality that did not belong to a gesture or an expression, which had the spiritual at its source. Vibration, reverberation, and abstraction of everything that is mundane all point to the transparence of pure hearts.

The African Contrast

Another form of transparence and vibration can be found in the contrast between black and white or between opaqueness and light. The paintings of Paul Klee show how gray, which is halfway between black and white and a mixture of the two, produces a lukewarm and banal effect, whereas the opposition and the mutual attraction of black and white produce an effect of the movement of life. Both Western and Asian religious art have emphasized at times chiaroscuro, which is a use of light and dark to contrast. African art, on the other hand, is marked by a violent contrast between the thick rays of the sun and the vigorous line of a statue or a mask. Although the climate and culture of Africa are different, the principle remains the same; but what shines through African art is the violent light of life, a life that is clearly victorious over the powers of death. African statues, with their living lines, are also in harmony with the rhythms and the dances of the religions of life.

Sacred images preeminently depict fertility, parenthood, and salvation or the restoration of health. "The tree has no symbolic value for me," a young person from Burkina Faso in West Africa told me. "It is there for its wood, and its wood is for heating. God is life. And life is dancing, the tom-tom, the full moon, the vibrant light of the sun." Dancing to the violent rhythm of percussion instruments under the burning sun or in a night of cosmic proportions, Africans are aware of the breath of the spirit and seize hold of the powers of life.

The Effect of Eternity

André Malraux said that the first mark of the supernatural is the imprint of eternity. Ancient Egyptian or Far Eastern statues bear this mark of eternity; the god is not worn away by time. The face of the god has a lasting value.[15]

The most primitive sacred image has this mark of eternity. God is the pole star, the fixed point in the sky. "I am constant as the northern star," Julius Caesar remarks in Shakespeare's play. This lasting, ageless quality is expressed in three ways: hieraticism; a perfect harmony of forms, which illustrates a perfection without a beginning or an end (in circles, for example); and a motionlessness of characteristics and gestures, which leads the viewer to the central point, the hub of the wheel.

The etymological meaning of "hieraticism" is "what belongs to the sacred or to the order of priests." The essential characteristics of this style are the absence of movement or a certain fixity, and an idealization of forms. Hieraticism's rigidity indicates a reality that is present, given, and established. Nothing is left to chance or to fantasy; God is not baroque. The beauty of such work is timeless. Jesus, however, challenged this fixity. Despite his challenge, every great religious expression of Jesus is rooted in the stability of the one who is. The eternal religious aspect of Jesus underlies the man Jesus, and the artist's composition goes back clearly to a perfect form.

Veronica by Georges Rouault. Used by permission of the Rouault family.

Indian child in a Bombay slum. The luminous spots in her eyes, her pouting expression, and her hair tossed by the wind all reverberate with a sense of an "elsewhere," a beyond. Photo P. Babin.

One of the finest examples of hieraticism, one that never fails to disturb us, is the shroud of Turin. We have all seen television films of the extraordinary face of a crucified man resting in supernatural peace. Science denies that the face is actually that of Jesus. But looking at the holy shroud, particularly under the radiation effect produced by television, I am quite spellbound. I feel I am looking at the face of Jesus, the man whom I seek in the depths of my being, the eternal one who was humiliated, the righteous one who was crucified, and who was hieratic and peaceful.

Religious music, particularly Gregorian chants, is also open to the effect of eternity. Its seriousness, its flowing rhythm, its rounded phrases, its held notes, and its gentle pauses all help to evoke the eternal and give the impression of the sacred. We should also note the sacred form of the big chorales, which are both strong and varied. Plainsong has recently become popular again in the Roman Catholic church. Young people naturally prefer singing what is familiar to them, but they also clearly like to join in the monastic offices.

It is worth pausing here to consider the songs sung at Taizé. They are symptomatic of a change in young people's taste in music and bear the imprint of a great power of interiority and peace. Many of them are in Latin. This is a clear sign of a need to go back to the church's roots and to a language that is outside time, transcending national frontiers. It is also a sign that rugged, primitive language is emphasized in the audiovisual world. Resonance becomes an essential element. In the end, it does not matter very much what is sung, so long as it "sounds all right." The Latin words resound, but what is even more important is that the songs sung at Taizé are songs that lead to the silence and the peace of God. They act like a mantra or canon.

These trends toward plainsong and a renewed use of Latin are indicative of a large need in the whole church for religious singing, for images and music that do not make sacrifices to the idols of the present age. There are modern alleluias and religious songs that are pale copies of rock and pop music. Musicians make their fingers sore on guitars and strain their lungs on wind instruments, only to produce false effects and very unconvincing sounds. The same criticism can be made of so many religious images and posters: they are soulless stereotypes, achieving overlapping effects, or simply ornaments or embellishments. They do not reflect the eternal.

We should try to keep fullness, transparence, and eternity in view as our ideals. Cheerful popular songs and posters are needed as a way to reach, by stages at least, the religious and the Christian quality. To reach this quality, we should follow the tradition of our older churches, where posters and magazine advertisements are often found outside, in the darkness of the porch, so that we pass these stages and approach the inaccessible that resides inside the church.

The Effect of Inaccessibility

Paul speaks of a God who "dwells in unapproachable light" (1 Tim. 6:16). Hidden in a cleft of the rock, Moses saw God only from behind:

"You cannot see my face; for man shall not see me and live" (Exod. 33:20). These biblical statements bear witness to the earliest expression of the sacred. The most common way of expressing the sacred is to create an effect of inaccessibility, emphasizing the distance between God and the believer.

God is presented as being elsewhere, infinitely distant. Solomon's temple was the architectural expression of this. Before one could penetrate into the holy of holies, one had to pass through countless walls, barriers, defenses, and enclosures. One had to be purified many times and many days had to pass. The high priest was the only one who was permitted to enter, and then only once each year. Another example of the god's inaccessibility is found in the mosque at Mecca, the sacred stone that is the goal of Moslem pilgrimage. There is also the Christian sanctuary in the valley of Los Caidos in Spain, which Franco had hollowed out of the mountainside.

The best example of the central principle's inaccessibility may be the Indian temple at Kanchipuram. To reach it, one has to go hundreds of yards, cross watercourses, and walk along dark paths flanked by pillars resembling trees, until one at last catches sight of the chapel from which the god's eyes gleam out of the darkness. There one is told, "Take off your shoes. Be silent. Do not take photos." This distance is material, created by the landscaping and a wealth of gold. But it is also created by age. There is a tree that is at least thirty-five hundred years old in the center of this temple. Above all, the sense of distance is created by darkness. Approaching the divine in Kanchipuram is leaving the light outside and going toward darkness. The most sacred place of all is a three-dimensional chiaroscuro, a misty darkness filled with tiny drops of light. All these distances, however they are created, say the same thing: "You cannot see. You cannot hold this. You cannot keep it. You cannot possess God. You can only adore God."

Audiovisual practice allows us to enter this sacred atmosphere. It is symptomatic of a change in religious attitude that, since the 1950s when churches were stripped bare, built of concrete, filled with anonymous chairs rather than pews, and made bright and cold with harsh electric light, young people have been returning to dark places of prayer, warm lights and flickering candles, stalls, and hangings. They are looking for intimacy and escape. They may also be looking for God in faithfulness to the demands of their bodies and their feelings.

Order and Beauty

A young Japanese woman was going up a mountain with a party of young people. When they reached a lake she said to the group leader, "It is so beautiful I would like to die!" Everything that expresses a higher order, perfect harmony, and beauty that transcends the imagination bears witness to a truth and a fullness in which we would like to lose ourselves and forget the burden of our earthly difficulties. Like this young woman experiencing the beauty of the mountain lake, we too, from time to time, tremble in the presence of the inexpressible beauty of the planets or the astonishing organization of microorganisms revealed to us by modern electronic instruments; or we may stand in simple admiration before a flower or a shell with its delicate lines. At such times, we have a sense of the sacred.

Young people, more than others, are conscious of the sacred. They find it in songs such as the theme from *Chariots of Fire*, in posters of the spotless perfection of Mount Fujiyama, or in photos of the effects of the enormous sun. They also know that the sacred emerges from things made by people. As the aircraft designer Marcel Dassault said, "Everything that goes well is beautiful."

Why was director Franco Zeffirelli's film about Jesus so successful throughout the world? Every image in it was a work of art. The formal beauty of the actors, their gestures, and the scenes in which they appeared were intimately connected with the unconscious desires of the universal imagination. The gospel was not the only thing that inspired Zeffirelli; he was also inspired by a visionary who saw the whole of Jesus' life in her imagination.

Peter Berger has pointed to another aspect of this reality. If it is to be religious, a document or an atmosphere has to convey a sense of order and stability—almost a sense of necessity—giving rise to a feeling of security. God is what underlies the power to move things. This sense of an order can, of course, be the justification for a permanent state of unacceptable injustice, but that is not the divine order as revealed by Jesus. His order is concerned not with the forms assumed by cultures and civilizations, but with the values that these forms embody. "Heaven and earth will pass away, but my words will not pass away," Jesus said (Matt. 24:35). The religious document, the photographic or musical composition, and the liturgical setting must all bear witness to the solid foundation given by divine order. Christians know that necessity is more important than fantasy.

In Chapter 7, Mercedes Iannone discusses the importance of the family home as framework for faith. The family home should not be a mess, nor should it be a cozy place filled with gadgets. Similarly, the liturgy should take place within a framework of beauty and greatness. This does not mean wealth and luxury, but it does mean that banal familiarity, free-and-easy attitudes, and a routine and unquestioning acceptance of things as they are must be excluded. There should always be fresh flowers and the home should be regularly cleaned and given extra attention before special feasts. All this helps create a framework to open people's hearts to the one who is beyond all beauty.

The Effect of Breaking Out and Death

The God who is beyond everything does not only make an impression in order and beauty, sacredness and the perfection of forms. It is because God is beyond everything that God's impression also can be found in negation, the state of trance, the boundlessness of the Dionysiac or voodoo cults, and the ecstatic dancing of certain African religions. Our ancestors respected insane people and believed that they uttered oracles from on high. All these forms of expression point to the fact that God lies beyond the limits of our human bodies and reason and transcends the forms and rhythms of our earth. God is not simply the perfect one but is also outside our perfections.

It is possible that, for some young people, negation and violence are a way of life. It may be the way of drugs, the way of radical solutions, the way of death, or even the way of the martyr who gives up everything in a single act. We can interpret this phenomenon by remembering that an extreme solution is required for an extreme evil, and that the only way that violent, marginal, and "insoluble" people may be able to know God is by breaking out, if only into excessive kinds of music. Those who experience these extremes can understand this. Like so many other modern paintings, Pablo Picasso's *Guernica* seems to proclaim a state of being beyond reason and history. In this, it is also an expression of an aspect of God.

All the same, because of its inhuman character and its rejection of human history and patience, this aspect of the divine can only outrage many people and be an exception for them. But Christians should never forget that the God who has mercy on all people is also expressed in these negative and radical forms, so that God may save violent, excessive, or marginal people, and indeed all those who long for the impossible and have an instinct for death.

WAYS OF EXPRESSING THE
CHRISTIAN DIMENSION

The great temptation for the authors of a Christian audiovisual document is to make it simply religious.[16] The sacred is, after all, popular. It is mass media and it sells well.

But there is Jesus.

The relationship between the sacred and faith is often the decisive factor in a drama. The story of Paul at Athens is a good example of this. When he arrived in Athens, he spoke first in the name of religious feeling and about the "unknown God" dwelling in every person. Then people began to listen to him. But, when he went beyond religious people and began to speak of the man Jesus, the man appointed by God and raised from the dead, many of the most religious among them left him (Acts 17:16–34).

The audiovisual document designed to lead to Christian faith those who see and hear it does not condemn or despise the religious element. On the contrary, it is based on it. But it is not reduced to the purely religious level. It goes beyond it and sometimes even challenges it: it is its salt.

Why does this distance exist between religion and Jesus? It exists because, with Christianity, we are no longer in the sphere of the old pagan gods or the world of myths and longings. We are confronted with a God who has entered our history. The Christian document does not confront us with the sun; it brings us face to face with Jesus. It makes us adopt an attitude toward humans: Abraham, Moses, and Jesus. The glowing red disc of the sun may stimulate a longing for the absolute, but the image of Jesus crucified asks people, "Do you agree? Do you believe in me?" and tells people "If you want to be my disciple, take up your cross and follow me." The Christian audiovisual document is one that calls us to conversion and commitment.

The image of the cross and the crucified Christ is a good example of the way in which the religious and the Christian documents overlap. In itself, the cross—as a bare sign—is a universal symbol. It is an archetype of totality. Its lines bring heaven and earth, the high and the low, the West and the East into communication with each other. It is a mandala,[17] something that is found in different forms in all the religions of the world. It is such a natural image that it has become a pendant worn as a decoration. But Jesus was stretched out on this cross and at once, far from being eliminated, this underlying natural symbol became ennobled and stylized. Its features were even exaggerated: the raised ground of Golgotha became a hill and the uplifted cross became a sacred tree on the top of a mountain.

Jesus is the fulfillment of the cross symbol. He is the absolute man raised up on the top of a mountain to unite all people and bring together heaven and earth. The point of intersection on the cross is the crossroads of restored communication. But the one who was crucified is not simply the fulfillment of a myth of universal communication. He is also a "species of God" that cannot be imagined, a "stumbling block" and "folly" (1 Cor. 1:23), the one who did not regard his relationship to God as "a thing to be grasped" but made himself "obedient unto death, even death on a cross" (Phil. 2:6–8).

So the cross of Jesus can no longer be just a gold pendant. It must be a question that astonishes us and summons us to follow the way of conversion and self-surrender in order to change both the world and religion.

Essentially two factors distinguish the Christian from the sacred. The first is that the Christian document always refers to a fact, namely, the historical event of Jesus Christ, in whom we recognize God made flesh. Saint Bernard insisted that, in the education of faith, the eye had to be purified by hearing. This means that the eye is more tied to the imagination or the pagan myth and that it is by the ear that we come to the word. In Hebrew, "word" (*dabhar*) means an event. The ear is less inclined than the eye to imagine what comes from the body, and is more receptive to what comes from outside, to the event, and therefore to the word. The ear is less self-sufficient than the eye.

This distinction inevitably emphasizes the unpredictable, unusual, and nonconformist aspect of the Christian document. It presents a God we cannot imagine, a God excluded from purely rational constructions. Tomorrow that God will put a napkin over his arm and serve us during the banquet in the kingdom. Christ will reveal a different order of things and a different type of priority.

The second way in which the Christian differs from the sacred is that the Christian document takes the person who uses it into a Christian community context. In one way or another, it refers us to a community in which the "new way of life" is made present and immediate. In other words, if it is to be really Christian, a film or audiovisual production must be based on the faith and generosity of Christian groups, and it must call others to the new life of Christian communities.[18]

An example of this is an image that has been very successful in the United States: the image of Jesus laughing (see page 134).[19] An image of this kind expresses a vigorous reaction to a sad and tearful form of Christianity. The image proclaims in a loud voice, "This is the Christ we believe in! This is how we want to be Christians in this world!"

If the Christian image is separated from its context within a historically committed Christian community, it may be severely criticized. We can legitimately respond, "To what evangelical message is this laughing Christ calling me? To laugh? But I do not need Jesus to make me laugh!" It is certainly possible to imagine a religious image of a laughing Jesus, but then the image would also have to call to mind a tense and anxious situation that Jesus transcends by a confident laugh. An image of Jesus asleep on a mat, like any other Jew of his time, would arouse no interest at all. But an image of Jesus asleep in a boat in a storm is interesting because it reveals a power and self-assurance that go beyond humanity's. Jesus in the Temple, laughing at the complicated rituals performed by the priests and the Pharisees—that is "revealing"!

The Laughing Christ.

In other words, the image of a laughing Christ bears the signature of a Christian community. It is an event, a revelation of the spirit acting in that community. Taken out of its context, simply because it is in itself more natural than Christian, it would have little chance of being a revealing event.

The Power of Appeal

What features can be marked out and identified as specifically Christian? As in the case of the religious dimension, five can be distinguished: the power of appeal, the sign of love, interiority, unity of opposites, and scandal.

Let us look first at the power of appeal. The religious document has the task of producing the same effect as Jesus. What, then, was the effect that Jesus had—the first effect on the person who met him on the way? He was obviously a fascinating man, but his personality was so complete and so unique that one who was confronted by him would not spend much time in discussion, but would simply join him or reject him. In this case, the medium and the message are absolutely one and the same.

Jesus was quite the opposite of an everyday, commonplace man. He was not worldly, artificial, or cringing. He was not diplomatic: "Let what you say be simply 'Yes' or 'No' " (Matt. 5:37). He called the Pharisees a "brood of vipers" (Matt. 23:33). The Pharisees themselves told him, "Teacher, we know that you . . . care for no man; for you do not regard the position of men" (Matt. 22:16), and Peter was told by him that he was "a hindrance" (Matt. 16:23).

The first characteristic of a Christian audiovisual document, then, should be that it does not leave us in a state of indifference. Like Jesus himself, it should be a scandal or "stumbling stone" (Rom. 9:32–33). A photo that does not make us react and a piece of music that merely soothes us are not capable of expressing Jesus.

The Christian document is the opposite of what we experience in the great shopping centers of our cities, where everything is displayed to send our minds to sleep and make us spend our money. In those places, there is hypnotic, trance-inducing, dream music. There are multicolored flashing lights and posters and advertising materials presenting us with an artificial paradise.

The Christian document is also the opposite of the nightclub. It is there not to make us forget, but to make us remember. It expresses the first petition in the prayers of Marcel Légaut: "Put us in the presence of ourselves and of God." Nor is the Christian document a drug. It aims to make us decide. It goes further than influencing our unconscious minds and our feelings and is directed toward our consciences: "Follow me." Many of the posters and statues in our churches and many of the illustrations in our religious calendars, as well as a great deal of our sentimental religious music, must therefore be criticized as ecclesiastical cotton candy.

Latin American producers have always insisted that a really good audio-visual product is one that makes the viewers and listeners react. It must be an appeal that is rooted in human ambiguity, a question asked with many different possible answers. What are the distinguishing marks of this appeal? I will confine myself to two: dramatization and vigor.

Dramatization

Dramatization, of course, is one of the key words in audiovisual lan-guage. If one draws a square on a piece of white paper and puts a dot inside the square, nothing happens. But if one puts a second dot quite close to the first, drama has been created—in other words, attraction and/or repulsion. Dramatization is created by the tension between reali-ties. Learning the audiovisual language is, among other things, learning the art of distance. If the distance is too great or too little, there is no vibration, no tension, and no drama.

In journalism, dramatization is the creation of the sensational. Only what is at a distance from the norm is discussed. But Jesus is not sensa-tional. In this sense, he embodies a certain distance and gives rise to drama—a distance, that is, from the worldly norm, the norm of custom or the norm of the Pharisees. Christ's standing at a distance is not of the superman order. It is of the order of the faith that makes all things possi-ble. It is a testimony to the power that is found in weakness. It is shown in resistance to the burden of things and to human hypocrisy.

The audiovisual document is Christian when it dramatizes the distance between the wisdom of the world and the foolishness of the cross. We could say, for example, that Dali's painting of the temptation of Saint Antony is Christian insofar as it reveals the contrast between the flesh and the cross.

Vigor

Another characteristic of the successful audiovisual appeal is vigor in the lines and rhythms, in other words, the firmness of the drawing and the development of the essential. If an expert reacts negatively to an audio-visual document, this is usually because it lacks vigor. "It is flabby," the expert will say, or "It is too nice; spineless; shapeless." All of these adjectives indicate that the appeal is insignificant and lacks energy.

A great deal of singing with guitar accompaniment at services is done listlessly and without precision. Sometimes, on the other hand, the music is quite complicated, and everyone has to go to great lengths to follow a talented leader. A document may also be full of unnecessary images and long, drawn-out phrases. It is better in every case when the singing is simple and repetitive and the document is brief and powerful.

Energy and dramatization do not imply tragedy or violence, even though these may sometimes be expressed. It must also be admitted that the sharp, abrupt, strident, and tense character of some modern pictures or pieces of music does not favor prayer or interiority.

At Taizé, the brother who was responsible for the stained glass told me, "You have to have rounded forms for prayer. You cannot stay long in front of sharp forms." The same could be said of songs or pieces of instrumental music that have violent accentuation or rhythms. It is possible to have recourse to such music in a service from time to time, but we need something else if the word is to penetrate our innermost depths: a force that will lead us to interiority.

The right environment is difficult to create, and it depends on the culture and the age of the image or the music. Think of the contrast between two images, the one a seventeenth-century print with unreal, dull colors, softened lines, and a childlike and euphoric representation of the presence of Christ (see page 138). It is difficult to imagine how it was ever possible for such images to be accepted! Compare this with another image that aroused great interest in the early 1980s. It was based on the idea of a young Canadian member of Parliament who later became a priest, and it was displayed along the highways. Its aim was to stimulate vocations to the priesthood (see page 139). You may like the style or you may not, but you can hardly deny that it is a powerful appeal, demonstrating vigor and dramatization. The fundamental idea is quite clear: you do not encourage vocations by using an affected, delicate, or commonplace style, but by creating a scandal or stumbling block, inviting those who see the image to give everything they have and are.

The Sign of Love

The sign of love is the Christian sign beyond all others, and it might be set against the symbolic system of tonality based on adoration and sacrifice. This sign is expressed in images by a preponderance of relational lines, rounded rather than schizoid forms, an absence of rigidity, warm

Seventeenth-century religious print.
Saulchoir Collection, Seita Museum, Paris.

Poster created by the Toronto Vocations Center for a campaign for vocations to the priesthood. Used by permission of the Archdiocese of Toronto.

colors, and a triumph of the good and the true over the forces of nihilism and destruction. Those who love give to their work, songs, or images a "positive vibration," a warmth, and a hope, all of which bear witness to a fundamental certainty and loving-kindness. They may well depict in their works failure and death, but not without tenderness and trust. The paintings of Chagall in the museum in Nice, for example, express the great dramas of mankind through a biblical fresco.[20]

I have already spoken about inaccessibility as a sign of the sacred, and also that Christ expresses a distance from the norm. It is important to add here that this distance, this "beyondness" of God, is not manifested in Christian terms by coldness, formalism, or aestheticism. The Christian sign of love must always give the architecture and the style of our churches a warm, personal, and welcoming character. It is this "high touch" that Christians today are looking for in their call to make the church a community rather than an institution.

But in the sign of love, perhaps more than anywhere else, forms are relative. In addition to warmth and welcome, love can be expressed by sharp signs, a certain violence, and the abrupt and oppressive character of some kinds of music. It depends on the people, the time, and the place— love can assume a thousand aspects.

The symbols of love in a work by Chagall are obvious from their archetypes and their essential sacredness. There is no doubt that in Christian renewal movements or in base communities in Latin America, the chief source is not the Song of Songs, but the first community described in the Book of Acts, in which there was only one heart and one soul. The signs of common sharing, putting everything to common use, and abolishing racial distinctions around the same table are undoubtedly carriers of the dominant spirit of our times. They are also, without any doubt, much more than the signs of forgiveness which, in the gospel, mark the pinnacle of love.

Interiority

Jesus was never satisfied simply when the crowds joined him. He did not want people just to keep to a doctrine but called them to intimate inner conversion—where God "sees in secret." He bore witness to interiority and called us to interiority. But what is that interiority and how is it manifested? This question can best be answered by comparing two images that illustrate two types of interiority (see pages 142 and 143).

In the first image (page 142), we do not know where the Buddha's eyes are looking. He is looking inside himself. The Buddha—at least the Buddha of the great tradition of Burma and Thailand—should be viewed from below; then his eyes appear fully, but they look at us without seeing us. Both the hieratical attitude of the Buddha and his gaze bear witness to his perfect stability. He is illuminated, totally balanced and unified, and totally transparent to his source, which is within himself. He is coincidental with his own mystery. This is certainly a perfect interiority, but it is outside time and history.

In the second image (page 143), Jesus' eyes, like the Buddha's in the first image, are wide open, but they look straight at us and we are troubled and fascinated by these eyes. On the other hand, unlike the body of the Buddha, Jesus' is a risen body. It has an aerial quality. Its harmony and its fineness reveal the perfect transparence of the spirit. The risen Christ is elsewhere. His clothing has a cosmic scope. But he continues to be historical and his eyes are sending the great procession of people toward the kingdom.

Interiority means that one is led by the intimate necessities within oneself. Its source is within, not in laws or social pressures or even in superficial instincts, but in the deepest movement of the person. There can be no doubt that the Buddha expresses this interiority, but the source that animates him seems to coincide only with himself. Christ's interiority, on the other hand, is different. Someone is present behind his eyes. That "someone" is God. And before his eyes are men and women. It is to this interiority that the Christian audiovisual document bears witness, by authenticity and creation.

What affects our hearts and inspires us to react spiritually in the Christian document are its authenticity and the authenticity of its authors. We can only express well what we allow to happen in ourselves by a humble and generous effort. The icon painter must be converted while painting the icon. Truth in mimicry, restrained emotional vibration, being reduced to bare essentials, the suppression of excessive verbosity or all artificial emphasis, simplicity as far as being stripped bare, and total honesty of expression all describe the main forms of authenticity.

Another characteristic of interiority is creation. This is the ability to form new connections determined by the most intimate aspect of a person's being.

In any production, what touches the heart is an encounter with the author: an encounter, in other words, not with a formal work but with the person behind the work. We react when we are surprised by the image and we find something unexpected in the text. At the New York International Fair, Protestant churches showed a little film—a "parable"—and the hall was always packed. The clown dressed in white was different from clowns that people were accustomed to seeing at a fair. It was a creation and the work of an author.[21]

Only superficial beings are captivated by those technical gadgets that are obviously quite artificial: fish-eye lens photos, electronic echoes, and other similar effects. They may be necessary in a variety show, but they are the wrong way of expressing God! If God is the creator, then God is expressed above all in "creation." Electronic devices and fake effects may be splendid in this context in the hands of a creator, but not in those of a conjurer.

We who work with young people in the production of religious audiovisual material have always been prepared to experiment over and over again with the same image. There was, for example, a young woman who wanted to express prayer in secret. "I could have drawn a religious image," she told me, "but your demands put me under pressure. So I began to pray. I saw myself sitting on the ground in the corner of a great empty room." This girl drew repeatedly until she had succeeded in producing the effect that revealed both her fear and her smallness in the world, and the power of her inner secret. In the end, she knew she had created something. She had entered into a spiritual mystery, and she was happy to speak about it.

The face of a Thai Buddha.

The Unity of Opposites

French mathematician and philosopher Blaise Pascal wrote:

> I do not admire the excess of a virtue . . . if I cannot at the same time see the excess of the opposite virtue, as in Epaminondas, who had extreme worth and extreme kindness. Otherwise, it is not going up, but falling down. We do not show our greatness by being at an extremity, but by touching both at the same time and filling the space between them.[22]

This can be applied both to Jesus and to the Christian actor. The ability to express greatness in terms of poverty, the flexibility of a face that is both authoritarian and gentle, the balance between violence and tenderness—all these contrasts are the test of a Christian work. Jesus is himself a contrast and, in that sense, he eludes our grasp. He is the opposite of an ideology in which everything begins with a point of view and then follows logically. He is the opposite of an ideology that always tells us the same thing.

"Christ the Pantocrator" of the Romanesque period. Monks' Chapel, Berzé-la-Ville.

Interviewing Mother Teresa, I was forcibly struck by the unpredictability of her replies. They departed from the accepted views. I took photos of her and showed them to my students, and asked, "Who is Mother Teresa?" In one, where her nose resembled an eagle's beak, she appeared authoritarian. She cannot be easygoing all the time! In another, where she looked tired and dreamy, her eyes appeared lost in infinity. In another, where she held a child, she was very tender, and in yet another she was tight-lipped and suddenly anxious. In one she sat on the ground in the midst of her sisters, listening like a disciple, and in another she seemed to say, with a kind of radical conviction, "Jesus is our secret." Her face is mobile and reveals a freedom and a range of feelings that go far beyond the hieraticism of the sacred. It shows "life in abundance," a life not hemmed in by theories of direction and the apostolate. Mother Teresa is entirely suited for photographs and the screen because she is totally herself, unpredictable and free. At the same time, she is also anti-mass media, because she will not conform blindly to the system's codes and constraints.

"If the salt has lost its taste, how shall its saltness be restored?" (Matt. 5:13). The unity of opposites may be, in an audiovisual document, what reveals this "salt" most clearly: the salt that is Jesus' freedom of spirit, what belongs specifically to the Son of man. A Latin American feminist movement was responsible for this slogan: Revolutionaries of every country— who will wash your socks? Jesus the revolutionary washed his disciples' feet. He commanded the storm and died on the cross.

Scandal

The French Roman Catholic bishops' communications commission brought out for Social Communications Day a poster showing Christ on a Peruvian cross, almost stripped of flesh and quite horrible to see (see page 145). Many people were deeply scandalized and protested, "They have no right to show that poster. It is not a picture of Christ. It is a frog." In saying that, they probably did not realize they were paraphrasing a text from Isaiah:

> He had no form or comeliness that we should look at him,
> and no beauty that we should desire him. . . .
> a man of sorrows, and acquainted with grief;
> and as one from whom men hide their faces . . . ,
> like a lamb that is led to the slaughter. (Isa. 53:2–3, 7)

In other words, Christ does not conform to the laws of beauty promulgated by the mass media. He does not have that kind of beauty. Sometimes he has the kind of beauty that makes us want to cover our faces.

The Christian scandal corresponds, I think, to that effect of breakdown and death that we have noted in the religious dimension, but with this difference: that what we have here is not a need to go beyond the limits, but a man, the man-God, historically humiliated and disfigured by the world, a man with "no form or comeliness" and "no beauty," who "has borne our griefs and carried our sorrows" (Isa. 53:4). The Peruvian Christ embodies the suffering of a people tortured in prison and disfigured by sickness, the people the media hide from us.

The Christian document cannot hide this scandal from us. A child certainly needs time to learn about the scandal of the cross, just as the disciples began with Jesus not at Golgotha but in the Galilean springtime.

The horror of Christ crucified does not always have to be the letter heading, nor does it have to fill the entire letter containing the Christian message. Our faith is above all in the risen Christ. But it is impossible to avoid the reality of the crucifixion. It is even impossible to avoid putting it at the center of our expression as the most deeply hidden mystery of Christianity and—in the last resort—its most deeply fascinating aspect.

The Peruvian Christ. Published by Chrétiens-Médias for Social Communications Day.

Art and beauty are not specialties or compartments separate from the communication of faith; they are an essential dimension of it. This is particularly true today. "Beauty is a logic that is perceived as a pleasure."[23] God makes himself known to the present music and television generation by the joy of being.[24]

6

THE SYMBOLIC WAY

Do you want to express the gospel today? Use symbolic language. That was Jesus' language, and it is the dominant language of the media today. It adds modulation to abstract words. It is the best way of putting thought on show.

Do you want to reveal the God of the heavens, the one who "dwells in inaccessible light"? Take the symbolic way. That was Jesus' method with his disciples. It is the oldest method of all, used in all religions. It is still the method used today on pilgrimages, in camps, and in group education.

But why choose this way? To what needs does it correspond? What is the process used in it? What are the consequences for religious communication and, above all, for religious education? Together with the way of beauty, the symbolic way is the royal way for communicating the invisible in our own age of sensory explosion. We move along this way from needs to methods.

The Religious Crisis and the
Need for Symbol

Carl Gustav Jung provided a very original explanation for the religious crisis of our time. In his view, a tragic gulf has been created between the religious forms and impulses that are more or less consciously dormant in every human being, and the churches' dogmatic and cultic modes of expression. Jung wrote:

> Christian civilization has shown itself to be hollow to a terrifying degree. It is only an external varnish. The inner man has remained apart . . . unchanged. Externally, everything is in its place, in images and words. But all of that is absent within. Inside, it is the ancient gods who rule.[1]

For Jung, a thinker and psychologist, one observation is obvious: there is in everyone a movement that cannot be forced toward a "total man, hidden and not yet revealed."[2] This impulse, this movement forward, cannot be explained without the presence, in the depths of everyone, of a certain number of fundamental directions and images, known as archetypes, which are rather like the programs designed for rockets and other computer-dependent devices. There is, however, an essential difference from these programs: the archetypes are neither so clear nor so decisive. They are only urgent and indicative, acting as intimate conditionings and necessities. They do not act by violence or by imposing external constraints.

Basing his observations upon his study of religions, Jung makes it clear that there is a deep affinity or parallel between archetypes and religious dogmas. "I know," Jung said, "because of an experience repeated a hundred times, that the counterpart of everything formulated in dogma is concealed in the soul. . . . The archetypes of the unconscious are empirically demonstrable parallels of religious dogmas."[3] So what dwell in us are confused longings, fragments of "foreknowledge," hollows that appear, through study, to connect with what all religions have established in clear dogmas, models, and cultic forms. "The soul is to God what the eye is to the sun."[4] The dogmatic content is not, of course, exactly the same: in the West, the image of Christ is dominant, while, in the East, it is that of the Buddha or Krishna, and so on. But the variants correspond with the ambiguity of the unconscious, with its contradictions and its fantasies.[5]

As a psychologist, Jung refused to opt for a God or a dogma, but this does not mean that his position was weakened. "When I say as a psychologist that God is an archetype," he wrote, "what I mean by that is the type of the soul."[6] He affirms the existence of an imprint, but not that of a being who makes the imprint: "The competence of psychology as an empirical science can go no further than this: to establish, on the basis of comparative research, whether, for example, the 'type' [the imprint] found in the soul can or cannot be called with good reason the 'image of God.' "[7]

It is not my intention to confirm the scientific value of Jung's statements, which were based on his practice as a psychologist. But his analysis is in accord with my approach, in two respects. First, as a Christian, I find that he echoes the words of Genesis about humanity being created in the image and likeness of God. In the second place, as an observer of the world of the media, I find that he explains the functioning of religious feelings. Archetypes, stimulated by the media, awaken religious feeling and a certain distant openness to religion. This leads to a type of rebirth of a "pagan" and fundamental religious feeling. But at the same time, because of poor education and inadequacy on the part of the churches, this religious feeling runs into a vacuum, unable to find any parallel in cults or dogmas. The ties between dogmas and cults, on the one hand, and archetypes, on the other, have gradually become looser, and the religious sense, which has its roots in the unconscious, has been repressed, set aside, and even scorned.

The Bible is full of fantasies, poetry, parables, dreams, miracles, prophetic signs, and speaking in tongues. For a hundred years or more we have subjected these aspects to critical analysis and rational investigation. Our only questions have been scientific. We have asked, for example, "Does the devil exist?" and our rational thinking has told us, "No." Symbolic thought, which would reply, "Yes," to this question, no longer carries any weight or explains any aspect of reality.

There is a wide gulf between religious feeling—in Jungian terms, archetypes—and the religions that determine the forms in the religious crisis of our age. Many people reject faith today because they find no connection between the present generation's great aspirations to justice, brotherhood, and the absolute, and the practice of the churches. How sad it is when one is conscious of a soul and there is no longer any God! Others continue to go to church, but their practice is often external and without any connection with the old pagan gods that are dormant in the depths of our consciousness.

If we accept Jung's analysis, we are bound to conclude that the essential problem of religious education consists of reestablishing the bond between the archetypes and dogmas. The most important task confronting those involved in religious education is to make people aware, not simply intellectually but vitally, of these connections. We have spent too much time saying, "The Trinity exists; here is the definition of it." Statements like that have no point of contact with anything in the depths of people's soul or in their experience. As Jung has said:

> It is not a question of proving the existence of light. . . . It is valueless to
> preach light when no one can see it. . . . It is more necessary to teach man the
> art of seeing. . . . I insist that the main task of all education is to enable the
> archetype of the divine image—or its emanations and effects—to enter man's
> consciousness.[8]

This brings us back, incidentally, to the central question asked in connection with moral education: How can the eye be aroused? In other words, how can the religious archetypes be stimulated in such a way that they form a slope leading to dogma or a preparation and an implicit longing for revelation? The symbolic way provides an answer to this question. In my view, it is the best way of joining the high point to the low, the archetype to its dogmatic counterpart. I would define it as an experiential process that, by stimulating fundamental religious feelings, leads toward their historical connections in revelation.

SYMBOLIC LANGUAGE

For many, the word "symbol" calls to mind a vague reality, something that is not to be taken seriously. Symbolic language is tragically misunderstood. Its exalted and special character, irreducible aspect, and radical difference from literary language or the language of information all have to be understood if we are to grasp the meaning of the symbolic way and audiovisual language.

The symbol was explained to me when I was a child through a simple metaphor. "If you see smoke, you will know there is fire." Smoke is the symbol of fire; it makes us think of fire. So, for most people, the symbol consists essentially of a mental operation. Later in my life, I began to use the words of the philosopher Paul Ricoeur: "The symbol makes us think." But it is precisely this intellectual character that I would call into question. It is not wrong, but it has become too dominant. This aspect is secondary in the audiovisual communication of modulation. Before making us think, the symbol acts as a transforming agent, which affects the whole person. In the language of young people, it is a drug that sends us on a "trip."

When I take a bath, I am not the same afterwards as I was before. I have been transformed by immersion in water, and this physical transformation gives rise to new associations of ideas and revives memories and longings. Similarly, there is undoubtedly a mental operation involved when I look at an advertisement for a well-prepared meal, but, before this takes place, there has been a bodily effect. The advertisement has somehow made my mouth water. Without ever concealing the intellectual aspect, Jung always stressed the global and vague character of the symbolic implication toward an elsewhere: "What we call a symbol is a term, a name, or even a picture that may be familiar in daily life, yet that possesses specific connotations in addition to its conventional and obvious meaning. It implies something vague, unknown, or hidden from us."[9]

Symbolic language, then, is a language of temptation before it is a language of explanation. It leads not only the spirit, but also the heart; it moves the body. It is a language full of resonances and rhythms, stories and images, and suggestions and connections, which introduces us to a different kind of mental and emotional behavior. The following "constellation" is a helpful way of describing it (see Figure 11).

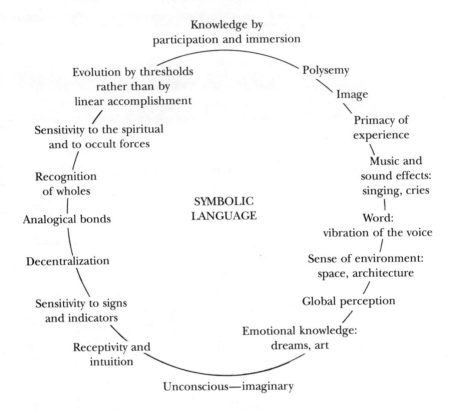

Figure 11

A person who has not entered into symbolic language will be unable to understand the extreme form of audiovisual language found in the video clip. For the literary person, the clip is nonsense, even a kind of destruction of the spirit. For the symbolic person, even if the clip expresses a disordered form of the symbol, it is still meaningful. All the characteristics displayed in the constellation above can be found in the clip. Yves Lever has described these clips in the following way:

What is the basic technique involved in video clipping? A large number of stimuli, many brief images, fleeting impressions, special effects (a divided screen, smoke, frequent use of accelerated motion, zooms, flashes of light, fade-outs, and so on), visual and sound punches, retakes, omissions, and repeats. . . . It represents the triumph of what is anecdotal, glowing, gratuitous, primary, ephemeral, and instantaneous and, at a different level, the triumph of the flash and of what is fragmented and scattered and spread out over a wide surface, rather than what is deep.[10]

The opposite of symbolic language is conceptual language. It is, in fact, very difficult to find an adequate term to characterize this form of language, which emerges in scholastic works connected with alphabetical communication. Conceptual language is that form of language that provides an abstract, limited, and fixed mental representation of reality. Its characteristics also are displayed below in the form of a constellation (see Figure 12).

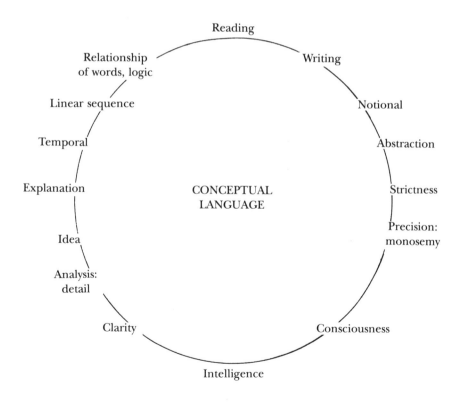

Figure 12

Words are at the center of conceptual language. W. Hamilton has called words the "fortress of thought." David Warrilow, an actor favored by playwright Samuel Beckett, was afraid of giving an incorrect rendering of the text by visualizing too much, and said that he recognized that the more restricted the field of interpretation is, the more the spirit of the writing is set free.[11]

It is certainly not possible to separate neatly these two forms of language, which are so intermingled in everyday life; and poetic language also mixes words with music and the image. The two forms of language can be compared to two waves, each one carrying with it its own sand. As we have seen, printing resulted in the victory of conceptual over symbolic language in the church and liturgy, and in the sacraments gradually losing their emotional force and resonances in the imagination. Instead of the baptismal font, we now have a few drops of water on the forehead, and many ceremonies have become complicated rites that cannot be explained without a great effort on the part of pastors or priests. The wave of conceptual language has carried with it commentaries, readings, the study of theology, and catechetical instruction based on intellectual effort and examinations.

On the other hand, the wave of audiovisual language takes us back to the symbol, like an artificial part replacing not a lost limb but defective senses. Every good audiovisual document is symbolic; due to the emotional impact of sounds and images, it has a "beyond"—something more than the reality it is speaking about, that becomes more important than the material reality proclaimed. What counts in audiovisual or symbolic language is not so much what it says as the effect it produces on us. It unites and pulls together. It belongs to us, but it is also that other part that eludes our grasp. It is a call to become closely associated with the mysteries that inhabit and orientate the universe.

That is why symbolic language and symbols cannot be dominated like a reality defined in a book. It has to be followed.

The Symbol Speaks to the Heart

The way of the parables, the way of the Song of Solomon, is a fascinating and astonishing way, arousing a longing for hidden treasure. And, however much we may challenge it in some respects, the way of so many images and films certainly moves the heart to love. After seeing Zeffirelli's film of Jesus on television, a six-year-old child was moved to tears: "He was so lovely. He was so right, but they killed him!" It is not theology or the catechism, but an open heart that makes Jesus lovable.

I asked an old catechist from North Cameroon what caused conversions among people of that region, and was told, "When they hear singing in the church. After the midnight service at Christmas, we have so many people asking for instruction. The dancing of the Gloria, the music, the feast—they are so beautiful!"

The Symbol Brings Knowledge
and Healing Together

The symbolic way unites the surfaces of reality. In particular, it brings together a Christianity of knowledge and a Christianity of healing. The second aspect is all the more important because, as we become more and more physically excited by the media, our sensitivity to factors of health and bodily fulfillment is increased. What so many young people today are looking for in faith is not so much knowledge as healing and spiritual fulfillment. The symbolic way includes the body, feelings, and sensations.

Because of their whole culture and their predominantly sensory and even audiovisual affiliations, African Christians are quite naturally more attracted to a Christianity of salvation than to a Christianity of knowledge. They therefore come more easily to knowledge along the path of healing. For example, a priest who is a well-known healer in Burkina Faso, Father Romain Dai, told me, "Healing is the way along which we take those who are to be initiated into faith. . . . Faith is closely linked to healing. Faith comes through faith in someone who heals. . . ."[12]

The old Roman ritual was full of blessings and exorcisms, which had the aim of healing, protecting, and purifying. Nowadays, of course, prayers asking God to free us from a plague of insects make us smile, because we have effective modern insecticides. But we should try to understand the deeper, lasting significance of these prayers. The world is still very sick because of an absence of strength, joy, meaning, and presence. The present generation is saturated with advertisements proclaiming youth, health, and happiness, and young people cannot be satisfied with a religion presented simply as true. It has to be presented as "good," even as the "good things" that can be given in symbolic language.

The Symbol Promotes Unity
between People

The special characteristic of the symbol, the image, and sound is that it produces effects that are not so much normative and cerebral as emotional and even physical and, because of this, tend to spread from one body to another and from one person's feelings to those of another. That is certainly the effect of African percussion instruments, rock festivals, or discos. And the dancer does not understand his dancing in his head, but in doing it. Rhythm is always contagious. All feeling, because it is rooted in our physical beings, tends to spread like a shock wave.

Do you want to set up a group? Arouse emotion! Create understanding by sharing. Run, dance, make music! Symbolic language does just that.

The Symbol Creates an Area of Freedom

The meaning of a thing is imprisoned in the word. Even if it cannot contain and set limits to the mystery, a doctrinal formula still tends to regulate it. Symbolic language, on the other hand, is suggestive and makes connections and parallels. For example, Christ is shown in the liturgy by the paschal candle and a focus of light in the church on Easter. This brings to the spirit or mind not clarity but the beginning of a movement, an appeal to us to go up toward the one who shines through the darkness.

This ambiguous language is essential to the life of the churches. A church—or any society—that does not give a place of honor to the discovery of images and poems, to popular forms of expression, and to music and symbolic ambiguity is bound to oppress rather than liberate our minds.

The Symbol Makes Us Open to the Spiritual

How does the symbolic way open us to the spiritual and the mystical? For Jung, the symbol is by definition the way by which we gain access to the beyond:

> As the mind explores the symbol, it is led to ideas that lie beyond the grasp of reason. The wheel may lead our thoughts toward the concept of a "divine" sun, but at this point reason must admit its incompetence, for man is unable to define a "divine" being. . . . Because there are innumerable things beyond the range of human understanding, we constantly use symbolic terms. . . .[13]

To this I would add that, just like the spiritual, symbols also call us to approach them in humility. One of Pascal's thoughts lends weight to these points. Speaking about faith, he wrote, "God wants to incline our will rather than our spirit. Perfect clarity may serve the spirit, but it harms the will."[14] Does a conversion of the heart, which is certainly the aim of the gospel, therefore follow a different inclination from an intellectual conversion? It moves from an awakening of a longing to look for total fulfillment, from a secret appeal to life itself, and to all things that go back to the symbol.

The Process of the Symbolic Way

The term "symbolic way" was created in order to define an approach and to insist on the vital experience that is inherent in the symbol. But it is not a new invention. For example, when he speaks about "occasions of special value for catechesis," Pope John Paul II gives first place to pilgrimages.[15] And there can be no better example of the symbolic way as a global activity capable of transforming us than such a journey to another self. Leaving home, walking together, conviviality, helping each other, the festive environment and discovery of an elsewhere, the nights spent in the open air, the pools of living water, the healings, the candles and pious objects, the processions, the singing, and the sermons—all this confusion of things, activities, and experiences makes up the symbolic way. There have been narrow definitions of the symbol, but the symbolic way is fundamentally a complex and ambiguous whole of sounds, images, words and gestures, relationships, rhythms, scents, and many other factors that bring about a physical conditioning and a psychic emotion, both of which help the deepest demands made by the person and his or her religious archetypes to be awakened.

The symbolic way has both an individual and a social effect. The effect is individual because it confronts the person with himself. Many people, walking in the silence of the woods, are able to find themselves again along the symbolic way. At Lourdes, for example, many sick people can face up to their illness and recognize it as a calling. If the symbolic way is followed by a group, it can also have a social effect, because it builds up a community. An example of this is Ramadan, the Muslims' fast. Gandhi also fasted, and, at the same time, he shed light on others and showed them a way of living that revolutionized the whole of his country.

The symbolic way is not just an object of thought. It is also an activity and an experience. It leads not simply to abstract knowledge, but to foreknowledge and longings. Whether it takes the form of yoga, zen, fasting, night vigils, or going on pilgrimages, the ultimate aim is always the same: illumination, knowledge of revelation at a higher level than simply intelligence or living for oneself or for others. Fulcanelli has shown that the architecture of many of the churches on the pilgrims' way of Saint James of Compostela is based on alchemic theories. Upon entering the church, the pilgrim went into a kind of alchemic egg that was a continuation of the pilgrimage and was thought to transform the old pilgrim into a new person. There was a movement from outside into inside, from darkness into the chiaroscuro of the deity, and there were also different optical effects.[16]

There are two major forms of the symbolic way: the symbolic way of everyday life, and the symbolic way of exercise, special times, or "shock." Here I shall describe the key process of the symbolic way in the special sense, the stages that take place with an inner logic and which give structure to the progress of experience. This process is in a certain sense normative, even if the times are diluted, cut back, or stretched out over a longer period. Fundamentally, the symbolic way, as a transforming experience, follows the classic pattern of all spiritual progress:

1. *Crisis*—consciousness of one's fragility, gaps, and longings, which cannot be fulfilled; solitude and listening to oneself.
2. *Experience of a death*—loneliness, insecurity.
3. *Experience of resurrection*—creation of a higher level of life and of meaning of life.

On the basis of many different experiences that we have had of the symbolic way, it is possible to outline the following scheme and the following stages (see Figure 13).

I now discuss requirements for the validity of the symbolic experience.

AN EXPERIENCE OF A BREAK

By the "experience of a break," I am not suggesting just any kind of experience. Going to a nightclub is also a symbolic experience, but where does it lead us? What I am suggesting are experiences that have a certain greatness and therefore can be interpreted as "breaks," and because of this they echo similar experiences in the Bible:

The Lord said to Abram, "Go from your country. . . ." (Gen. 12:1)

"I will . . . bring her into the wilderness, and speak tenderly to her." (Hosea 2:14)

In this age, when "mortal sin" consists only of being "in" and tossed about by the need to conform, the symbolic experience should mean a real break: a change of place, timetable, and habits. Such a break might mean going off into the mountains very early in the morning. But the break also calls for a recognition of certain needs and a longing for these, so that it brings about introspection and communion with the self. For example, in the 1983 prize-winning film at the Cannes Festival, *La ballade de Nayaiama*, the pilgrim had to respect the following rules in his final

The Symbolic Way

Crisis

1. Setting the scene: *presentation of an inspiring theme* on the basis of the state of the group. Each member is helped to enter into himself or herself, and to welcome his or her shortcomings and calls.

Resurrection

5. *Liturgical celebration:* each small group is invited to celebrate its experience with the help of gestures, songs, and key texts.

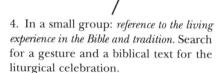

4. In a small group: *reference to the living experience in the Bible and tradition.* Search for a gesture and a biblical text for the liturgical celebration.

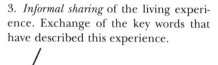

Death

2. *Symbolic experience* in the strict sense— in silence, breaking with everyday life. "Plunged into archetypes." Here, feeling and emotion are priorities, and from this will come other, particular feelings and reflections.

3. *Informal sharing* of the living experience. Exchange of the key words that have described this experience.

Figure 13

ascent of the mountain: "When you go to the mountain, do not speak"; "When you leave home, go in such a way that no one sees you"; and "When the time comes for you to return from the mountain, do not under any circumstances turn back."

The necessity for an impetus to introspection is reflected in these words by Paul Valéry, on the façade of the Palais de Chaillot:

> Whether I am a tomb or a treasure
> and whether I speak or am silent
> depends on the one who is passing by.
> Do not come in here, my friend,
> without longing.

It is only when longing has been aroused that we can choose and appreciate the treasures within the museum.

The part that group leaders have to play in this aspect of the symbolic way is very important. They are responsible for the choice of an inspiring theme that combines the group's hidden needs (for example, rest and fear) and the atmosphere of the time (for example, autumn leaves), as well as the events that are taking place and deeply affecting people's condition (such as illnesses, strikes, and unemployment).

To carry out the task of helping all members of the group to enter into themselves, group leaders have to be serious without needing to dramatize. The religious approach is intimately connected with our becoming aware of our basic weaknesses and deficiencies. A symbol is only effective if we do not look for that other part of ourselves that is lacking. Acceptance of myself as a being that is an insoluble problem is the prerequisite of every spiritual journey. Animators who have tried to make the experiences of the symbolic way a reality with various groups generally say the same thing: with today's young people, caught up as they are in the glitter of the modern world, it is essential to make the first period of the approach as long as possible in order to achieve the necessary break.

CONVIVIALITY

The symbolic experience is strictly individual and unique, like each person's soul. It does not mean that living together, even thriftily and uncomfortably, is not an important aspect leading to each one's experience being enriched by the experience of the other, so that community is brought about. Tongues are gradually loosened by the shaking of the bus, the annoyance of changing buses, and the shared meals, and people begin to talk about themselves more truthfully than they do in group discussions. They tell the stories of their lives, speak of their hidden sufferings, and share their dreams. The situation becomes a mixture of tedium, loneliness, and exchange. They listen to each other and even begin to listen to themselves. They become sheep in the same fold.

It is by coming together that we travel elsewhere, and the first elsewhere that we encounter is the other person, the one who is quite different. Every real departure is at the same time an experience of encountering others in the desert and of encountering God on Sinai.

Silence and Being Plunged
into Archetypes

Because of people's spiritual characters, it is not possible to force anyone to have a symbolic experience. As soon as one is committed to it, however, certain rules must be respected, if only for the sake of other members of the group. The most important of these rules is that of silence. This will be usual at the beginning of the experience in the strict sense of the word. It will be a rule with no exception. And the longer the silence, the deeper the experience will be. It is advisable to have something to write with and possibly even a camera, but any technical practice will only follow a period of "emptiness." It is because of the period of silence that being plunged into religious archetypes—those primitive forms and impulses that wait at the bottom of our imagination—can take place.

To begin with, *the plan is to try not to think, but only to feel.* You have the inspiring theme at the bottom of yourself. This may, for example, be, "I am going to the water to be reborn." Leave it in the background of your consciousness. Gather your longings and your problems together and go there without thinking. Open your senses as wide as possible. Follow your inclination to touch, to look at this, and to go there. Gradually an image, a reflection, a proverb, or an impression probably will rise from the bottom of yourself and will appeal to you. At this point, let yourself begin to think. It is from feeling and emotion that thought will be born and, in contact with things, that thought will gradually become "revelation."

It is this approach made from emptiness and feeling that I have called "being plunged into archetypes." This means that, because of a physical experience, such as going up a mountain, we feel basic needs, we let our longings and dreams rise up in us, and we become united with our instinctive roots. At the same time, this experience makes us encounter objects or brings about states of the soul that suddenly say to us, "The blade of grass and the wind are secretly uniting with my weariness and suggest an answer to my questions." That is precisely what the symbol is. It reveals itself when that part of ourselves that is waiting in us encounters some "beyond." "Symbol," in the etymological sense, is the coming together of two separated pieces: me and nature, me and a slum.

Let us consider a symbolic experience. A tired man is troubled by the precarious nature of life and the end of things. Climbing a mountain, he has the experience that, although he is exhausted, he can go on walking, because he is drawn along by the group. Even more than this, he suddenly becomes aware that "there is breathing going on in him" and "there is walking in his legs," and that he is animated by a life that transcends his own life. This discovery may seem to the reader to be merely an everyday consideration, but for people who have experienced it, it is an illumination that will accompany them definitively. Later, meditating on the Bible, they will say: "It is the first time I have ever understood the word 'creation.' Creation is that every moment the breath has been given to me, that breath leads me. It is mine and it is greater than me. It is me breathing and it is a principle that goes beyond me, which makes me breathe. I can hand myself over to that breath that goes ahead of me."

The Bible is filled with examples of symbolic experience: Jacob at the ford of Jabbok (Gen. 32:22–31), Elijah at the cave (1 Kings 19:9–18), and Moses on Mount Sinai (Exod. 19:16–25; 24:15–18). In each of these cases, the person descends into the depths of himself. He is "plunged into archetypes." This is followed by an emergence of the unconscious longing, which will suddenly encounter the symbolic object that is appropriate to it. And, in the secret of freedom, the person is illuminated and meaning is created.

Word and Celebration

The final stage of the symbolic way makes the word intervene—a word that is not artificial but is produced by seeking in the Bible or looking for analogies in the lives of the saints. This word will be in tune with experience and it will usually come from the group itself. It is specific to symbolic experience that it enables one to come to faith without that break that characterizes anthropological approaches. Unlike reflection about life around a table, it has a "beyond" within itself.

The exchange is interrupted with silences or personal searches. Experience has shown that the decisive context for the symbolic experience has been the liturgy. It is in the liturgy that we move from what is implicit to action, from reflection to prayer. This liturgy is certainly sober, but it is one in which some compromise is desirable in the gestures. In such a way, for example, after the crossing of the Red Sea, Miriam sang in celebration of the tragic and yet marvelous experience of the exodus (Exod. 15:19–21).

The Audiovisual Expression

Sometimes the experience ends with a last stage: an audiovisual expression. This will be the group's memory. On the basis of their emotions and feelings, some members of the group will feel the need to write a poem, story, or parable. This is a typically audiovisual approach, moving from the experience itself to expression of that experience, from emotion to the idea.

For some time, then, the members of the group will gather their thoughts and memories together, go back to the places of those memories, embellish and dramatize the situations, and go further with what they want to say. Surely that was the approach that ended in the Bible?

The Great Symbolic Experiences

In the descriptions above, I have been careful to indicate that not every symbolic experience leads to the kingdom of God. I have several times mentioned the great experiences of departure, pilgrimage, community, and the desert and mountain experiences in the Bible. All the archetypes that are particularly suitable for arousing a sense of God and for leading us to faith can be found in the Bible. From the purely pragmatic point of view, working with young people has led me to give prominence to seven experiences, but the list can be developed and, by adding other experiences, become part of an especially powerful group experience.

First of all, there is *the experience of nature.* Nature can be harsh and immense and it has enormous force. Indeed, its violence is so unpredictable that it acts as a stimulus to our human strength and leads people to strip themselves of everything that is not essential. The souls of Moses and so many other prophets have been forged in the desert and the mountains. Nature is also a mirror that enables people to know themselves. It brings their intimate disruptions back to them within a splendid order. Finally, it is a teacher of wisdom. It teaches people the patience of time, the essential rhythms of life and death, the end of all things, and the abundance of life that cannot be forced. The trees will last longer than a person; the flowers grow and open, but then fall and scatter seeds. In beauty and in the chaos of its storms, nature gives us a foreboding of what is beyond everything.

Even if we are much taken up with the world and modern technology, we cannot dispense with the sources and the teachings of nature. Examples of the educational value of nature in awakening faith are plentiful in the practices of the saints. In his training of his novices, Saint John of the Cross would send them out alone to spend a whole day in the fields and the woods. Basil of Caesarea believed that the heart had to be awakened by contemplating the sky, and that this had to take place before the gospel could be understood. He explains this in a splendid text:

> If, at any time during a calm night, you have fixed your eyes on the inexpressible beauty of the planets and thought of the author of the universe and wondered who embroidered the firmament from these flowers and how, in the visible world, necessity has precedence over pleasant things; and if, on the other hand, you have [asked these questions] during the daytime thought, in a reflective frame of mind at the wonders of the day, then you will come prepared as a listener. . . .[17]

Second, I would point to *the desert experience,* the experience of solitude and nakedness that leads us to confront ourselves: not just the desert of nature, but also that of illness, rejection by others, and hidden suffering. In this way we get rid of the universal distraction, that great ill of which Pascal spoke and which prevents us from becoming fully human. Nothing can be established outside our presence to ourselves. It is impossible to achieve interiority without experiencing that radical loneliness into which our deepest demands are finally able to penetrate. The desert is more than an artificial exercise. It has to be looked for and longed for, like an aspect of life itself.

Serving the "poor" is a particularly important experience. Training camps concentrating solely on personal achievement may possibly lead to the Olympic Games, but they seldom lead to the gospel. If we are to find the "pearl of great value," in one way or another we have to "lose our lives." In other words, we have to be responsible for those who are not valued by society, strangers, the sick, elderly people, the poor, and people with mental and physical disabilities. This experience has been a revelation for many young people. Opening themselves to it, they have discovered the higher value of the "poor" that is truth and love. Giving themselves, they have discovered what is best in themselves and their greatest possibilities. All young persons ought to go through this experience, at home or abroad.

Another experience is *the shared life in camps and other communities*, working together in an atmosphere of thrift and simplicity and sharing this with older people and spiritual awakeners present in the group. Certainly, there is a danger that a purely "flat" or "horizontal" comradeship in the long run may prove to be hollow. But what a grace it is in conviviality to encounter awakeners and share with them! Awakeners are people who remain standing on their own because of the sources, who know what is good and true not because of laws and reasoning but because of an intimate conviction. They are key persons in the symbolic experience. What they *say* is of secondary importance; it is what they *are* that matters.

Experiences of creation and responsibility are also fundamental aspects of an awakening of oneself. After identification with the leader and the actions taken in his or her footsteps, apprenticeship in real responsibility and autonomous creativity takes precedence. Creation entails the overcoming of anguish, fear of failure, impatience, and loneliness, and it is essentially a solitary activity. We are made free and become like God the creator through human creation and responsibility.[18]

Of all human experiences, *love* is the most ambiguous, but it is certainly the most important as a vehicle of faith. The problem in the experience of love is that of its depth. All people love, but how and how far do they love? I shall simply try to determine the conditions of the depth of such experiences. If the experience of love occurs in a climate that is too relaxed and easygoing, perhaps one of drugs and meaninglessness, it is unlikely to have any religious dimension. If, on the other hand, it takes place in a climate of responsibility and prayer, in the proximity of people with high ideals who are demanding, then we may hope that this love will develop a longing for fullness and the religious absolute.

Finally, it is impossible to ignore one special aspect of the symbolic experience found in music, singing, or, in a much more general way, the universe of sound, especially when it becomes celebration. From this point of view, gospel music, using gestures, songs, and poems, developed in the African-American Christian tradition of music, is obviously very successful among young people. It makes them enter into the spirit of protest of the gospel.

Music also plays a creative role and functions as a collective act. "Music is my way to God," said Indian musician Ravi Shankar, and there is no doubt that, for many people, music also opens the way not only to oneself, but also to God. Music not only accompanies us, but it also expresses the inexpressible. It makes us feel the presence of the one who is beyond words. Music and singing must be integral to each symbolic experience, to prepare the way for it, to amplify it, to interiorize it, and sometimes even to create it.

RELIGIOUS EDUCATION AND THE SYMBOLIC WAY

Our task is not just to sprinkle our catechesis with "symbolic way" exercises such as those I have outlined above. The problem is primarily not one of methods and activities, but one of spirit and approach. We have to go back to a communication of faith in which the key concepts are contact with an awakener; Christian environment; constant recourse to gestures, images, and stories; community and liturgical life; spiritual experience; ground emphasized over figure; process emphasized over speech; and so on.

In recent years, the approach of experience, usually known as the anthropological approach, has been very popular with teachers of religion. It differs from the symbolic approach in the following ways:

1. The point of departure for the symbolic way is not reflection upon an isolated lived experience, but an experience that is lived together with others and that has a real emotional impact.

2. It is not just any experience, but the very experience that is capable
   of stimulating religious archetypes. Advertising arouses the archetypes of a paradise on earth, flight, or domination. The dominant
   characteristic of symbolic experiences in religious teaching is the
   awakening of the soul, Jung's "self," or the archetypes of God.

This last point draws a clear distinction between the symbolic way and
the anthropological or "experiential" approach, which is based on human
experience in general, with the result that in the symbolic way an attempt
is made to move from life to faith. The symbolic way was necessary at a
time when faith seemed to hover high above life itself, but it is less necessary at a time when the religious sense is being reborn. Above all, it is an
approach that is difficult to sustain, because it is not easy to move from life
to faith. Very often true faith is not reached at all, beyond a development
of particular abilities on the part of the listeners or a charisma on the part
of the catechist. We have all heard remarks such as, "You can talk as much
as you like about friendships between people or about work—that's all
right. But as soon as you talk about seeing love or God acting in love and
want to make me see that, I can't take it! You have no business making
that kind of leap."

This is an understandable reaction. Listeners of this kind do not have
the intimate abilities that enable them to see or to make the transition.
The way of religious sense and of archetypes cannot automatically make us
move to faith. There is always a great abyss between the religious factor
and faith. All that I would claim is that, on the basis of a stimulation of the
religious sense and the religious archetypes, there is an inclination in
people's hearts that makes them tend toward God and, if it is a time of
grace, toward faith. I have observed that, if a group is a community that is
powerful in the human and spiritual sense and if that group is invited to
have the kind of symbolic experiences outlined above, it will not accuse
me of making that artificial leap to God.

There are many differences between the way of the catechism and the
symbolic way, the primary one being their different relationships to the
Christian message. In the catechetical way, we are confronted with the
message in the dominant form of dogmatic truths and theological pro-
nouncements. In the symbolic way, we are confronted with the message in
the dominant form of stories, key sayings, and modulation. Whether it is a
symbolic experience worked out on the basis of being plunged into religious archetypes or a video film on the parables or an audiovisual religious

lesson on baptism, the symbolic approach is full of images and stories that have an emotional impact. Its aim is not primarily intellectual understanding, but a participation of the heart and conversion. It relies not on explanation, but on the communication of an experience.

Perhaps I shall be accused of falsifying catechesis. However, isn't this above all a stage in our reflecting about faith and our structuring of it? As I shall say emphatically in Chapter 8, there can be no question of our abandoning the way of the catechism, but we have to operate on two tracks. It is, however, important for us to recognize that the symbolic way also has its own logic, its own structure, and its own synthesis. It is not modulation in a void.

In catechesis, we can be perfectly sure of establishing an initial structure for faith if we rely on the following four elements: (1) a knowledge of history, (2) memorization of key texts, (3) a deep assimilation of the fundamental images of Christianity, and (4) participation in the liturgy. This structuring can take place by means of a dogmatic synthesis. It can also be achieved by using the history of salvation. This was the way followed by Saint Augustine in his treatise on the instruction of the "unlearned" *(De catechizandis rudibus)*. In Chapter 9 I shall try to show how well adapted audiovisual language is for providing us with a history of our Christian inheritance: not "what is baptism?" for example, but "how did baptism originate and how was it constituted throughout the ages?"

History can provide this structure not only by means of its narrative flow and internal connections, but also because it places, even in our unconscious mind, images, directions, and forms that determine our ambiguous archetypes. This is a kind of prerational structuring, but how important it is! How many times is our concrete life determined by fundamental schemes, proverbs, and key words that for a long time permeated our beliefs and attitudes? There can be no doubt that stories and history itself play a key role here, with their long line of images, emotions, and dreams.

The following scheme may serve as an example to show how the history of salvation itself can structure faith in symbols (see Figure 14). I have placed the key persons at the head of this scheme, because it is around them that history has become crystallized. It is through them that God has become clear and it is with them that we identify ourselves with the aim of entering into the movement of faith. Beneath the names, I have listed several key images that belong to the iconographic tradition. They are stained-glass windows in the style of Salvador Dali's *Bible* and express our Christian inheritance in terms of contemplation and longing.

STRUCTURING A SCHEME OF FAITH
IN THE SYMBOLIC WAY

KEY PERSONS	*Abraham*	*Moses*	*Jesus*
KEY EVENTS	Leaving for Ur	The exodus	The last supper
	The sacrifice of Isaac	Mount Sinai	The trial and crucifixion
			The resurrection
KEY WORDS	"Abram, leave your country"	"Take my people out"	Love
	Earth	Yahweh	"This is my body"
	The covenant	The Ten Commandments	"I will send you my spirit"
			"I shall be with you always"
KEY IMAGES	Abraham the nomad	The Red Sea	The manger
		The burning bush	The last supper
		Mount Sinai	The cross
		The tablets of Law	The resurrection
		Moses the seer	
ARCHETYPES (Religious Symbolic Experience)	The break	The desert	Sharing with the outcasts
	Setting off	The mountain	The meal
	Pilgrimage	The crossing	The mandala
	The moon	The sun	
	The way	Water	
	The seer	The horse	
		The serpents	

Figure 14

Underneath the key persons, I have given a number of examples of key events or symbolic experiences that might be capable of opening young people and others to the reality of faith. My inspiration here has been various key words both in the Bible and the symbolic vocabulary of Jung and, drawing on these, I have identified several symbols that might be suitable to live out the symbolic experience and later to express in catechesis. This list can be extended: for example, night, the cave, the desert, the journey, the crossing of the water, the mountain, the tree, the cross, the house, the city, salt, the meal, and so on.

I am quite sure that there is a response in the gospel to the hidden expectation of so many people today who have been both uplifted and disappointed by the many images of an earthly paradise that are imposed on them. But, before trying to analyze or find an explanation, we have to offer a spiritual experience and speak a symbolic language that will act as stimuli to the most profound religious archetypes and aspirations that lie dormant in human beings. Both the symbolic approach and symbolic language, on the one hand, and audiovisual resources, on the other, should be dominant nowadays in the communication of faith.

7

THE FAMILY: THE CRADLE
OF THE SYMBOLIC WAY

MERCEDES IANNONE

The family is the cradle, even the womb in which the symbolic way is born in religious education. For Christians, it is the first and the most powerful awakener of faith. It is the community cell in which the child is able to hear for the first time the message of Jesus and the call to his kingdom.

To be more precise, the family arouses faith by means of its own interpersonal relationships and interactions with the environment surrounding it. Because they believe in the grace of God in their lives, the members of a Christian family have, among themselves and outside the family group, relationships overflowing with hope and freedom. They are able to reflect for each other the unconditional love revealed by Jesus. In the same way, their reaction to the culture and the material environment in which they are living is modeled by their faith. This expresses the fundamental goodness of creation, but it is also moderated by a consciousness of human freedom and the presence of evil in the world.

INTERPERSONAL RELATIONSHIPS

The human relationship is the first source from which our experience of love springs. Let us consider an example of this relationship between a mother and her child.

"I love to kiss," Amy giggled as she snuggled into her mother's shoulder. "I love to kiss you too," her mother said. That night in bed, her mother savored that moment. She could almost feel that warm, wet smack. She wondered how long it would be before the innocence of being five years old would give way to the distance of being ten, twenty, thirty. And Amy would learn that kissing is not always a joy, is not always possible, and is not always even true.

On the other hand, she was reminded by her husband's arm around her that Amy could look forward to a depth of meaning in her future kisses that she could not now understand. At a certain level, Amy's kiss was a ritual symbol of her feeling for her mother, which was literally beyond words. Moreover, it "taught" her mother by touching her whole being. In its very communication it demanded a response. At another level, this symbol also offered a threshold of meaning that went far beyond human meanings. The kiss is a universal symbolic act of great power. It tells us in a different way what John says again and again in his Gospel: "God is love." God is relationship.

Our experience of God cannot take place outside human interaction, since no one has ever seen God. It takes place at the heart of our activities, not in words but in the word of God made flesh. This means that the symbolic way can use the particular history of the family as it is lived every day as a source of reflection both about the meaning of life and about relationships between the human and the divine.

The first family "love story" is marriage. This is an experience that illustrates in depth the possibilities of the relationship, because, through sexual intimacy, it comes into contact with the very mysteries of life. Our interpretation of this love as a symbol of the relationship in Jesus between God and humanity derives its power not only from our living experience but also from the associations brought about under the influence of archetypes. These archetypes raise this experience from the level of the personal symbol to that of the collective, religious symbol.

In Christian marriage, the partners awaken each other to faith in two ways. First, they are for each other the causes of those primordial experiences of ecstasy that Peter Berger has called "signals of transcendence." Second, due to the value that they share together through a myriad of indirect means, they give a meaning to that experience.[1]

Apart from the power they have to arouse faith in each other through sexual intimacy, marriage partners also have the power to create new life and to mold it from its very beginning. The action of bringing a child into the world is perhaps the most profound renewal of the experience of relationship in their marriage. Everything begins with a shared longing and continues in an intimate experience, in which one partner loses himself or herself in the other in order to complete himself or herself in a new creation, the symbol of the fusion of lives. Each time a child is born, it has been said, God is telling us, "No, I have not given up on you. Try again."

If the parents are living in faith, they can light the spark in their child in many different ways. First of all, they provide the child with the fundamental images of life. By their smiles, their contacts, the mother's milk, and their hugs and kisses, the child can feel the fullness of life and learn the basic religious convictions of hope and love.

The child's memory and imagination are filled with stories of frequently heroic ancestors, parents who have been through great trials and have overcome, a savior who has come as a baby. These images are called to mind repeatedly by family rituals. It is in these rituals that the child's first image of God and first movement toward life are modeled. Only much later are dogma and institution introduced into this picture.

The parents, then, are the arousers of wonderment in their children, and their first catechists. But the children also have the power to reach their parents and stimulate their faith. In a world that is often cold and dark, the presence of children becomes a sign of hope. In their powerlessness, children call on their parents to go beyond themselves. In their innocence, they are a challenge to the temptation to compromise. In their playing, they lift up their parents' hearts toward a renewal of their being. Finally, they make old memories rise in the hearts of their parents, and this gives mothers and fathers a chance to tell their stories—stories that they may not have thought about for a long time.

Relationships between brothers and sisters have great power to arouse faith within the family system. Learning to share, to recognize their gifts and limitations, to be different, and to forgive are all lessons that are first learned among brothers and sisters. As children learn to love each other in deed and in truth, they will grow in wisdom, age, and grace. They will be disciples of the gospel who, unlike the elder brother in the parable, are able to rejoice when one of their brothers who was lost has been found again.

The way in which the family enters into relationships with other families can be a confirmation of and a challenge to its faith. Today especially, when there is so much mobility and the family no longer acts as a protective cover for the human community, a network has to be created between families. From the point of view of the social sciences, a family begins to function badly when it becomes a closed, inward-looking system. It is healthy when it is open to interactions beyond itself. Jesus calls us not to put up a tent on the mountain in the light but to build the kingdom. A family that is favored with good health can learn a great deal by associating with another fully believing family that is at grips with a mortal illness. A single-parent family can be given a great deal of support by one in which both father and mother are present. An elderly widower or widow can overflow with hope when young children come into his or her life.

It is hardly surprising that countless small communities of faith can be found in the world today. What is surprising, rather, is that families are often not aware of the influence that these groups have on the development of faith. They forget the profound religious dimension of their actions when they give food to the poor, when they bury the dead, and when they counsel the unknowing in their daily life.

Finally, the family can be awakened to faith by entering into a relationship with those who are outside the family circle. The Gospels are full of stories in which Jesus for one reason or another forms a friendship with outcasts, the poor and the underprivileged, the sick, those who mourn, adulterous women, tax collectors, and the homeless in the towns and country. Nowadays, for the Christian family, the gospel's challenge to welcome the stranger may be traumatic. Every time it takes the risk, the family has an archetypal experience of fear. It learns how to unmask it. It learns how to assume the ambiguity of the human response, which is both the joy of the encounter and the sadness of feeling exploited. In fact, the virtue of hospitality is perhaps the cornerstone of family spirituality, because it puts into practice in the concrete Jesus' challenge: Love one another.

To sum up, faith is aroused, above all, by the variety of relationships in the family system, an arousal that is subsequently extended and amplified because of interaction with other family systems and even with strangers. These relationships are concretized through rituals, symbols, and stories, which express them and interpret them in time and space.

RITUAL, SYMBOL, AND STORY

Ritual, symbol, and story are the main factors that convey meaning, especially in rites of passage such as birth, parenthood, marriage, and death, the great moments that affect the family in its relationships between generations. The meaning that the family ascribes to these sacramental times to a great extent determines our longing and our way of perceiving the rites by which the church interprets these events. For example, if the birth of a child is perceived by the grandparents as a mistake or by the parents as a crushing burden, and if the family rites that surround this event signify resentment, the rite of baptism will have very little meaning. If, on the other hand, the child is welcomed as a gift, then the ritual acts of caressing, nursing, bathing, and changing the child will speak of welcome, faithfulness, and hope. The official baptism of the child in that case becomes a public affirmation of what has been experienced in the home. It marks the birth of a new generation of faith and provides a point of departure for the grandparents and the parents in their mutual relationships.

It is the same at the time of marriage, when several generations interact with each other. Some family counselors have observed that the rites surrounding marriage call for important changes that will later affect each generation. Thus, the event of marriage acts as a stone thrown into calm water, the shock producing waves that constantly increase. In the mystery of this event, each person can once again come into contact with the most profound questions about the meaning of life. For a believing family, this experience is the occasion for a renewal of hope. Old loves are renewed, new decisions are taken, parents are reconciled with each other, brothers and sisters move away from one another, and grandparents retire into the background. Memories of earlier marriages make the belief rise again that "God is with us," and give birth to a new creative energy.

Death is also a family event. Here, too, the scheme that goes from disintegration into an indefinable phase finally ends with a new integration around a different center, finding meaning because of the death and resurrection of Jesus. Christians can let grief be grief, in the knowledge that this pain is real and profound but that it is not the last word. They can re-member in a very real way, which means that they can make those who have departed present again through ritual song and story.

One family in which the father had died, leaving a widow and seven children, invited those present at the vigil to tell a story about their father. After sharing these stories, the family sang and danced a folk dance they had often danced with their father. It was he who had taught them to dance. From that point on they had to dance without him but, in some way and at a different level, they felt his presence in the ritual gesture. After having made the coffin themselves, the older boys placed it in the family van and made the journey to the church and cemetery carrying their father's body with them—a united family. The celebration of the Eucharist confirmed and sustained the hope that they had first found in each other.

For family catechesis, there is also an occasion that is certainly less dramatic than the rites of passage but no less important as a point of impact: mealtime. The center of our faith, the mystery of the saving action of Jesus in his death and resurrection, is ritualized in a meal. The meaning of the Eucharist is communicated according to whether those taking part have or have not experienced meals as an event that sustains life. Families break bread together many times each week. Christians find this a means perfectly adapted to teaching each other respect, joy, solidarity, and hope. They do this in their preparing the food, serving each other, and eating together. Meals can also be the occasions for telling stories in which each one's day is given a value, so that each one's burden is taken seriously and hope is rekindled. Such meals are the fundamental ritual expression of the family as a community of faith.

For the Christian family, meals on feast days are the special means for celebrating the cycle of life-death-resurrection. From one year to the next, Christmas is the same feast, but the stories of the past revive images that are often forgotten. The smell of the festive dishes reminds the family of its inheritance and of the faith of earlier generations. So each Christmas can be a new beginning, a new opportunity. The Savior came into history and still comes again each year. The meaning of time and our relationship with time are expressed in our life by turning-point acts—by fasts and abstinences, by Lent and Easter, and by Pentecost. Even in tropical climates, where the seasons are not marked by changes, the rhythm of planting and harvesting, death and resurrection, can be identified in family meals.

THE PHYSICAL ENVIRONMENT
OF THE HOME

An aspect that contributes a great deal to the soil of faith is the physical environment of the home. As an archetypal symbol, the home offers important possibilities for touching the heart and arousing love. Although families live in houses of every kind, from thatched huts to luxury apartments, there should be one common concern: the beauty of the home.

A Christian home can be evaluated as a Christian painting, on the basis of its ability to call those who live in it to full life. In the first place, the home of a Christian family calls on that family to form a community. The memories of the family's past history, such as pictures and mementoes, can play a part here, just as in the Far East, a place of honor is given in homes to the altar of the family's ancestors. As for the importance of sharing, this is symbolized by the family table.

More than anything else, however, the Christian home forms a space for the inner journey, a space of silence and reflection. More than an ostentatious shop window, the home symbolizes the simplicity of life, a state of harmony with the environment rather than a state of being dominated by the environment. This climate can be achieved by a reflective use of color and space. A garden, whether it is a beautiful space of the Eastern kind or simply a window box, recalls the cycle of life.

It has been said of the Christian image that it has to maintain a unified tension between opposites. A Christian home shelters young and old people, new and old, memories and dreams. It is a place both of conviviality and of intimacy. It contains memories of times of suffering and times of joy. A home that is simply a museum full of antiques could not be in the Christian spirit. The home reflects the daily struggle of those who live in it to find light in the darkness.

Finally, the Christian home speaks of the creative genius of the family. It reflects the talents and interests of each member. It excites the imagination. Even more than a painting by Picasso, the portraits of the children will have a place of honor in the living room. Books and pictures will bring about relationships and urge the family to action in the world. Thus, enlivened and stimulated from within, the home can be the door that opens the hearts of members of the family to love.

THE FAMILY AND TELEVISION

I have spoken about the family insofar as its members arouse one another to faith through their interaction against the backdrop of their domestic environment. I have also noted the powerful impact of emotional, physical, and temporal realities in creating a home and bringing about religious images.

In our own time, there is a reality in competition with the family in creating new images that affect mutual relationships and radically transform the environment of the majority of homes. This is the audiovisual medium. In the first place, the auditory sphere of the home is affected by stereo networks. Their vibrations are felt as far as they are heard, and they awaken the old pagan gods in the young people who listen. And what are we to say about the repercussions on parents, whose feelings about these media are frequently different from the children's? The message of music is communicated more by vibration than talk and more by indirect impression than teaching. Music is there. It is a fact. Its power is undeniable. How can we pass over it in silence when we are speaking of catechesis by the symbolic way?

But in today's families, there is an even more pervasive medium: television. According to a 1980 study made by the National Institute of Mental Health:

> Television can no longer be regarded as an occasional part of daily life or as an electronic toy. The results of research have long since destroyed the illusion that made a simple, innocent distraction of television. Even though it may be true that the teaching it provides is to a great extent indirect rather than direct and formal, it still plays an essential part in the total process of inculturation.[2]

Two questions arise here: First, how is television in competition with the family as a source of religious images? Second, what strategies do Christian families have at their disposal for making television a positive force instead of an enemy that cannot be grasped?

FAMILY AND TELEVISION:
VEHICLES OF RELIGIOUS IMAGES

Because of its intimacy and the continuity of its action, the family finds itself in a special position to create and make renewing images of hope appear, images that are the primary matter of faith. Nowadays, it would seem that television also has this power, which is derived from intimacy and continuity. Television enters our living rooms and even our bedrooms. It is as close to us as a member of our own family. It keeps us company when we are alone. It is there day after day, in our good times and in our bad times. So television can claim a family role as the first producer of images, as the first criterion of value. According to Gregor Goethals, "The commercial has become a kind of visual, musical catechism, which affects the way persons see themselves and the world."[3] What is there in television that makes such a phenomenon possible?

TELEVISION AS A STIMULUS

In catechesis, the awakener is someone whose very presence opens us to a more intense consciousness of the mystery of life and calls us to enter into that mystery. Television affects us in the same way. It brings about a state of general stimulation. It also gives rise to an atmosphere of intimacy similar to that produced by the family. For example, when newscaster Dan Rather looks into our eyes through the medium of our television screen and says, "Good evening" to us, he sets a personal questioning in motion.

Sometimes we are invited to eavesdrop on a conversation in the bedroom of another person, or we are given advice about personal hygiene. These are things that give us a feeling of intimacy without, however, making us feel the slightest need to respond.

But it is not only the content of television broadcasts that suggests intimacy. The mere placing of the set in the heart of the home symbolizes its status as a full member of the family, a member we trust. Very soon after birth, the child is introduced to the television. From then onwards, it will form part of the child's life. It will be more present to him or her than most relatives. By its familiarity and lack of external control, the television becomes a powerful producer of images. This, however, is only true insofar as the family cannot or does not want to recognize the limitations of this medium.

What those limitations are is a source of confusion. Dorothy Singer has said, "The television is essentially a system of images that tell other peoples' stories by substituting them for our own stories, our current affairs, and the worries and troubles of our private life. Is it possible for our daily dependence on this medium to bring about a change in our way of thinking, in the very object of our thoughts, and even in the great effort that we make to find our information elsewhere?"[4]

Our response to this concern should not be to banish television, but to determine the place of television in the home. In a word, families must learn how to use television rather than let themselves be used by it.

THE ABILITY TO
MAKE RELATIONSHIPS

The fundamental message of Christianity is that we are loved unconditionally and we must in turn love one another unconditionally. This message can, as we have seen, be experienced and practiced in the conditions of family life. What role can television, with its special ability to visualize the symbols of a happy life, play in integrating the Christian message in people's lives? Goethals has written:

> Today, commodities such as churches continue to provide their members with myths and visual symbols. At the same time, however, commercial television, especially as it has developed over the last twenty years, has played a major role in expressing and shaping our values. It has done so by weaving a web of easily understood and accessible images, which provides fragmented groups with public symbols. In a highly complex society, television has begun to

perform one of the oldest, most traditional functions of images: visualizing common myths and integrating the individual into a social whole.[5]

Television speaks, expresses, models, and integrates, but in fact it does not involve anyone in dialogue. Although we do not have to make any effort of involvement, however, we can have the illusion of a relationship—even the illusion of control. Television seems to obey us. We set it in motion and stop it, and we choose our programs as we choose our companions. We cry, we laugh, we learn, and, according to our whims, our hearts beat with what we watch. In truth, our human companions are neither so docile nor so flexible. Is it so surprising, then, that divorced couples say that they can trace the failure of their marriage by counting the number of times each week that they have eaten their evening meal in front of the television?

But what seems true is not entirely true. Although television is our servant, it can, at another level, become our master. It creates a dependence. Various studies have been made of families who have decided to do without television for a certain period. These families have shown the same symptoms of loss as have subjects who have been on a diet or have stopped smoking. Similarly, it is difficult to control the impression made by the images saturating our imagination when we watch television. Advertising slogans run through our minds, and a longing for Big Macs or Bud Lite becomes implanted at a subliminal level in our consciousness and cannot be uprooted.

Another aspect of the modification by television of personal relationships is the element of participation in the cultural and religious celebrations that provide the family with a context for its own rites and beliefs. Looking at the Olympic games on television, we have the illusion of taking part in them. We see and hear the event, and we become very close to the participants. All the same, the human context, the feeling of a related physical contact, and the sounds, smells, and tone of the event can only be re-created in us by suggestion. The event is packaged in such a way that what is perceived as participation is in fact only a private representation. The resulting psychic effect is that we can settle for this as life by regarding ourselves as committed and in a close relationship, while we are at best no more than just spectators.

Finally, television creates the illusion of a relationship because it appeals to a basic human need to ask questions and give replies. In thirty seconds, an advertising spot can raise a question: for example, What do you have to do to get rid of dandruff? And we are given a quick and definitive reply.

Every week, the program *Thirtysomething* asks questions about relationships and, in one hour, claims to provide a satisfactory reply.

News and information programs also raise questions and provide answers. We become accustomed to quick answers and solutions. A trick is being played on us, however, because the questions raised are not really our questions, so the replies only give us an illusion of satisfaction. All the same, television acts as the key to the basic human need to ask why. That need has always been the point of departure for most family conversations; Why? is the question the children always ask. And the question provides the opportunity to tell stories, impart values, and show love. Could such a role not be given today to Kermit the Frog?

Another crucial element in the symbolic way of family catechesis is concerned with the style of the home and its impact on the members of the family. The home proclaims a powerful message about the meaning of life. Television, with its power to provide replacement experiences, can affect the perception that the family has of its environment, if the family has neither awareness of the medium's power nor concern for it.

First, television can create uneasiness with regard to the affirmation of the values honored in the home. If the home does not have every commodity, elaborately prepared food, and all the appliances publicized in the commercials, its value is called into question by television. Second, in bringing scenes of war, destruction, and despair into the home, television succeeds in taking the edge off these scenes and making them banal. People are made harder and less sensitive. Our feelings are diminished. We reach the point where we no longer grasp the unspoken tensions, the gratitude, and all the nuances in family life.

A third way that television has of changing the family environment for the worse is physical. If the center of convergence in the family's living room is the television screen, the medium's declaration is made to everyone. But, if television sets are placed in every room in the house, including the bedrooms, the world is privatized and the family is separated. This can lead to extreme individualism. It cannot lead to community. In this extreme case, the house begins to resemble a hotel rather than a home.

STRATEGIES FOR THE USE
OF TELEVISION

What is the family to do when confronted with a rival such as television? The key to answering this question is to understand that technology, even if it may give the illusion of replacing the influence of the home and the family, cannot in fact be a substitute for persons. In reality, it increases the need for great personal involvement. This is shown by the development of human potential in the first generation really affected by television. High tech creates a renewed consciousness of nearness, a dynamic tension that John Naisbitt has described in the words "high tech—high touch," by which he means a "counterbalancing human response."

As a result, "the appropriate response to more technology is not to stop it, Luddite-like, but to accommodate it, respond to it, and shape it."[6] The key word is "balance": "We must learn to balance the material wonders of technology with the spiritual demands of our human nature."[7] That is the solution. Television becomes tyrannical as soon as abilities that are not its own are conferred on it. We then make a god of it, instead of seeing it as a good thing. We look at it in an unreflecting way, settling down to the illusion of stimulation and relationship. The fault lies not with technology, but in our abdication of responsibility.

Welcoming

The first step to be taken by parents with regard to television is to affirm that they are the first producers of images. The family does not have to adjust to television; television has to adjust to the family. Television must conform to the family's values, beliefs, and ways of life, not the opposite. In plain terms, looking at television in the home can be very constructive, as long as our looking is subjected to discipline.

Because it is the image of our world, television can in fact be extremely useful to the family in developing a critical sense of culture. The family that analyzes, in the light of the gospel, the attitude of extreme consumerism broadcast by the commercials can find in this a marvelous opportunity to unmask the illusion that makes us look for happiness in "bread alone." In the same way, talking together about the program *Dallas* gives us an opportunity to discuss subjects such as faithfulness and love, loyalty, and, above all, the meaning of the family.

For the family to use television to develop a critical sense, two conditions have to be satisfied. First, the family should agree after discussion what programs are to be watched, and second, it should decide that these programs will be watched together. There is a great deal of evidence to show that healthy families watch television together and that what is perceived by the children is all the more profitable if they talk about it with the adults. Of course, this last point implies that television cannot baby-sit the children. Parents must understand how important it is to be active in the lives of their children when they are young.

In the same way, several studies have shown that the gap between the generations most often results from parents refusing to involve themselves in what concerns the young people. Watching television actively together can provide young people with the opportunity to narrate their experiences to their parents. They are led in this way to raise serious questions without feeling too threatened. In return, the parents will also be able to tell their own story and to affirm their values and their beliefs without lecturing. This is one of the ways of balancing high tech with a high level of personal, human response.

Reacting

Television can go beyond discussions of programs in the family and also act as a catalyst for action. For example, after discussing a reconciliation scene seen on television, one of the parents kisses the child and in this way engraves this image deeply in their hearts; or, after seeing scenes of ungrateful children, the children react by baking a cake for their parents.

Television helps us know that we are living in a "global village." Reacting to the evening news program, families write to their members of Congress about an unjust war in Latin America, do voluntary work visiting the elderly or disabled persons, or telephone family members who live alone in other states. In this way, it is possible to enter into the reality of human interaction under the stimulus of television.

Modeling

Understanding that television is not a god and that there is a way of giving it form is a liberating experience. We have control in pressing or not pressing the button, choosing the network and the programs, and turning the volume up or down. We do not have to let just anyone and anything come into our home. But it is also possible to model the television at the other end of the broadcast. Like any program, advertising reacts to the desires of consumers. In this respect, Christian families should engage in the modeling process actively by praising good broadcasts and criticizing negative broadcasts. They should also support certain religious broadcasts that correspond to their needs, and criticize those that are not of good quality.

Finally, families can influence the media by encouraging their children to choose a career in television. And why not? It is ultimately the quality of the television production staff that is the best guarantee of the positive influence the medium can have.

It is the family's task to balance the television images, those venerable icons of our culture, with a strong and vibrant family life. The hypnotic power that television possesses is in inverse proportion to the loving contact provided by the family circle. It is for the family to choose what role television will play in family relationships, and how it will respond to that medium.

8

STEREO CATECHESIS

When he was invited to France in 1983 to speak about the conditions of faith, Cardinal Ratzinger said, "The catechism should never have been abandoned." This statement elicited a variety of reactions, in particular from all who had worked so that catechesis no longer would be an empty formula but would become a doctrine of life in a deeply secularized society. The study of modulation or of alphabetic language and knowledge of the historical development of catechesis according to media changes illuminate the debate about catechisms in a remarkable way. We are on the threshold of a new age in which the mixture of printed and audiovisual media will require us to adopt complementary rather than opposite positions regarding the use of these media in catechesis.

I would like to suggest that priority be given to the symbolic way and, at the same time, to functioning in stereo. Stereo has the specific attribute that two modulations, with different sources, result in a unified effect. For example, with the first modulation, known as the right-hand channel, we have more specifically the melody, frequently provided by the brass instruments. With the second modulation, or left-hand channel, we have more specifically the sounds of the percussion instruments. Between the two there is a certain amount of interference; otherwise, we should have very bad stereo with an effect of emptiness in the middle. The fact remains that each channel follows its own path and provides a distinct sound. Applied to religious teaching, stereo means that we can speak two languages in a simultaneous but really quite different manner: the language of Gutenberg and the symbolic language:

Functioning in stereo means that two times, two modes of being, two "tracks" are established in the system of education. In a sense, a decision is made in favor of both hemispheres of the brain and their special ways of functioning. . . . Sometimes the artistic, global, intuitive, and "taste" register dominates and, at others, the analytical, rigorous, sequential, and abstract register dominates. There is a movement from the one to the other, but it is dependent upon perspective and which register is dominant.[1]

CHANNEL 1: THE SYMBOLIC WAY

The symbolic way should and does have priority in communication because it corresponds to the language of our own times. Even more important, it represents the best possible way of arousing people's interiority and is the only solid basis for all education in faith today. I should like to define this central point more precisely here.

In an audiovisual apprenticeship, we learn how to recognize an important distinction between the ground and the figure.[2] For a photo to be powerful and striking, there must be an optimal distance creating relief and contrast between the main subject (the figure) and the ground or complete atmosphere. The same applies to radio: this distance must exist between the word (the figure) and the music (the audio ground). When a picture is overloaded with images and words, the viewer no longer reads anything. This condition also applies strictly to faith: in our own time, the word of God is expressed in an overloaded picture in the whole of which there is no relief.

Consider as an example a child living in a village fifty years ago. Growing up, the child would have seen the great "figure" of the physical church, towering over all the houses, and soon would have learned that the pastor's voice was the main voice expressing God. The church steeple was a finger pointing to heaven, far above the "ground" of the village. Half a century later, things have changed a great deal. The real image of our times is the interior of our homes, where it is neither the crucifix nor the photos of our ancestors that are enthroned, but the television set.

Therefore, we can draw up this rule: when there are too many figures in a limited space, everything becomes ground and there is no more figure. Under these circumstances a figure can only emerge if a choice is made, from foreknowledge or preexisting subjective tendencies. If we listen carefully to some things that young people say to each other—"Have you seen those jeans?" "I heard this album the other day. It's great! You ought to buy it." "I hate that teacher!" "My parents—ugh!"—we find the talk goes through a forest of unrelated things. What principle would make the young person today in this universe of thousands of voices, many of them violent and perverted, pick out the treasure from the imitations? The church is small and the banks are skyscrapers. On television, young people receive the commercials and films of the whole world. What place can Jesus Christ have in this?

Only by arousing interiority can the challenge of a space filled with "figures" be resolved. In the past, the communication of faith was based principally on solid, systematic teaching, and it did not matter very much if a child ten or twelve years old did not understand everything. The dominant figure of the church inclined people toward the religious choice and guaranteed that the catechism eventually would be assimilated. There was no question of criticizing this structured teaching, which was in accordance with man's intellectual demands. In the age of the multiple media, however, when everything is figure, the catechism is no longer enough. Faith today must be founded on an awakening of the eye, in other words, on an awakening of interiority. Only a faith built up on an awakened interiority can survive.[3]

When there is no distinct figure because everything is figure, the key to Christian education is to emphasize an arousing of the most intimate and absolute demands made by the individual, in conjunction with the figure of the word. To do this successfully, we have to follow the symbolic way. This does not automatically lead to an arousing of interiority or to some secret correspondence between interiority and dogma; that goes back to the mystery and grace of each individual. But the symbolic way is still the most suitable for giving ground to the word of God, for modifying that which affects, and for fashioning desire for knowledge leading to the Christian revelation.

CHANNEL 2: THE CATECHETICAL WAY

I have already suggested at the beginning of this chapter that we should no longer function on the basis of a single source that embraces everything, but in stereo. If we are to have stereo, then Channel 2 has to be added to the dominant symbolic way or Channel 1. Channel 2 is the way of the catechism.

If we were to abandon the catechism, we would lose one of the greatest historical methods of teaching known, a form of teaching so popular that it has, in a sense, been reintroduced recently into teaching programs that make use of computer technology. Learning with computers, like the catechetical method, functions on the basis of question and answer. If we were to abandon the precision of language, the strict linear sequence of words, analysis, abstraction, and synthesis, we would also lose the datum of human intelligence.

There are people who are unwilling or unable to accept symbolic language and the way of religious feeling. Moreover, at certain times in life, the language of strict reason is recognized as the necessary dominant language. Finally, in the chaotic period in which we live today, it is essential to keep the catechetical way to preserve the unity of the church and to give Christians the security of a number of reference points.

After World War II, teachers of religion turned to a form of catechesis based on "life," mainly because they were convinced that abstract dogmatic formulas had to be embodied by human experience. No one would dispute the cogency of and urgency for this orientation in the postwar period. But that time has passed, and children and young people growing up today are without the protective covering of religious teaching and practice prevalent in the 1950s. People today are conscious of this absence and, at the same time, have a need for information to a degree that was unknown in the past. Finally, many Christians are so alarmed by the changes taking place in today's society that they are asking for secure points of reference. It is in this context that we have to reconsider the catechism.

NEW FORMULAS

The catechism has to respond to two kinds of need: the need for unity in the church, and the need that both Christians and those outside the church have for clear information and guarantees.

Two examples from Canada may shed light on these needs, providing new formulas to approach them. The first is a little book about the Roman Catholic Church and the pope, written in preparation for the 1984 papal visit to Canada.[4] The second is a program on baptism, intended for videotex or teletext.[5]

These new formulas are distinguished by five primary characteristics.

1. The questions are based on a survey. What questions preoccupy the "person in the street"? What questions are Christians asking? From a great range of questions asked by Roman Catholics surveyed in Canada, a few include: "What use is a pope?" "Is the pope rich?" "What is the Vatican, really?" "Is everything the pope says true?" "Is the pope going to put the church here in its place?" and "Where shall

we see the pope, and when?" Many general questions also were asked about other Christian churches, different cultures and nations, progress, capitalism, Marxism, and so on.[6]

In the case of the videotex on baptism, several questions have been added that the Roman Catholic Church insists on asking because it regards them as essential. In the present age of information, it would be impossible, however, to confine oneself simply to the questions asked by the church and to the church's way of asking them. On the other hand, an official church has to ask its questions. A balance has to be preserved between the two sources of questioning.

2. The text was prepared by people who were qualified in two spheres: theology and the media. "I am an engineer," the man in charge of the program on baptism told me. "I studied theology and scripture at Montreal University. All my work consists of presenting dogma in essential formulas that will be clear to the viewers and understood by them, and which can hold their own on the television screen. Second, I am always looking for an attractive presentation with pleasant graphics that are easy to memorize."[7]

3. In the case of the videotex, the presentation of the whole, the structures, and the final edition were studied by a committee where members, bishops, and diocesan pastoral organizations were represented. In this way, the text was given official sanction.

4. In addition to questions and answers, selected texts and key quotations were included.

5. Finally, pieces of practical information, such as addresses, telephone numbers, and recommended procedures, were given.

Of course, a formula of this kind cannot be entirely satisfactory, and a more systematic doctrine could be provided. But these attempts undoubtedly point the way to the future. In the age of information, catechism has to give satisfaction above all in two areas: There must be a close relationship between the questions asked by the church's hierarchy and those asked by the people, and there must also be a close bond between theological and journalistic language.

THE STEREO WAY OF FUNCTIONING

What does it mean to function in stereo? The two channels have been mixed recently in much religious teaching. Within a school context, attempts have been made to adopt the symbolic way by using discs, magazines, and images. The formula could be instructive, and sometimes, with young people in a situation that is barely Christian, nothing else can be done. We should not accuse those responsible for attempting this approach of failure. But in fact the formula has been found to produce few results. It is not really serious either at the intellectual or at the symbolic level. In the long run, not much has been achieved so far by this kind of teaching.

In using stereo, we have to respect both kinds of language. We have to produce symbolism thoroughly, and this calls for places, times, and a special context. Sometimes it even calls for different animators! We also have to be thorough in following—as soon as we can—the catechetical way, with its demands of intellectual application and reflection.

This leaves us with the problem of harmonizing Channels 1 and 2. Stereophony produces a unified effect. There are not many rules governing this unified effect: no overmodulation of one channel, no marked preponderance of one channel over the other, and no void between the two channels. Good mixing really goes back to the art of being faithful to the need for harmony and human integrity. This form of teaching implies a few simple rules, but it comes down finally to the art of being human. The teaching itself has to be illuminated by faith, prayer, and a sense of the universal church, and then it has the task of harmonizing the catechetical way with the symbolic way.

How can we fail to give clear information about faith in the age of newspapers and computers? How can we fail to speak the symbolic language in the age of audiovisual modulation? How can we fail to make the luminous figure of Christ understood and presented as the central figure of light, in an age with countless figures? The symbolic and catechetical ways are not at opposite poles. They are dialectical ways of entering the one truth. They are two complementary languages, expressing the one and same Jesus. They correspond to the two hemispheres of the brain in the same person.

I believe that, in catechesis, the time has finally come for us to function with both hemispheres of the brain. Until the sixteenth century, catechesis functioned essentially in "mono 1," with the right-brain hemisphere predominating. Since Gutenberg and the Council of Trent, it has functioned essentially in "mono 2," with the left-brain hemisphere predominating. But these times have passed and, although there are still preponderances, we ought now to function definitively in stereo, both in order to enter into the truth of Christ and to respect human wholeness.

9

MEDIA FOR
EVANGELIZATION

In this final chapter, I intend to go beyond a limited framework of catechesis or religious education and consider evangelization as a whole. After all, communicating the gospel through the whole world is surely the fundamental basis of our activity as Christians! Politicians and those who manufacture and sell communication devices engage in often acrimonious competition for the huge market for their goods. Even the church is asking itself whether it should follow Hollywood, the model of the electronic churches, or the way of the underground media struggling against the establishment. In recent years, two fundamental questions have preoccupied Christian communications in many different countries:

1. Mass media, group media, or self-media?
2. What kinds of programs and media for evangelization?

There are no definitive replies to these questions. We live in a world where pastoral demands are closely related not only to the differences between individual situations but also to rapid advances in technology. All the same, certain useful clarifications can be provided, bearing in mind the various life situations and responses to faith, the probable development of technology, and the demands made by evangelization itself.

MASS MEDIA, GROUP MEDIA,
OR SELF-MEDIA?

It is very significant that teachers of religion in the United States, unlike those in Latin America or Europe, have continued to use films rather than audiovisual montages. Is this because of their emotional response, technological developments, or their pastoral orientation? In communicating faith, in other words, should we opt for huge missionary advertisements and posters "proclaiming on the housetops what we hear whispered" (Matt. 10:27) or should we concentrate on small communities? Should our standard be that of the West or should we react by investigating approaches in other cultures' communications that often appear simpler? Should we protest against the mass media, which are of necessity dependent on the god of money, or should we enter this secular fortress?

Before we can answer these questions, we must survey recent history. This will enable us to throw some light on the concepts as we go along and to detect some orientations for the future.

Pope John Paul II, in an official document published in 1979, showed an early initiative to take group media seriously into account:

> From the oral teaching of the apostles and the letters circulating among the churches down to the most modern methods, catechesis has not ceased to look for the most suitable ways and means for its mission, with the active participation of the communities and at the urging of the pastors. This effort must continue.
>
> I think immediately of the great possibilities offered by the methods of social communication and the methods of group communication: television, radio, the press, records, tape recordings—the whole series of audiovisual media.[1]

The history of our age of communication begins with the development of mass media. By mass media, I mean the audiovisual products dominated by the imperative of profit and/or political power. They aim to satisfy the fundamental needs of a vast public, and thus they are faithful to the imperative of public demand. Their commercial spread follows the strict application of the laws of marketing, which have as the object the creation and the sale of products based on certain scientifically determined targets and needs.

Not all the producers of mass media accept this strict definition as pertinent to their industry, and some reject the philosophy of the mass media in favor of a more human philosophy of "social communication," to use the church's terminology. For such producers, the economic and political imperatives exist, but they are not the only criteria and do not always predominate. Strict adherence to marketing is tempered in their case by their personal convictions, their devotion to their cause, and their sense of human relationships.

In reaction to the mass media, the group media began gradually to appear between 1965 and 1970. They were, in fact, a merging of two great movements, the group movement and the audiovisual movement, and there was some fluctuation and interaction between the two.

The basic locus for training, action, and Christian life itself in the group movement is the group or, in the language used by the church, the Christian community, or "basic community." From this perspective, group media are those media able to encourage the life of the group. They may be catalysts, leading to an exchange or a search, or they may even be the fruit of a creation by the group itself. Many media producers in Latin America have been outstanding in this respect, creating short montages or programs with a dramatic basis. A parallel "photo language" is used by people of many widely different cultures in Africa and Asia. What really counts here is not so much the affirmation of a doctrine as the process set in motion by the group to enter the truth and to stimulate Christian commitment. Manuel Olivera, one of the Latin American leaders of the group media movement, stressed that ambiguity and the evocative character of the message are important features of these media. The shock caused by a montage ought to make it possible for us to react, seek, and discuss.

In the other movement in group media, there is great insistence on audiovisual language. Clubs and small groups have formed and are investigating using audiovisual techniques without either becoming too professional or using too expensive or sophisticated material. Photos, sound tracks, audiovisual montages, and similar products have become simple means of expression, corresponding to the language of today.

Apart from those media that emphasize audiovisual techniques, group media as a whole are characterized by four main aspects. First, they are "minimedia," in other words, lightweight media that are reliable but simple, usually readily available in shopping centers and stores, and easily transported and repaired. Second, these media appear to limited groups of people, who aim to create them and make them react and progress, with the result that they use special scenarios and methods. Third, the creators of group media also aim to make audiovisual language joyful and of high quality. But, finally, group media are also a cry. In them, we can hear a battle call: the cry of protest raised against mass media professionals who jealously guard the keys to knowledge and power, the cry of the poor against the alienation created by the rich countries, the cry of minorities who want to preserve their own cultures, and the cry of the church for the kind of living communities that Jesus wanted.

The positive achievement of these group media and their diversity can only be explained by the different contexts that have led to them. I will mention three of these here. The first is the movement in Spain in the

1970s. When the Spanish Roman Catholic bishops set up their National Audiovisual Center, they gave the director, Max Escalera, the following instructions: "Christianity in Spain has been very sociological for a long time. Our pastoral orientation now is to develop a more personal and committed faith. So we would ask you to create a movement based on the ability of audiovisual media to bring about and encourage groups and active communities."

In the case of Spain, the orientation of the group media returned to a precise and national pastoral program. The second context is one that is often encountered in Africa and Latin America. Group media there almost always originate with spontaneous and traditional organizations and among people who participate actively in community exchanges. In such a situation, a few simple and basic electronic media are added to the traditional media of the local culture—dancing, theater, puppet shows, and so on. Sometimes, in the name of the group and the local culture, these people even reject the foreign electronic media, regarding them as alienating. Through these group media, however, they rediscover their own identity, and the church finds the basic communities that it needs.

The third context exists in Europe and, perhaps, in North America. Group media in these continents have been above all the work of educators reacting to groups of people who have become indifferent to and out of tune with society. The reason for choosing group media is essentially to help them become conscious of themselves, express themselves, distance themselves from everyday conditioning, find a space of freedom, let themselves be called into question by others, and rediscover themselves within the group.

The differences between these three contexts may help us to understand how different the methods and the pastoral implications of group media are, depending on the places, the people, and the culture, even though they may have a number of characteristics in common. There is no question of defending or rejecting one formula; rather, one must grasp the fundamental fact that group media express a protest and that the Holy Spirit is concealed in that protest. Is the weak growth of group media in the United States connected with the church's powerful internal and social structure; with a societal attitude that is inclined more toward the success of the whole than toward group creativity; with a mere coincidence of circumstances, or with the dominant influence of textbooks and powerful means; or with the absence of leaders promoting new ways? These questions are often raised at international conferences of Christian communicators, but no answer has so far been found to them.

THE SELF-MEDIA—UNOBTRUSIVE
AND PERVASIVE

The self-media are the most recent media in the history of our age of communication. They are not disruptive or protesting; they are, rather, insinuating. The term "self-media" was first used by Jean Cloutier of Canada between 1970 and 1975,[2] but no one was prepared then for the great wave of cassettes, videocassettes, and personal computers that would follow and be embraced by the definition. In 1984, the CREC-AVEX group, with which I am affiliated, had ten thousand cassettes on gospel training distributed through mailing societies and personal contacts. The witness borne by the Roman Catholic archbishop of Lyons ("I have had cancer") was promoted through self-media by the League against Cancer. In the hospital, the doctor and the nurses had the cassette played during his radiation treatment and chemotherapy. Another example of the appeal of self-media is the catechist who listened to the same cassette on "Keys to an Understanding of the Gospel" fourteen times! And a garage mechanic who was a militant communist heard cassettes on the gospel twice and said, "If that's Christianity, I'll go along with it."

It is still difficult to define self-media precisely. Without being too limiting, I would suggest that they are characterized by four aspects: they are simple and cheap; they tend to be addressed to limited and well-motivated groups; they become the objects of a search, and bought and used by individuals; and they are distributed paracommercially and can be bought, hired, or circulated systematically.

WHAT IS THE WAY FORWARD?

It is obvious from the many different terms used to describe communication techniques—group media; minimedia; local, participatory, and alternative media; and self-media—that the situation is not fixed and is rapidly evolving. In what direction is it going? Apart from considering pastoral demands on the direction of the media, we must also be aware of the evolution of the techniques and the market.

There were countless "prophets" in the 1940s and 1950s who foresaw a society subject to the omnipotent rule of a handful of great information trusts. More recently, with the acceleration of computer technology, the alienation of individual freedoms has been frequently denounced. There is certainly every reason to be afraid, because there are sufficient machines to flatten us into a shapeless mass. But what had not been so clearly foreseen was an additional rapidly accelerating invasion of the market by machines designed to make us more individual: minicassettes, photocopiers, videocassette recorders, and others. According to statistics, one family in every four in Malaysia has a videocassette recorder; television programs in Islamic countries are very strict, and the people of Malaysia use video-cassette recorders to evade the Islamic television monopoly, which is easy as they are not far from the great Asian program producers and prices for equipment are falling rapidly.

In the short term, a fairly safe prediction would be that the tendency to make us into one mass will diminish. The production of professional cine-matographic and television materials will not be reduced, but, on this basis of mass media, we will probably move toward a great diversification of methods and audiovisual products. The result of this will be that the definitions used in the recent past will become confused. Cinema film already is obtainable on videocassettes and audiocassettes, and these self-media will become mass media, through promotion on the part of the producers. There is every reason to suppose that, because of the reliability of the material and rapid reduction in purchase prices, there will be an increase both in the number of small production centers and in duplica-tion. At Saint Paul Church in Minneapolis in 1984, the Roman Catholic Catechetical Center distributed about eight hundred videocassette titles, most of which were produced and copied there. As McLuhan said, "Everyone will become a publisher when photocopiers become more numerous."

The whole phenomenon of developing self-media and, at the same time, the mass of people, both the group and the individual, are pro-moted by the evolution of electronics. As those developing and marketing this technology have increased power to make us and everything into a mass, nonetheless, because of the development of pocket calculators, home computers, and all the electronic gadgets available, we are becoming increasingly individualized and associating more and more with each other. So, on a basis of mass production, an alternative means of communication is developing. By this communication, I mean a form that is not totally dominated by political and economic forces. The mass media will con-tinue like a landscape; but in this landscape, various forms of communica-tion will develop on the basis of diverse situations and aspirations. And surely this provides the church with a great opportunity! Group media, self-media, and mini-media: the church does not have to select on the basis of these media themselves, but on the basis of their ability to stimu-late faith and the *agape* of Christian communities in a given context. The struggle ahead will be dominated by the need to promote the media that can best express the gospel and build up the great community of men and women, proclaimed by Christ.

PROGRAMS AND MEDIA FOR
EVANGELIZATION

In recent centuries, the church has developed a special pastoral and missionary effort that has been based in print media and has resulted in church schools, seminaries, and the catechism. There are great libraries in many of our institutions and religious houses, collections of books that have cost a fortune. Should we now convert these into television studios and produce audiovisual materials? Should we redirect our financial resources and invest them in a pastoral policy based on the audiovisual media? Should the church try to join the national television networks, or should it set up its own independent organizations? And what programs should be produced?

In an interview printed in the French newspaper *Le Monde*, Roman Catholic Cardinal Wyszinski said, "The church must give up its book-shelves. It must set itself free from the technology of theology and casuistry."[3] Does this mean that churches should deliberately choose to embrace the new barbarians: the electronic media?

If we are to answer these questions, we have to make a careful distinction between two territories: the church *ad intra*, that is, the circuits of education and communication within the church itself; and the church *ad extra*, the circuits of missionary communication. I shall concern myself here only with audiovisual communication.

Ad Intra

As the historical stage when the church was a very powerful society has now waned in the world, it seems to me irrelevant to make habitual use of the mass media for communication within the church itself. In my opinion, to do this would not only be a mistake from the financial point of view, but would also be a misinterpretation of the gospel. *Priority should be given to group media and audiovisual methods within the church.* Bearing in mind the idea of "church" itself, we should aim at a community production that will allow each member of the church to go to a deeper level (self-media) and the church community to create itself as such a community, to grow, and to communicate with others (group media or media of social communication). Cassettes and videocassettes, radio clubs, or private television productions would be the best way for the future. Finally, we should prepare programs for videotext, providing Christian information for the expansion of cable television.

This orientation is bearing fruit already in almost every country in the world. Audiovisual montages, cassettes, and community radio broadcasts are being developed, for example, in Latin America, India, the Philippines, and France. Rather timorously, videocassettes are being implemented by groups—timorously, because productions of this kind are hardly profitable financially. In some Roman Catholic dioceses in the United States, the bishops' pastoral letters about nuclear power have been reviewed in diocesan television studios. In an interview, a bishop gives explanations and replies to objections. This has not taken place on the great television networks, but, despite that, videotape copies of such interviews circulate among many families and groups. The written document, knowledge of which had been restricted to only a few people, was thereby made available to everyone. Similarly, at Man on Africa's Ivory Coast, the sounds of choirs reach even those parts of the bush that are farthest from the center via cassettes, and church officials' statements are translated into different dialects and tribal idioms by the catechists.

Programs of this type must be multiplied in small centers of training, production, and distribution that are linked to church institutions and existing pastoral centers. They are an expression of regionalization and the autonomy of basic groups. At the same time, they are also links in a great chain or network. So, going beyond the audiovisual media that are still firmly centered in the traditional pattern of communication, another way of communicating is developing.

Ad Extra

Turning now to communication *ad extra*, in other words, to the work of evangelization outside the church, we are confronted by two different orientations, depending on the meaning that we give to the word "evangelization." For some Christians, evangelization is defined more in terms of message, an intellectual and doctrinal content to be transmitted. For others, it is defined more in terms of life, attitudes, salvation, and healing that all must be communicated. Bearing in mind the characteristics of audiovisual language, we are bound to be conscious of an affinity between that language and evangelization in terms of life and salvation. Our first option, therefore, will be to evangelize less in terms of doctrine and more in terms of experience of life in fullness.

I personally favor the definition provided by the theologian Martin Marty:

"Evangelization is saving people by situating them in the context of a Christian community, in such a way that their lives are given value in fullness."[4]

If evangelization means essentially giving the "right word" or "true doctrine," then television interviews would take priority as the media for evangelization. But it is precisely this interpretation that is criticized by J. W. Bachmann, who quotes Ecclesiastes 5:2: "Be not rash . . . to utter a word . . . let your words be few." Too many gadgets, too many audiovisual effects, too many words, he has said, are used as a substitute for the inner movement of faith. Instead of producing Christians of faith, we produce in this way only nominal Christians. In insisting on fullness of life, the aim of evangelization becomes the Christian community, and its main medium is also the Christian community. Recognition of this is essential in defining our pastoral options: the medium is the community of believers themselves. It is their dynamic faith, their life-style, and the witness they bear to having been healed and saved by Christ. All these are things that can be translated into electronic media, which are ideally suited for transmitting this type of message.

What are the consequences of an affirmation of this kind? First and foremost, religious programs on television and all audiovisual productions must appear to emanate from living Christian communities rather than being a simple expression of institutional functioning. If a televised service shows a community at prayer, convinced priests or pastors, and Christians acting as free and happy people, that service will evangelize. If, on the other hand, it presents practicing Christians dressed in their Sunday clothes and behaving formally and a perfect sermon without a soul, it will not evangelize. One viewer, after watching a parish service of the latter kind for a little while, commented, "I switched on, then switched over to the second network and watched an aerobic display. That was really living."

Before even deciding on what means to use, we ought to recognize that a preacher standing alone, however gifted he or she may be, will not evangelize if we do not see into the individual and beyond him or her, past the institution of the church to the living community. The electronic churches may be criticized because of their message, but they have fully understood that there can be no program unless it expresses the life of the Christian community and returns the viewers to that community. That is why they give priority to singing; free, convinced actions; vigorous testimonies; and even miracles. They stress in their broadcasts what will touch people's hearts, as did the apostles in the Book of Acts, and, following the celebration, they urge people to be converted and to write or give something and in this way to share in the full life to which the Christian community bears witness. A good program, then, places the listeners or viewers in the context of the full life of a Christian community, and it therefore calls them to go beyond the clearly fragmented life of the great shopping centers.

This insistence on the living community raises new questions concerning organization. What can we do to produce a unified service that is a true expression of the church as such and, at the same time, to allow different initiatives to emerge that will express the basic communities that bear witness to the action of the Holy Spirit? This question can be answered by considering the development in several countries of private religious radio services. Unity does not mean centralization. If we want to express life, we shall find it both in various small basic communities and in those great gatherings in which Christian people—church leaders and technicians—come together for celebration.

WHAT PROGRAMS?

In politics, the aim of the different parties at election time is to win over those who are undecided. In evangelization, the churches, using the media, have very much the same aim: to win over those who are looking for God, believers who are without a church, the "poor in heart." For this reason, the media the churches have to promote are the great media: press, radio, cinema, and television. I would emphasize in particular three types of production that are especially suitable for evangelization using the great media: the Christian happening, the history of our Christian heritage, and parables, stories, and testimonies.

THE CHRISTIAN HAPPENING

By "happening," I mean the kind of show that becomes an event because it is direct and realistic, contains a number of unforeseen incidents, and involves the audience personally. The happening is intimately connected with the word of God. According to the Bible, the word is not just a theory; it is an event that brings about a people. This, then, ought to be the first aim of any religious program, especially a television program: to be an event that touches the viewers and calls on them to participate.

This means, first of all, that radio or television program producers should emphasize the realities of the church that are, in themselves, events. The correctness of this emphasis is confirmed by facts such as the coverage of the journeys made throughout the world by the present pope. There are certainly many Christians who find displays of this kind disconcerting, to say the least. But we receive a different perspective from the Chinese, the Japanese, and the two-thirds of humanity's population who live in Asia. For the first time in history the church is on the screen. In a sense, therefore, for the first time the church exists! The church is word, not primarily because of its texts, but because of a presence that makes the event. And it is that event that creates the unity of the church today.

Services should therefore be chosen for television not primarily because they provide information or are spectacular, but rather because they are *events*. These can be great church convention services, ordinations, or the Roman Catholic Christmas Mass in Rome. But such official liturgies are not in themselves enough. There are also other events that must receive coverage, such as protest marches and great gatherings of charismatic Christians, missionary congresses and youth festivals, and cultural events such as the jazz concert in Westminster Abbey, given in memory of soprano saxophone innovator Sidney Bechet, who died in 1950. In a word, we ought to be able to apply the slogan "Something is happening here!" to religious broadcasts on radio and television. There should be praying and singing, not just with good technique, but with real faith. There should be bearing witness: that is an event and it carries well over television. Time and money should be spent on finding and preparing the best possible place for God. What should appear on the air or on the screen is the discovery of the heart that is the unforeseeable mark of the Holy Spirit.

Seizing hold of the event is one thing; creating it is another, and no less important. The event is created above all by involving the actors. An airplane accident can be described in a neutral and objective tone of voice or the story can be told emotionally, conveying the trauma of the moment. In the first case, the reporter is giving information; in the second he or she is transmitting an event. Religious broadcasts call for witnesses and actors. Jesus was himself a star living his words, expressing his life, and, thus, able to attract people. Our religious broadcasts will continue to be weak so long as Christians do not agree to be represented on the great media by great actors. At the National Congress of Christian Social Communications in 1984, several journalists addressed the assembly deploring the church's fear of "stars." We have more need today of actors with a deep faith than of professionals. Whether "holy" actors will be found among the professionals is uncertain!

THE HISTORY OF OUR
CHRISTIAN HERITAGE

At the end of the Middle Ages, a great reformation took place. This marked a turning point in the history of the church, when the catechism appeared for the first time. Christians were generous but confused in their faith, and that little book provided the solution by clarifying what they ought to believe and do. What the great and inspired religious thinkers of the sixteenth century invented at that time could be revived today, and it would be an enormous gain for the church. But we really have to invent another form today for the corpus of our Christian faith: an audiovisual form. The catechism derived its original form from the printing press and its potential, and the new presentation of the corpus of faith that we need today will derive its form from the audiovisual system and its great potential. It should be able to suit both Christians and those who are searching for God.

Of what should this new presentation of the corpus of faith consist? It should essentially consist of slices of history. It could be a film or a videotape, a document produced in the most professional way with all modern resources and the best actors available. It should also be the result of collaboration between the churches, at least at the theological level. It will be a document accredited by the church and will consist of at least two different parts: one common to the universal church, expressing our Christian heritage in the form of a history, and another relating to the local churches, expressing the traditions of the community, the forms of its present existence, and the questions arising from that life. This second part, which would have to be reviewed quite frequently, can be realized without great professionalism, but it must always echo the basic realities.

The object, then, of this kind of production is faith as it has been expressed in the course of history. Protestant Christians have certainly grasped this technique and its object. They were the first to discover the value of catechetical teaching—Luther's *Kleiner Katechismus* of 1529 was the first catechism—and later, in the twentieth century, they led the field in great film productions based on biblical history.[5]

A great deal of work remains to be done in developing audiovisual materials for the church, especially in connection with sacraments such as baptism. How did baptism originate? How was it shaped throughout the ages? What needs and struggles surrounded its development? Who were the great leaders and what were the great events influencing the teaching about baptism? The professionals know, of course, that it is not simply a question of constructing a detailed, linear history to answer such questions; that would just mean a return to the book form, and the result would simply be dull. It is rather a question of pinpointing the key moments in the historical development and giving them a dramatic emphasis: for example, Jewish baptism and the baptism of Jesus, family baptisms, the catechumenate, and so on. How good it would be for the whole church if we could have really outstanding productions on our common heritage! Several leaders of the African and Asian churches have said, "This would be a contribution of inestimable value for us, in a missionary context. Discoveries and parables, yes—but we have so much need of the essential. Our people would like to know faith in terms of history." Those who commit themselves to this venture would certainly be the greatest missionaries of the present.

A fundamental reason for historical form is obvious. The revelation and word of God consist primarily in events, persons, situations, and living attitudes; in a *history of salvation*: God acting and people reacting. Further, the historical form is completely in accord with both the audiovisual language and what the mass public expects. We have only to think of the great films and television dramas of recent years. History in an audiovisual form is certainly the best way of making the great actors and those who most inspire us with faith, together with the message of salvation itself, physically present. In the audiovisual form of narrative, the listener/viewer is led to measure a personal history against the sacred history presented audiovisually. The listener's involvement in the longings of Moses, for example, gives a broader basis to the individual's aspirations. He or she is made conscious of Moses' trials, strengths, and shortcomings, and this enables the listener/viewer to accept the human adventure and be aware of God's grace. In following Jesus on his journeys, an individual recognizes his or her own destiny as Jesus' disciple.

History dramatized by actors is the best way of extending Christ to all people. The ingredients that are needed for this narrative include a dramatic scenario, star actors, an exemplary story of a human adventure, a symbolic environment, and highly symbolic situations. The importance of the actors cannot be overemphasized, at least where the cinema or the television is concerned. Claude Brasseur has said of French historical dramatizations:

> French people give first place in history. That is, I think, because of our whole literary background. . . . We work exclusively on history. What counts most in America, in other words, what people there work on for seventy percent of

the time, are the characters, the personalities. Work on history is in second place. There are, of course, rather frightening expressions in France, such as "psychological research into a personality." But to act a person's present we have to know his past, his motivations, and many other things about him.[6]

These comments can also be applied to the communication of faith. History is not so interesting in itself as the causal development of facts and events. It is interesting as the best way of revealing individuals. At the center of history there is the person, his or her character and personality; little secrets; and a way of shaking your hand, keeping slim, and concealing an inner self and his or her reactions to events.

The unity of faith will not be achieved in the age of the media by clinging to intellectual formulas. The best way of ensuring unity is by keeping to a common heritage of persons, stories, events, and key words. That is why we have to discover—not only for ourselves, but also for the world—a new audiovisual type of catechetical corpus.

PARABLES, STORIES, AND
TESTIMONIES

Why do teenagers go to the cinema? Above all, because they are "looking for themselves," according to educational theorist and psychologist Bruno Bettelheim. No one has pointed out more clearly than he the great value of stories: "fairy stories to make the consequences of our actions visible," and the cinema, "which can have the function of the great art of every period—the moral function."[7] Even the most questionable television series have provided young adolescents with material for self-identification and moral discussion. Works of the imagination, testimonies, or stories of the saints—using audiovisual methods, we can rediscover all these paths followed by our ancestors, when they were lovingly telling the stories of their dreams and fears that form the living foundation of our intellectualization and prepare the way in our unconscious for our future attitudes.

With India's population of seven hundred and fifty million people in mind, the Roman Catholic archbishop of Calcutta once said, "There can be no question for us of choosing between group media and mass media. Even though the church in India has the right to only thirty minutes on the radio at Christmas, we have to try to be at the very heart of the mass media, just as we also have to promote the group media." It is, in other words, a question not of one or the other, but of both. That is our first conclusion.

Our second conclusion is this: the media provide us with an unprecedented opportunity to reach all those who are outside the church, including purely nominal Christians. The media can cross walls and be secretly
present, touching the hearts of those who are seeking. There is an urgent
need for Christians to become aware of what is at stake and therefore to
renew their way of being missionaries. The media are not just for specialists: they are for the whole of the Christian community. When all
Christians are involved in the media, there will be a sufficiency of specialists and an astonishing appearance of faith in the world.

FORMATION
COMES FIRST

What task lies ahead of us? We live in a difficult interim period between two ages and have insufficient people at our disposal to help us both to respond to the needs of the past and to confront new needs. In my opinion, the most important task is not to plug holes, but to launch a program of formation and training in both understanding the present and mastering the new modes of communication. So far, we have hardly even begun to do this.

Since the 1950s, documents coming from Vatican II, the pope, and official church organizations have stressed the increasing importance of social communications and the need to devote energy and means to them. Among these means, formation comes first. The pastoral instruction *Communio et Progressio*, which was promulgated in 1971 following the Decree *Inter Mirifica* of Vatican II (1963) on social communication, stated formally that priests and religious and lay people had to be trained to prepare themselves for apostolic activity in the media. At the 1980 Manila and 1983 Nairobi conventions of the General Assembly of the great international Roman Catholic radio, television, and cinema organizations, this formation was defined as having the highest priority of all. What has stood in the way of this policy?

In the 1980s, the superior of a major seminary covering several dioceses was urged to include in his curriculum a course of training in social communication, consisting of at least one session per week. His reply was, "Everyone is asking us to add a new course. We have to protect ourselves —if we did not, there would be no place on the syllabus for theology."

What is happening to make us respond so halfheartedly to such interest? Why is there such indifference to media studies in centers for the training of clergy? Why is there such suspicion generally with regard to new techniques of communication? When I introduced a university course in audiovisual practice, a colleague asked me with a smile what had happened to make me have to stoop so low!

The main difficulty seems to be that those in charge of the training are book people. They have been formed by a literary upbringing and are going backwards into our new civilization of information and communication. Priests and religious persons in the Roman Catholic Church are traditionally celibate men whose lives consist of personal contacts, family visiting, aural confessions, and class and group teaching. They are not well adapted to anonymous media contacts.[1] The church leaders have gradually developed their message in the form of doctrine, which is expressed in literary terms. In brief, the leaders of the churches come from the world of the school, and they find it difficult not to reproduce the school. If, on the other hand, we think of the leaders in the business world, most of them have very quickly grasped the importance of modern communications and have immediately invested in the new technologies. This is because they are primarily concerned not with making known a doctrine, but with selling products to make people healthy and happy. These are things that can best be expressed through images, music, and advertising.

Religious communicators, because of five centuries of catechetical and theological training, are so imbued with and conditioned by the values of the alphabetical, literary form of communication that they have remained very close to the culture that stems from this formation. A fish does not stand back and judge the water that it lives in. We are similarly uncritical about the school culture in which we remain. We criticize the school, of course, but not the great cultural models underlying it. We do this so unconsciously that other cultures are called prescientific and prerational. They are regarded as imperfect preparations, even primitive, and having no intellectual weight.

In my view, this is the fundamental reason that we resist modern symbolic and audiovisual communication. It represents a culture that is not considered equal to the scientific and literary culture. It is not another aspect of culture itself, but is only a subculture. And as for the message of faith, if it is not presented in terms of doctrine but in terms of life and modulation, it becomes a submessage.

HOW ARE OUR TEACHERS
TO BE CONVINCED?

How can we convince those in charge of training—those who have, from their earliest years, been immersed in the literary culture—of the value of and the urgent need for the audiovisual and symbolic approach? There is only one way to do this: to immerse them in the other culture. These literary people must, in the words of the gospel, reenter their mother's womb. It is, after all, not just a matter of knowledge. They have to experience the symbolic approach themselves, something quite difficult for a teacher who is a very long way from the concept of having to understand through participation, contact, synchronicity, and the emergence of affectivity and the imagination.

There is no doubt that some people, who have an active and curious temperament, will not need to be immersed in the symbolic approach to grasp this new mode of understanding. Experience alone, a sense of action, and intuition may free them from their own school formation and make them open to a bond with the media people. But the majority of our teaching staff and their leaders will not be convinced of the value of this other way of understanding until they have been through this immersion stage. It is, in other words, not a matter of proving a formula but of making another aspect of man appreciated. It is also not a matter of asking church leaders to abandon the communication of doctrine in the school or book forms but of balancing one approach against the other.

First, however, one must understand what is meant by immersion in another culture.

FORMATION BY IMMERSION

Formation by immersion is a training, the content of which is expressed primarily by the medium and our living experience of it, and only secondarily by the lessons themselves. In other words, what takes precedence in formation by immersion is the daily timetable, the dominant activities, the building and its atmosphere, the way students are welcomed and their relationships to the staff and each other, and the place of prayer and the liturgy. In formation by immersion, the ground is more decisive than the figure; the atmosphere counts as much as the formal instruction. Was this not also the case in our family life? Weren't the attitudes of our parents and the atmosphere in the home a much more powerful language than the words themselves?

In the process of formation, in audiovisual language, the student learns first from the machinery, the group, and the producer. Everything is merged together: the life of the group and the production itself. The austerity of relationships; the discipline of time; and how to learn roles, submit to technical requirements, respect the creative act, and be alert to the quality of the final expression are all things learned in the patience and "suffering of childbirth." The vibration and the expression of our body plays a vital part in this symbolic formation. We live the symbols, and the lessons themselves take second place. But, although they come second, they are no less necessary, because they provide meaning and an explanation of how symbolic formation functions.

It would not be wrong to apply to this formation by immersion what Jesus said to his apostles after they had experienced his washing of their feet: "What I am doing you do not know now" (John 13:7). The aim of the lessons that follow the experience of immersion is to ask, Do you know what has happened to you? Do you understand why the group has to be interdependent, even though it cannot always be sustained through inter-dependence? Do you have a better understanding now, since you have this experience of electronics, of the way the world is going? Do you under-stand why there are such things as regionalization and racial conflicts? Do you understand why all the chiefs of state or church leaders are charis-matic? The aim of the lessons is to reveal our experience and to extend it to include an understanding of the whole of our civilization.

Prayer and liturgy should be at the heart of this formation—prayer as experience of Christ. The characteristic of the language of the media is, as I have already said, not to illustrate ideas but to provide an experience. But how can we provide an experience if none is proposed? The heart of formation or training by the catechism is the school and the classroom. The heart of formation by audiovisual communications is the studio and the chapel. What we build up in the studio is developed and corrected in prayer. If this does not happen, it will not be an experience of Christ that we are providing but illustrated texts.

As in business training courses, the formula of immersion presupposes a break with the normal conditions of life, a separation from the usual frames of reference, and a change in the generally accepted ways of func-tioning. We must operate elsewhere, in a different way, and with other people. It is not simply a matter of just following lessons together. We have to live together.

Jean-Marc Chappuis, a Protestant theologian and media proponent, in his description of the modern types of pastor, has described the characters of the school of wisdom in Israel. It is interesting to note the relationship between that school's type of formation and what I have called formation by saturation. Chappuis claims that formation in the Israeli school of wisdom consists of three parts:

> The first component is its initiatory aspect. . . . This is a formation to which we have to subject ourselves entirely and which we can describe as psychosomatic. . . . The second component is knowledge formed by experience. . . . This is an empirical kind of knowledge . . . a search for balance, a mystical act. . . . The third component is the acquisition of a knowledge of how to conduct oneself. . . . Wisdom is acquired by an initiation that is both psychological and corporeal. It is total education.[2]

But is this kind of formation not manipulative? Yes, it is. It is only acceptable under certain conditions. First, those of us in charge of this kind of training must always be sensitive to its implications. Second, although we must remain united in our attitude and not lose sight of our vision, we must make sure that ideas put forward by different animators circulate freely and that affective polarities are not allowed to form but are broken up. Third, this kind of formation will be intensive but relatively short in duration. The best way of relativizing a powerful experience is to change it. The risk involved in immersion is like the danger not of living in a closed village community but of never leaving it. Finally, the critical aspect should never be forgotten. It is important to preserve a critical distance by means of abstraction and personal reflection. Not only the lessons, but also our own written work should be subject to this process. If we respond to teachers' initial requests for models to analyze, we shall find ourselves entering the audiovisual world with eyes trained only for the alphabetical, book form of communication. On the other hand, analytical grids will be necessary for formation and training.

WAYS OF FORMATION

Countless questions arise about the practice of this kind of formation. First, if the formula of immersion is so important, should we reject those short sessions and lectures in which, for example, a talk followed by discussion inevitably plays a dominant part? No, they should not be rejected! For people immersed in the literary culture, such sessions form a necessary bridge connecting two worlds. They do not provide an intimate knowledge either of the language or of how to handle it, but they may lead to a new and sympathetic way of looking at what is happening on the other side of the river. In these first encounters, the aim is simply to remove obstacles and state the real problem quite clearly. That problem is not one of means, but of language and civilization. Finally, we have to arouse a longing to go further. To achieve this result, the lecturers or animators will, above all, be awakeners and "link people," that is, create people who are at home in both cultures.

Should we promote a formation through language or through audiovisual methods? If we begin too early with language, we run the risk of being frustrated in many ways, especially if we have not provided welcoming structures with formation in mind. People who have been stimulated in this way may well feel cheated, insofar as what they have understood cannot be achieved in their context. Powerful personalities may be able to create transitional structures and may even be able to revolutionize a pastoral situation, but less strong personalities will find themselves deprived. If the training sessions in audiovisual work are normally given at the base, it will most usefully begin formation through audiovisual methods. Care then has to be taken to ensure that those methods are not completely remote from the local culture but are, rather, designed to amplify that culture and respond truly to local needs. For example, in a part of Africa without electricity, we have to begin with photo language, which is linked to the ability of the local people to tell stories about the photo or photos shown.

One of the dangers of using audiovisual methods is that of going no further than simply building and equipping a little studio and having its products circulated. There is a risk, in other words, of getting bogged down after making a good start. A whole country can find itself in a dead end, however well it has begun the journey. Technology may continue to develop, but education remains embedded in the past, without any vision of the whole.

It is worthwhile, therefore, to introduce not simply animators and technicians but above all "awakeners of language" into these necessary sessions of stimulation and audiovisual training. And finally, it is from these basic sessions that the leaders, producers, and artists who are able to achieve success in the media will emerge and be spotted. These are the people who should be offered professional training, formation at a deeper level, or even both kinds of training at the same time.

Who are these people who are capable of receiving training at a deeper level? They will not be technicians, who, concentrating almost exclusively on techniques, can make a center completely unproductive. They will instead be leaders and animators who are sensitive to communication.

Elizabeth Thoman has defined the "qualities of a good communications person" as follows:

> We think there are at least seven:
> 1. Good communicators are questioners. . . . They are not content with "pat" answers.
> 2. Good communicators are confident. . . . They are not easily intimidated.
> 3. Good communicators are creative thinkers. They are the people who say, "Hey, wouldn't it be a good idea if. . . ." or "Why don't we try it like this?" . . . Their cross is that time doesn't permit them to try everything.
> 4. Good communicators think and express themselves clearly. . . .
> 5. Good communicators must have a sense of quality about their work. They are willing to rewrite and rewrite. . . .
> 6. Good communicators should be good organizers. In fact, possibly ninety percent of any communications job is administrative. . . .
> 7. Finally, good communicators are bugged—by poor communications. . . . Somehow, they have a vision—of how things ought to be. . . .[3]

The characteristics outlined above apply especially to journalistic communication. They describe quite well the qualities that a national or regional director of a department of religious communication should have. In religious communication by the group media, attention will also have to be given to quality in animation, group reflection, and artistic creation.

There is a final matter to be considered: training in institutions, seminaries, and universities. There is, at present, an urgent need for a new spirit of communication, new methods, and a new course. A fairly classical type of formation can be integrated into the normal course of studies. The traditional university approach can be preserved by giving regular instruction concerned with the culture of the media, audiovisual language, schemes of communication, the impact of the different media on the life and pastoral activity of the churches, and the philosophy, sociology, and theology of communications. Moreover, outside the regular university system and according to the pattern of saturation that I have just described, training sessions of varying lengths should be inaugurated. In the course of these sessions, participants will be able to experiment among themselves with the new modes of communication and will be encouraged to create an audiovisual production. At the end of these sessions, the student will not have become a technician or a producer of programs but will have developed some intuition of the new language and, if the student has discovered in himself or herself some special talent, will have become conscious of an appeal to go further. To sum up, this training will express both aspects of our culture today—Gutenberg and McLuhan in stereo.

Telmo Meirone, founder of the Communications Center La Crujia at Buenos Aires, said that we have to form the "third person to come." That third person will be not only an animator of private radios but also a regional religious animator, in charge not only of religious broadcasts on television but also of formation sessions or training centers; not only a producer of audiovisual materials, including cassettes, but also responsible for catechesis, religious education, and liturgy; not only a leader of opinion but also a person with spiritual experience. It will be a person not only of interpersonal but also of media communications: a person exposed both to the breath of the Holy Spirit and that of people today. It will be a person who amplifies the word of God.

With the vision of such a person before us, we inevitably become convinced that our most important priority is formation and training.

HOW TO EVALUATE AUDIOVISUAL TEXTS

TWO METHODS, TWO AIMS

To give concrete expression to my discussion of beauty, and to help religious animators to build media libraries, I provide two methods of evaluation. The first evaluates the validity of an audiovisual text for general religious education. The second assesses a text in terms of its ability to communicate faith. Each method assesses what I call the "strong positive charge," that is, the specific ability of an audiovisual text to touch affectivity and imagination, thereby changing attitudes and providing greater understanding of faith or the "religious."

THE RELIGIOUS VALIDITY OF AUDIOVISUAL TEXTS

Assessing the value of audiovisual texts for religious education can be done in a fairly objective way by surveying a given group. Of course, a relatively large sampling must be taken in order to obtain valid results. In the field of religion, personal and cultural factors seem to play such an important role that it is naive to claim universality *de gustibus et coloribus non disputatur.* For the religious animator, what is important is to evaluate the document according to communication with a concrete group.

The Test

The method of evaluation proposed below has been used on more than a hundred texts. Is it faithful to the criteria of traditional science? Probably not. But each time we sought a more scientifically rigorous evaluation, the results were so much less significant that we preferred this more global method, despite its dependence on the people responsible for interpreting the results.

Following is the procedure for evaluating photographs. (For texts involving sound, seek a reaction to a dozen or so pieces of music, suggesting (1) a period of silence after each one and (2) the writing of reactions and captions.)

1. Give the group twenty numbered photographs to examine.
2. Ask the group to look at them carefully for at least seven minutes. The group should not discuss the photographs.
3. Invite each member of the group to note on a piece of paper the three photographs they like most and the three they like least.
4. Ask each member to write whatever caption comes spontaneously to mind for one or another photo. This caption is to be written on the bottom half of the page, indicating the number of the photo.

Studying the Results

The results should be analyzed by several people who have expertise in communication and psychology. To determine the religious validity of the text, two criteria are important:

1. The *number of reactions:* First, separate the photographs that elicited reactions from those that did not. A photo might be aesthetically beautiful, but if it was given neither a positive nor a negative reaction, set it aside. Such a response meant that the photograph lacked a *strong positive charge.* Do not set aside reactions of rejection or even anger: on the contrary, these photos are good for discussion. The devil is a religious character just as is God.
2. The *number* and *quality of religious connotations* must then be evaluated. Some photographs may have received a number of captions that bear no relation to what is religious or moral. Reactions that are valid in themselves but not on the religious level are set set aside.

Scoring

Score photographs in the following way:

No value: 0. There was no positive or negative reaction, or no caption for the photograph.

Weak value: Adding up all the reactions—negative, positive, captions—yields less than a 10 percent reaction from the whole group.

Average value: 10-30 percent reaction.

Great value: 30-60 percent reaction.

Very great value: 60-100 percent reaction.

(Specific intentions apart, we reject from our media library those audio-visual texts that do not have great value or, at least, average value.)

0	1	2	3	4
no value	weak 1-10%	average 10-30%	great 30-60%	very great 60-100%

DOCUMENT VALIDITY

1. *Reaction value*
   Did the text produce a reaction?

0	1	2	3	4

2. *Religious connotation value*
   Did the text provoke any kind of religious reaction?

0	1	2	3	4

REACTIONS
Phrases or key words

STRONG POSITIVE CHARGE FOR FAITH

Subjective Nature of the Evaluation

Evaluating an audiovisual text's ability to awaken or communicate faith is a delicate matter. There are numerous variables, most important, how does one judge faith? More than ever here, we depend on the assessment and experience of animators who have a sense of faith, of beauty, and of communication. The evaluation proposed in the table below is based on the criteria defined in the chapter on beauty.

Several people may evaluate a text according to the criteria listed below. One can also carry out a simple, personal assessment based on personal experience. In either case, the assessment remains subjective, although such subjectivity will be based on analysis and reflection.

Interpreting What Is
"Religious" and "Christian"

For a text to have a strong positive charge for faith, it must have a religious dimension of 60 to 80 percent. Of course, faith cannot be added to what is religious like blocks on a pile. A text has a strong positive charge for faith when its Christian explanation is saturated, impregnated, and surrounded by the religious.

Moreover, the criteria of what is religious and what is Christian vary; some are even contradictory—harmony and scandal, trance and the sign of love. In the end, the evaluation must include all criteria to enable the determination of which ones dominate in a particular text, and the measuring of how far the religious and the Christian are present, how far they penetrate each other, and in what proportion.

Method for the Evaluation Grid

Evaluation begins with the following evaluation grid. It includes main criteria (Transparence, for example) and lesser criteria (vibration, reverberation, etc.). From this, for each criterion, mark the relevant box, indicating for each item: "No" (= 0, this characteristic is not found in the document), "Doubtful" (= 1, which means "don't know," "I hesitate"), and "Yes" (= 2, this item best describes the document). At the end, add up the number of points given.

Sample: For the Buddha image, the main criterion might be **Transparence:**

	No 0	*Doubtful* 1	*Yes* 2	*Total*
Transparence				
Vibration			✔	
Reverberation			✔	
Beyondness			✔	
Purity		✔		
Welcoming signs	✔			
Totals	*0*	*1*	*6*	*7*

RELIGIOUS DIMENSION

	No 0	Doubtful 1	Yes 2	Total
1. Transparence				
Vibration				
Reverberation				
Beyondness				
Purity				
Welcoming signs				
Totals				
2. Being Eternal				
Sacredness				
Stillness				
Stability				
Totals				
3. Being Out-of-Reach				
Distancing				
Separating				
Light and shade				
Richness				
Age				
Greatness				
Loftiness				
Totals				

	No 0	Doubtful 1	Yes 2	Total

4. Order and Beauty

Harmony				
Hierarchy				
Perfect shapes				
Essential shapes				
Unity				
Totals				

5. Creation

Unique character				
Unpredictable shapes				
Elusive power				
Inspired				
Freedom of shapes				
Outrageousness				
Totals				

6. Signs of Worship

Gestures—Adoration, prostration				
Sacrificial gestures				
Human humbling (low)				
Raising up God (high)				
Decor—liturgical action				
Totals				

	No 0	Doubtful 1	Yes 2	Total

7. Breaking-Out Effect

Trance				
Ecstasy				
Fright				
Outrageousness				
Violence				
Totals				

CHRISTIAN DIMENSION

	No 0	*Doubtful* 1	*Yes* 2	*Total*

1. Reference to Historical Revelation

Evoking Christian history				
Evoking Christian communication and church				
Realism in shapes and appealing power				
Totals				

2. Symbols of Charity

Evoking fraternity, gift, charity, forgiveness, etc.				
Commitment— protest against disorder and injustice				
Feeling of presence, community				
Totals				

3. Interiority

Authenticity of characters and positions				
The mix of weakness and power				
Presence of opposites				
Totals				

	No 0	*Doubtful* 1	*Yes* 2	*Total*
4. Scandal				
Signs, shapes, gestures, or contrasts confirming a certain love madness—Christ crucified				
Expressions of the world's violence against the just—torture, disfigurement, etc.				
Opposition to the powers that be, to the law—Revolution				
Totals				

WHY SUCH A MINUTELY DETAILED EVALUATION?

The aim of this type of evaluation is not to identify what is good or bad in religious education, what is going to sell or not, but rather to help us discover if a particular text can be a pathway for faith—beginning with the criteria for the way of beauty.

Such a study will affect our judgment, and it is essential for a Christian communicator, particularly today when commercial advertising and pseudo-charismas can easily interfere with our seeing. That said, I measure what this evaluation grid can tell us that is important or barbarous. To someone whose heart is open, a child's look is sufficient to reveal Christ! And a banal image of the crucified Christ can lead to conversion! There is the objective value of the text, but, far more importantly, there is the *internal light* in the eye of the beholder.

NOTES

INTRODUCTION. THE BIRTH OF CONVICTION

1. Pierre Babin, *Crisis of Faith* (New York: Herder & Herder, 1963); idem, *Faith and the Adolescent* (New York: Herder & Herder, 1966); idem, *Options* (New York: Herder & Herder, 1967); and idem, *Teaching Religion to Adolescents* (Palm Publishers, 1967).

2. With these characteristics in mind, a work written by an ecumenical team, *Audiovisuel et Foi,* appeared in 1970. It was translated in the United States as *The Audio-Visual Man* (Dayton, Ohio: Pflaum, 1970).

3. Pierre Babin and Marshall McLuhan, *Autre homme, autre chrétien à l'âge électronique* (Paris: Editions du Chalet, 1977).

4. Ibid., 58-63.

5. Cf. Claude Bailblé, "La musique et le corps," *L'Audiophile* No. 3 (n.s.) Bimestriel; No. 46 Feb/Mar 1989: 92. See also Michel Imberty, *Les écritures du temps* (Paris: Edition Bordas, 1981).

6. Speaking about the way sound can induce colors, Olivier Messiaen explains, "It is childish to attribute a color to every note. It is not single sounds that engender colors, but chords or, rather, blocks of sound. Each block has a definite color. That color is apparent at all octaves, but it will be normal in the middle register, fading into white (that is to say, more clear) moving towards the treble, shading into black (that is to say, more somber) moving towards the bass" (Bailblé, "La Musique et le Corps").

7. Alvin Toffler, esp. *The Third Wave* (New York: William Morrow, 1980); and John Naisbitt, *Megatrends* (New York: Warner Books, 1984).

8. Naisbitt, *Megatrends,* 2-3.

9. J. M. Albertini and A. Silem of the IRPEACS Laboratory of CNRS, Lyons, researchers in economics, data processing, and audiovisual, study the conditions under which knowledge is transferred between specialists and nonspecialists.

10. "Economie mondiale 1880–1900: la fracture? Rapport du Centre de prospectives et d'information internationales," *Economie* (1984).

11. Jacques Séguéla, *Fils de Pub* (Paris: Flammarion, 1983), 174.

12. Ibid., 21.

13. Ibid., 218.

1. RELIGIOUS EDUCATION FROM GUTENBERG TO THE ELECTRONIC AGE

1. Pierre Chaunu, *Le temps des réformes* (Paris: Fayard, 1975), 21.

2. J. Fedry, "L'Afrique entre l'écriture et l'oralité," *Etudes* (May 1977), 584-85.

3. J. Jungmann, *Catéchèse* (Brussels: Lumen Vitae), 16-19.

4. Chaunu, *Le temps des réformes*, 172.

5. François Rapp, *L'Église et la vie religieuse en Occident à la fin du Moyen Age* (Paris: Presses Universitaires de France, 1971). "The church attempted to strengthen the effects of preaching by extending them. It employed three principal means to achieve this aim. First, the priest repeated to each individual member of his flock, inside the confessional, what he had said to the whole congregation in the pulpit. Second, those who enjoyed the privilege of literacy could read at home, in works of piety, the reflections that had been introduced in sermons. Finally, all Christians, the uninformed as well as the educated, were surrounded by a great number of pious images, illustrating what they had heard in sermons" (p. 137).

6. J. Delumeau, *Le christianisme va-t-il mourir?* (Paris: Hachette, 1977), 41.

7. E. Germain, *Langage de la foi à travers l'histoire* (Paris: Fayard, 1972), 76.

8. Ibid., 24. This is according to thirteenth-century statutes of the city of Angers, Rodez.

9. Ibid., 20-21. Mendicant orders also played an important part, at this time, in the apostolate of preaching. According to the evidence available, their preaching was often earthy and included stories, pieces of verse, mimicry, onomatopoeia, and outbursts of laughter.

10. This form of popular religion still is found in certain rural countries that are not influenced by modern industrial and technological developments. For example, a Corsican village resident placed Saint Anthony on the same level as Jesus. The only reply I could make was, "The saint showed his mettle. When Jesus showed his mettle, he was believed!"

11. François J. Casta, "Eveques et curées corses dans la tradition pastorale du Concile de Trente" (Ph.D. diss., Institut Catholique de Lyon, 1964), 113.

12. Rapp, *L'Église et la vie religieuse en Occident à la fin du Moyen Age*, 140.

13. Chaunu, *Le temps des réformes*, 324-25.

14. Evidence can be found in the Musée de l'Image at the Épinal commune, France.

15. Fulcanelli, *Le mystère des cathédrales* (Paris: J. J. Pauvert, 1964).

16. L. Febvre, *Au coeur religieux du 16ème siècle* (Biblio Essais, Paris: Hachette).

17. J. Delumeau, *Naissance et affirmation de la Réforme* (Paris: Presses Universitaires de France, 1968), 366-67.

18. *Horizons protestants* (June 1975), 3.

19. Germain, *Langage de la foi à travers l'histoire*, 31. The most important documents referring to the origins of the catechism will be found in Germain's book

and in J. C. Dhôtel, *Les origines du catéchisme moderne d'après les premiers manuels imprimés en France* (Paris: Aubier, 1967).

20. See the General Congregation of April 5, 1546. The so-called Roman Catechism of the Council of Trent did not appear until 1566.

21. Germain, *Langage de la foi à travers l'histoire*, 36. Calvin's "Ordinances" appeared in 1541. After 1551, the Genevan Catechism was being used everywhere in France.

22. Chaunu, *Le temps des réformes*, 171.

23. *De Veritate*, q.14, a.11.

24. Delumeau, *Naissance et affirmation*, 196.

25. Alain Peyrefitte, *Le mal français* (Paris: Flammarion, 1977), 162, 166-74.

26. It would be an absurd oversimplification to reduce everything to the "message" of printing. What characterizes above all the Greco-Latin way of speaking and thinking, and in particular the philosophy of Plato and Aristotle, is a constant effort to elucidate intellectually. But printing emphasizes and generalizes this way of thinking and imposes it on the public. Reading establishes contact with a reality via signs that have been made abstract twice: first, by focusing our eyes on words, and second, by fragmenting our understanding. This is achieved by looking from above at bits of sentences linked to each other by punctuation marks and coordinating conjunctions. It is hardly surprising, then, that we have become people with a linear, temporal, analytical, and abstract form of intelligence.

2. A NEW APPROACH TO MORAL LIFE

1. R. Pucheu, *Presse Actualité* (Paris: Bayard Presse, 1974), 39.

2. Fernand Seguin, *Forces* (Dorchester Montreal: Hydro-Québec, 1973), 10.

3. Ibid., 9.

4. Michel Souchon, *Education 2000* (Paris: La Cité, 1974), 6.

5. Max Laplante, *Jalons pour une psycho-sociologie des moyens de communication sociale*, Cahier d'études et de recherches, no. 2 (Montreal: Office des communications sociales, 1965), 16.

6. Cohen Seat, Gibert and Pierre Fougeyrolles, *L'action sur l'homme: cinéma et TV* (Paris: Editions Denoël, 1961), 39, 110.

7. Séguéla, *Fils de Pub*, 21.

8. Harvey Cox, *The Seduction of the Spirit* (London: Wildwood House, 1974), 222.

9. It is unusual for those who own and work in large vineyards to get drunk. There are, of course, numerous exceptions to this rule. Certain factors, such as alcoholism, a particular physical disposition that doctors still try to define, or an unhealthy environment make it impossible to stimulate a taste of the kind described.

10. Marcel Légaut, *Intériorité et engagement* (Paris: Aubier, 1977), 53. Légaut was a university teacher in Paris for many years. At forty, he became a sheep farmer in the mountains of southern France. At eighty, he began to write novels and essays. His demanding reflections about the conditions of contemporary spiritual life have deeply influenced religious thinking. See esp. *L'homme à la recherche de son humanité* (Paris: Aubier, 1971); Eng. trans.: *True Humanity*, trans. David Smith (Ramsey, N.J.: Paulist Press, 1982).

3. THE IMPACT OF ELECTRONIC MEDIA
ON FAITH

1. For the theory of the two hemispheres of the brain, see Pierre Babin and M. F. Kouloumdjian, *Les nouveaux modes de comprendre* (Paris: Centurion, 1983), 79-90. There is an interesting case of overlapping in California, where a school in Palo Alto also bases its explanation of communication on the theory of the two hemispheres. See E. Marc and D. Picard, *L'école de Palo Alto* (Paris: Retz, 1983), 106-12.

2. The average time spent viewing television in the United States in 1985 was seven hours and ten minutes a day, according to the BBC (London, 8 March, chap. 2). French young people, on average, spend fourteen hours a week watching television and fifteen hours listening to the radio. This is based on studies of young people between the ages of fifteen and twenty-four, made by the French Ministry of Culture in 1985.

3. For Saint Bernard, the churches "will be bare stones, . . . devoid of all orna-ment and systematically stripped of all claim to distraction to the detriment of the word." To make even more certain that the ear has priority, the lighting is restricted. There are few windows and no stained glass. In the Abbey of Thoronot, the echo in the vault lasts for four seconds. This calls for a particular way of singing and a special rhythm. The stone sings and "the echo represents the hearing of the sound that has already passed through the present of the lips." See H. Larcher, "L'acoustique cistercienne et l'unité sonore," *Encyclopédie des musiques sacrées* (Paris: Editions Labergerie), 2, 10.

4. Jean-Paul Dubois, "La Pub se rebiffe," *Médias* (6 June 1983): 40.

5. Jim McLaren, "Sounds of Silence" (1975), Studio 24, Festival Records.

4. A CHRISTIAN APPROACH TO
COMMUNICATION

1. Virginia Stem Owens, *Media Development* (London: World Association of Christian Communication [WACC], 1984), 35.

2. The Greek word *agape* was first employed by Homer, but Christians were quick to adopt it. It means love and charity as experienced and celebrated in the banquets shared by the first Christians—a love that gathered them together in a single body in Christ.

3. In his treatise "On the Soldier's Laurel Wreath," Tertullian states that the Christian should pray while standing, especially from Easter Sunday to Pentecost.

4. I speak here without distinguishing between "friendship" and "love." Both terms go back to the same source and the same movement, even though, depending on the culture and the situation in question, they may be differently expressed. There is in both a fundamental personal inclination that has no justification apart from itself.

5. Naisbitt, *Megatrends* (New York: Warner Books, 1984), 35-58.

6. Saint Augustine, *Soliloquies,* Book 1, Chapter 12.

7. Légaut, *True Humanity,* 171-72. There is also an excellent analytical chapter on this subject, "Encounter and the Spiritual Life," by Thérèse de Scott, in Lé-gaut's *L'oeuvre spirituelle* (Paris: Aubier, 1984), 191-208.

8. Légaut, *True Humanity*, 174-75. I do not deal here with this special model, according to which an audiovisual director, in particular in the liturgy, in a sense takes the place of the priest or the catechist. In his study of liturgy on television, Johan G. Hahn went so far as to speak of two messages. See "Liturgy on Television or 'Television Liturgy,' " *Media Development* (London: WACC, 1984), 9-12.

5. THE WAY OF BEAUTY

1. Olivier Clément, interview with Pierre Babin. Cassette Novacom, Lyon. *La Vie Spirituelle* (1984). Clément teaches at the Catholic University of Paris and is the author of many theological works. See *Sources* (Paris: Editions Stock, 1982).

2. Nsambi e Moula Bokulaka, *Etude dans éveil et croissance* (Kinshasa, Zaire).

3. Saint Augustine, *Homily 26 on Saint John*.

4. Pierre Babin, A. Baptiste, and C. Bélisle, *Dossiers Photolangage* (Paris: Editions du Chalet, 1969). See esp. "Situations limites," a file of 96 photos showing intolerable situations of injustice, poverty, racism, sickness, loneliness, and other forms of suffering; "Groupes," a file of 48 photos showing various group situations, faces, and individuals (included is a booklet describing the ways in which these photos can be used in group-centered research); and "Valeurs en discussion," a file of 96 photos about money, nature, freedom, forms of love, and other themes, which contains questions that can be used in group work.

5. It is debatable whether images that mock religion are religious. They certainly have an objective relationship to religion and, in that sense at least, they can be included within our definition. On the other hand, they have been created to be used against religion.

6. By denotation, I mean the material and objective description of realities. By connotation, I mean the whole complex of characteristics surrounding the material realities and giving rise to special feelings. A connotative reading moves from impressions, the impact, or what is felt to the material reality.

7. On the basis of this general notion, we instinctively make use of terms related to religion and the sacred, in the knowledge, however, that the sacred has a more primitive connotation of fearful and fascinating power. See R. Otto, *Le sacré* (Paris: Payot, 1949).

8. The World Association of Christian Communication (WACC), London, devoted an entire issue of its journal, *Media Development*, to "Silence in Communication" (1982), no. 4. On the subject of spiritual masters, Michael Traber has written, "The spiritual masters who lived in solitude and silence have throughout the centuries been the great teachers of communication, and some of them were the greatest communicators the world has ever seen. . . . A silence expressed primarily in music, poetry, and prayer. . ." (4:1).

9. A. Wathen, *Silence* (Washington, D.C.: Consortium Press, 1973), 10.

10. Otto, *Le sacré*.

11. Marcel Jousse, *L'Anthropologie du geste* (Paris: Editions Gallimard, 1975), 165-68.

12. What is certain is that the "religious" quality of the voice, as described here, is reproduced better by a sensitive microphone than by one that is only able to pick up a limited range of medium- and high-pitched sounds.

13. Cf. chapter 3, n. 3. "The vault of heaven, where the music of the spheres plays, eternal and powerful in the image of the Father, and the vault or roof of the mouth, where the word vibrates, modulated in the flesh in the image of the word. . . . And, corresponding to these two, a vault of stone, reflecting the word and fertilizing the ear like the Holy Spirit. . . ." See Larcher, "L'acoustique cistercienne et l'unité sonore," *Encyclopédie des musiques sacrées*, 9.

14. Carl Dreyer, as quoted in *Media Development* 4 (1982), 27.

15. André Malraux, *Le surnaturel* (Paris: Editions Gallimard, 1977).

16. Another temptation for such authors is to make simply a "church" document, a purely catechetical document with a negligible affective impact, strictly defined intellectually, and unambiguous. The choice is justified by the ultimate aim of belonging to the group and keeping the group together. If it is contested here, it is contested not in and of itself, but with regard to the option of revealing beauty.

17. The mandala is a diagram calling to mind both the cross and the concentric circles that represent the universe. The universality of the mandala as an archetype has been studied by Jung.

18. In this sense, however hesitant we may be about the message and life of the electronic churches, we must admit that they have understood that a Christian television message is based on a community and takes us back to a community in which life breaks out. See Chapter 9, "Media for Evangelization."

19. "The Laughing Christ" became a kind of manifesto in the 1970s for many American Christians, who wanted to leave behind a dark and immature form of Christianity.

20. "If the whole of life is moving inevitably toward its end, we have to color it during our own lives with love and hope. The social logic of life and the essential aspect of every religion is to be found in that love. For me, perfection in art and life has come from that biblical source. . . ." See Marc Chagall, *Message biblique par Pierre Provoyeur* (Paris: Cercle d'Art, 1983).

21. Before his famous concert in Westminster Abbey, Duke Ellington said, "I am not worried about how much this may cost. I want the best I can get. I want the best musicians, the best singers and the best directors, amateurs and professionals. I want them to give the best of themselves. I want all the help I can get. I want to express my hope in this way, because it will be the show of shows—if it is God's will. We all have a soul, a secret dwelling in us that we depend on and that upholds us, a soul, a source of survival and creation."

22. Blaise Pascal, *Pensées* II, frag. 575 (Paris: Editions Gallimard, 1977).

23. R. de Gourmont, *La culture des idées*, no. 1595 (1983), 10–18.

24. For discussion and example of how to evaluate audiovisual documents, see Appendix.

6. THE SYMBOLIC WAY

1. Carl Gustav Jung, *Psychologie et alchimie* (Paris: Editions Buchet/Chastel, 1969). I refer repeatedly in this chapter to this work, in which Jung provides a remarkable synthesis of the crisis and problems of religious education. See esp. 14.

2. Ibid.

3. Ibid., 23.

4. Ibid., 13.

5. Ibid., 21.

6. Ibid., 19.

7. Ibid.

8. Ibid., 20.

9. Jung, *Man and His Symbols* (New York: Doubleday & Co., 1964), 20.

10. Yves Lever, *Relations,* Special Culture, Montreal (July-August 1985).

11. As quoted in *FNAC Journal,* Paris (1983), in connection with the play *Solo.*

12. Romain Dai, interview with Babin (February 1983), Cassette. Novacom, Lyon.

13. Jung, *Man and His Symbols,* 20-21.

14. Pascal, *Pensées,* 219.

15. "I am also thinking of various occasions of special value which are exactly suitable for catechesis: for example, diocesan, regional, and national pilgrimages, which gain from being centered on some judiciously chosen theme" (*De catechesis tradendae* [1979] 7:47).

16. Fulcanelli, *Le mystère des cathédrales.*

17. Basil of Caesarea, Hom. 33. See D. S. Sterckx, *Le monde des symboles* (St. Léger-Vauban, France: Zodiaque, 1972).

18. See Légaut, *True Humanity.* Légaut has shown how fatherhood, love, and creation are fundamental experiences opening the way to God.

7. THE FAMILY: THE CRADLE OF
THE SYMBOLIC WAY

1. Kathleen R. Fischer, *The Inner Rainbow: The Imagination in Christian Life* (New York and Ramsey, N.J.: Paulist Press, 1983), 10-11.

2. Quoted by Eli Rubinstein in *American Psychologist* (July 1983).

3. G. Goethals, *The TV Ritual: Worship at the Video Altar* (Boston: Beacon Press, 1983), 137.

4. Dorothy Singer, "A Time to Re-Examine the Role of Television in Our Lives," *American Psychologist* (July 1983): 815-16.

5. Goethals, *TV Ritual,* 2.

6. Naisbitt, *Megatrends,* 41.

7. Ibid., 40.

8. STEREO CATECHESIS

1. Babin and Kouloumdjian, *Les nouveaux modes de comprendre,* 150-55. I first applied this concept of stereo to intellectual training in general.

2. The word "ground" means more than simply "background." It also means territory, basis, environment, context, and matter. In fact, the relationship between "ground" and "figure" is a subjective one. The "figure" is what we are clearly conscious of, here and now. It is what occupies our minds.

3. For the concept of interiority, see *L'homme à la recherche de son humanité* (Aubier, 1971); and *Interiorité et Engagement* (Aubier, 1977). Marcel Légaut is an author who has tried more successfully than others today to define interiority in terms of consciousness of and faith in oneself. See esp. *True Humanity.*

4. Guy Marchessault, *Le pape chez nous* (Ottawa, Canada: Novalis, 1984). The author is a journalist.

5. A videotext is a presentation on an ordinary television screen of information in the form of texts and graphics or simplified images. This type of presentation can be obtained on request.

6. These questions can be found in Marchessault's *Le pape chez nous*. In the case of the videotext, the questions and replies are a little more formal.

7. Bertrand Ouellet, director of the Télec service at the Office des Communications Sociales, Montreal, Canada, in a personal interview. See *Le videotex, un nouvel outil pour la pastorale*, Cahier d'études et de recherches, no. 32 (Montreal: O.C.S. 1984). Vincent Guillon has presented a full document on the videotext—churches and telematics—in *Chrétiens medias*, Paris (September 1984).

9. MEDIA FOR EVANGELIZATION

1. Pope John Paul II, Apostolic Exhortation, *De Catechesis tradendae* (1979), VI: 46. In its official documents, the Roman Catholic church has always used the term "social communication" rather than "mass media," thereby rejecting the materialistic connotations that might be implied in the word "mass."

2. Jean Cloutier, *L'ère d'Emerec ou la communication audi-scripto-visuelle à l'heure des self-media* (Montreal, Canada: Presses de l'Université de Montreal, 1973).

3. "Sélection hebdomadaire," *Le Monde* (12-18 October 1978).

4. See the special edition of *Media Development* (London, WACC, 1981), devoted to the theology of communications.

5. In the period between 1980 and 1985, there was, e.g., the enormous "Genesis Project," which aimed to cover the whole of the Bible.

6. Claude Brasseur, *Première* (March 1984): 48.

7. Bruno Bettelheim, *Psychologie* (1982). Bettelheim was thinking of the school in this case.

EPILOGUE. FORMATION COMES FIRST

1. It is interesting to note in this context that the most popular form of pastoral ministry in the church in the United States is counseling.

2. Jean-Marc Chappuis (University of Geneva, Switzerland, photocopied notes). Chappuis was vice-rector of the University of Geneva.

3. Elizabeth Thoman, *Medias and Values* (January 1981).

INDEX

Abstraction (in art), 124
Acoustics. *See* Reverberation; Vibration
"Affectivity," 44
    framework of, 63
Affinity, 90-91
    communities, 51-53, 99
African Christians, 153. *See also* Art, African
Agape, 72, 76, 193, 225 n.2
Alphabet(ic), 56, 85
    church, 89-90
    language, 182. *See also* Communication, alphabetical
Amplification, 58, 62
Anchorites. *See* Contemplatives
Anthony, St., 120, 136
Appeal, power of, 135
Archetypes, 63, 132, 147-48, 159, 161, 164, 165, 169
    and dogmas, 148
    plunged into, 160
Architecture, church, 139, 155
    steeple in, 183
Art, 145
    African, 124-25
Atmosphere, 58, 65. *See also* Liturgy, atmosphere of
Audiovisual
    culture (new), 3-4
    discovery of, 3
    education, 206-7
    expression, 160
    images, 13
    language, 3, 11, 64, 190
    methods, 3
    participation in, 21
    text evaluation, 211-21. *See also* Communication; Media; Photo language.

Augustine, St., 22, 67, 93, 94, 113, 165
Aural sense
    and liturgical development, 62
    faith framed by, 58, 60-65
    perception, 59, 60, 61, 79
    preponderance of, 58
    superior to visual, 61
Authenticity, 141
Authority, 35, 38
    in village, 40
    on value, 38
"Awakeners," 35, 49, 114, 208

Bachmann, J. W., 196
Background, 58
Baptism, 74, 107, 152, 165, 172, 185-86
    audiovisuals on, 199-200
    videotext on, 186
Basic communities, 140, 190, 191
Basil, St., 118
Beauty, way of, 35, 60, 110-14, 145
    and order, 130
Beckett, Samuel, 152
Belief, as "being in," 67
Bellarmine, Robert, 26
Berger, Peter, 130, 169
Bergman, Ingmar, 72, 117
Bernard, Saint, 61, 123, 133
Bettelheim, Bruno, 201
Bible, 160, 161, 167, 197
    return to, 61
    Vulgate, 28. *See also* God, word of
Books. *See* Media, print
Borromeo, Charles, 25
Brain, hemispheres of, 55-56, 87, 183, 187
Break, experience of, 156-58
Broadcasts, religious, 198

Calvin, John, 26
Canisius, Peter, 25, 26
Cartesianism, 87, 89
Cassettes, 192, 194
Catechesis, 3, 20, 106, 165
  audiovisual form of, 31-33
  based on life, 185
  development of, 182
  by drama, 22
  in family, 173, 178
  by immersion, 22
  memorization, 22
  notional form, 31
  stereo, 32, 182-87
    harmony and integrity with, 187
Catechetical way, 27, 184-85
Catechetical movement, 30
Catechism, 18, 28, 76, 86, 164
  method of teaching, 184
  result of printing, 18, 26, 199
Cathedrals, 20-21, 24, 40, 155
Celebration, 160
Chagall, Marc, 113, 139
Chappuis, Jean-Marc, 206-7
Charismatics, 88. See also Tongues, gift of
Chaunu, Pierre, 23
Chiaroscuro, 125, 129, 156
Children. See Families
Christmas, audiovisual communication of, 32-33
Church, ad intra/ad extra, 194-97. See also
  Alphabet, church; Architecture,
  church; Cathedrals; Modulation,
  church
Clément, Olivier, 110
Cloutier, Jean, 192
Communication
  adaptation by Christianity, 18, 70
  alphabetical, 84-90, 204
  by color and form, 24
  Christian
    aim of, 75-76
    approach to, 70-100
    features of, 135
    formation by immersion, 204-8
    resistance to audiovisual, 204
    paradox of power and weakness, 108
  first, 78-79
  of friendship, 91-94
  function of, 4-5
  ideological, 87
  language of, 4
  lasting, 98
  of love, 91-92, 104
  modes, 88
  oral, 19-20, 86
  personnel, 209
  and the poor, 82, 100-105
  purpose of, 62, 97
  social, 189, 203
  of spirit, 94-97

technology, 5
training, 209. See also Faith,
  communicating
Community, 20-21, 51-52, 74, 94, 158, 162,
  171, 190, 193, 197
  and electronics, 51, 194-95
  essence of Christianity, 52, 133, 135
  participation in, 78. See also Affinity
    communities; Audiovisual,
    participation in; Basic communities
Computer(s)
  counterbalances to, 93
  personal, 192
  and precision, 184-85
  technology, 12, 63-64. See also Data
    processing
Conversion, 73, 153, 165
Conviviality, 158
Cox, Harvey, 47
Creation, 141, 162
Cross, 132-33
  sign of, 22-23. See also Jesus, crucifixion
Cult of leading symbols, 63
Cults, voodoo, 131
Culture
  and media, 90
  American, 16
  oral, 19-20
  pop, 12

Dai, Romain, 153
Dali, Salvador, 120, 136, 165
Dance, 125, 131, 191
Data processing (media), 12-13
  information and calculation in, 31
Death, 97, 172
  and resurrection, 156-57
Delumeau, J., 21, 28
"Desert experience," 161
Destructuring, 41-43
Distance, art of, 136
Document
  audiovisual, 132
  religious, 122
Dramatization, 136
Dreyer, Carl, 117, 124

"E" factor, 41, 43, 47
Ear, 133
  as dominant organ, 59, 86
  as symbol of body, 58. See also Aural sense
Ecumenism, 88
Education, religious, 13
  atmosphere of, 205
  by experience, 49, 163-64
  denied the faithful, 27. See also Symbolic
    way and religious education
Educators, religious, 14
Electronic church, 188. See also Media,
  electronic
Emptiness, 159

Environment, sense of presence within, 61
EPCOT, 11-12
Eucharist, 172, 173
Evangelization, 20, 54
  as message, 195
  media for, 16, 188-91, 194-97
  to/from community, 196
Externalization, 45
Eye, 133
  message received by, 58, 86
  of spectator, 47. See also Image

Faith, 107, 164
  abstract correctness of, 29
  affective, 29
  approach to, 56
  and emotion, 23
  and healing, 153
  communicating, 1, 5, 6-7, 8, 13, 15, 29-31,
    106-9, 191, 201
    agents of, 35
    feeling and background, 9, 184
    in audiovisual form, 199
    oral, 18, 19-20
    print, 24-28, 36-37
    symbolic actions, 18
  crisis of (1950s), 30
  Dionysiac foundation of, 30, 131
  framework of, 69, 131
  message of, 6, 7
  mystical approach to, 79, 113
  perceived, 55-56
  personal and committed, 191
  relation to primitive religion, 63
  scheme of faith, 166
  "strong positive charge" of, 215-19
  taking part together, 69
  triggered by consciousness of self, 61. See
    also Belief; Immersion; Symbolic way
Family
  as framework of faith, 131, 168-81
  and television, 174-75, 176, 178-81
  values, 178, 179
Feedback, 77
  Christian, 73-74, 81-82, 98
Feeling (religious), 63, 148, 185
  test of, 66-67
"Figure," 8, 64-65, 183, 184. See also
  "Ground"
Films, 189, 199
Formation, 203-9
Francis of Assisi, 97
Freedom, 110
Freud, Sigmund, 78-79
Friendship. See Communication of
  friendship
Fulcanelli, 155

Gandhi, Mahatma, 155
Gerson, Jean de, 25
Gesture, 121

God
  as "abba," 74-75
  as absolute transmitter and receiver, 73
  and beauty, 112
  "beyondness" of, 139
  communication in love (agape), 72
  experience of, 169
  frame of reference for, 57, 61
  grace of, 110
  in history, 132, 200
  as love, 169
  mysterious presence, 90, 112
  and negation, 131
  not self-sufficient, 105
  and reason, 106
  spontaneous approach to, 61
  unknown, 132
  word of, 65, 76, 107, 112, 160, 183, 197,
    200, 210. See also Jesus, message of;
    Image; Revelation
Gospel
  "good news," 2, 54
  symbol, 2, 146
Gregorian chant, 123, 128
"Ground," 8, 64-65, 89, 183, 205. See also
  "Figure"
Gutenberg, Johann, 18, 24, 187
"Gutenberg crisis," 30, 209

"Happening," Christian, 197-98
Harmony, 60, 130
Hearing. See Aural sense
Hieraticism, 125, 127
"High tech/high touch," 93-94, 114, 179
History, teaching, 199-201
  salvation, 200
Holiness, 107-8
Holy places, 89. See also Cathedrals
Holy Spirit, 61, 95-96, 191, 197, 210
Home, environment of, 173-74. See also
  Family
Hymns. See Music

Icons, 124, 141. See also Images
Illusions. See Television, illusion of
Image, 183
  civilization of, 58
Images, 23, 124, 125
  of Buddha, 119, 140 147, 215
  of Christ, 147
  Christian vs. religious, 115-22
  emotional impact of, 165
  of Krishna, 147
Imagination. See Symbols; Television and
  imagination
Immersion, faith by, 20. See also Catechesis,
  by immersion
Inaccessibility, 128-29, 139
Incarnation, and technology, 17, 18
Indians, North American, 56-57

Information
  age of, 11-12
  as audiovisual media, 11
  pollution of, 120
  society of, 12, 14
  transmission of, 64
Interiority, 48-50, 99, 122, 135, 140-41, 184,
      220
  awakening, 48-49
  of Jesus, 49
  surrender of, 108

Jesus (Christ), 118
  Abraham, Moses and, 166
  appeal of, 135
  in art, 137
  and audiovisual language, 65
  as communicator, 64-65, 68, 71, 88, 109,
      198
  crucifixion, 105, 114, 132-33, 144
  eyes of, 140
  face of, 127
  film about, 130, 152
  historical event of, 133
  lack of interest in, 32
  laughing, 133-35
  message of, 64
  miracles, 80
  and religion, 132
  portrayal of, 63
  poverty of, 101, 142
  use of place, 119
  words of, 14
Joan of Arc, 50-51, 60
John of the Cross, St., 97, 161
Jousse, Marcel, 121
Jung, Carl Gustav, 146-48, 154, 167
Jungmann, J., 20-21

Klee, Paul, 124

Language
  in audiovisual, 128, 206
  Latin, 128
  poetic, 152
  schemes, 77-79, 88
  union of words and silence, 119. See also
      Audiovisual language; Photo
      language; Symbolic language
"The Laughing Christ," 133-35
Learning
  by environment, 24
  by salvation, 24. See also Education
Légaut, Marcel, 45, 50, 93, 98-99, 135
Leisure, 13
Lever, Yves, 150
Life
  inner, 45
  quality of, 13
Light, 124-25, 154
Liturgy, 20, 107, 152, 160

atmosphere of, 13, 65
framework of, 131
heart of formation, 206
modulation in, 81
participation in, 165
Logos of God. See God, word of
Lord's Prayer, 23
Love
  ambiguity of, 162-63
  and friendship, 225 n.4
  sign of, 137, 139. See also Agape;
      Communication of love
Lucas, George, 43
Luther, Martin, 25
  Small Catechism (Kleiner Katechismus), 26,
      27, 199

Malraux, André, 125
Mandala, 132, 227
Marriage, 169, 172
Marty, Martin, 195
Mass. See Eucharist; Liturgy
Mass media. See Media, mass
Meals, ritualization in, 173
McLaren, Jim, 67-68, 121
McLuhan, Marshall, xi, 4-6, 7-10, 46, 55-56,
      193, 209
Mecca, 129
Media,
  audiovisual, 189
  electronic, 9
    and psychological times, 35
    basic, 191
    characteristics of, 41
    effect, 41, 44, 54-55
    efficient causes, 9
    environment, 9
    formal cause, 9-10
    impact on faith, 54-67
    language of, 54
    role in society, 54, 193
  group, 188-89, 191, 201
    as expression of protest, 191
    for church ad intra, 194-95
  mass, 188-89, 193
    profit and power, 189
  narrative, 10
  multiple, 184
  print, 18, 86
    and audiovisual, 182
    and church institutions, 194
    and faith, 25
  self, 188, 192
  techniques, 90
Meditation, 83
Medium, the
  is Christ, 7-8
  is the message, 6
Mimicry, 124
"Minimedia," 190
Miracle(s) and healing, 20, 65

Missionary
    advertisements, 189
    movement, 25. *See also* Evangelism
Modulation, 6, 58, 80-81, 108, 149, 182
    and/as word(s), 80
    aural and visual, 56, 187
    church, 89-90
    communication of, 77-78, 87
    criticizing, 83-84
    and overmodulation, 62, 83
    vibration, 6, 86. *See also* Liturgy,
        modulation in; Vibration
Montages, 189, 190, 195
Moral life, 117
    new approach to, 39-53
    formal cause of, 41
Moses, 166
Music, 112, 174-75
    African-American, 163
    as approach to God, 61, 77, 112
    as audio "ground," 183
    "becoming," 44
    conversion by, 153
    effect of eternity, 128
    hymns, 90
    plainsong, 128
    role of, 89, 90
    sentimental, 135-36
    simple and repetitive, 137
    as substitute for religon, 31
    symbolic experience in, 163
    videos, 59, 112. *See also* Gregorian chant
Mysticism. *See* Faith, mystical approach; *See
    also* God, mysterious presence
Myth(s), 79, 176

Naisbitt, John, 11, 93-94, 179
Nature
    authority of, 40
    electricity and, 40
    experience of, 161
Negation. *See* God and negation

Order. *See* Beauty and order
Otto, Rudolph, 120
Owens, Virginia Stem, 71

Parables, 201
Paradise, artificial, 135
Parents. *See* Families
Participation. *See* Community
Pascal, Blaise, 91, 109, 142, 154, 162
Paul, St., 97
Petit, Guillaume, 27
Photo language, 115, 117, 190
Picasso, Pablo, 131, 174
Piety, 61
Pilgrimages. *See* Symbolic actions,
        pilgrimages
Plainsong. *See* Music, plainsong
Plato, and beauty, 110-11, 224 n.26

Pleasure, 110-14
Poor. *See* Poverty/poor. *See also*
        Communication of the poor; Jesus,
        poverty of; Poverty
Pope John Paul II, 63, 80, 155, 189
Poverty/poor, 95, 100-105, 162, 190, 197
Power, overcome by weakness, 120
Prayer, 74-75, 94
    at heart of formation, 206
    as transmitting and receiving, 75
Presence, 60
Presentation, manner of, 14
Printing. *See* Media, Print
Proclamation, 20
Psychopedagogy, 2

Rapp, François, 21, 23
Ratzinger, Cardinal, 182
Receptivity, 60
"Religious," 115-31, 183-85
    expressions of, 120
    opposed to "Christian," 132
Religious education. *See* Education, Sunday
        schools
Repentance, 73
Revelation, 71-73, 104, 113, 114, 159, 200
    by sounds and images, 115-16
Reverberation, 122-23, 215
Rhythm, 154
Rites of passage, 171
Ritual, song and story, 171-72

Sacred, The, 118-20, 130
    and faith, 132, 133
    atmosphere, 129
Sacraments, 152. *See also* Baptism
Salvation history. *See* History, salvation
Sartre, Jean-Paul, 44
Satan, 105
Sauli, Alexander, 26
Scandal of Christianity, 135, 144
Scripture. *See* Bible; Koran
Shankar, Ravi, 112, 163
Shrines
    Compostela, 24
    Epinal, 24
    Lourdes, 24, 155
    St. James, 24
Silence, 90, 95, 118-19, 120, 158-59
Singing. *See* Music
Society of longing, 14
Sound, 44
Space, multidimensional, 60
Spirit. *See* Communication, of spirit; Holy
        Spirit
Spiritual families. *See* Affinity, communities
Stained glass, 124, 165. *See also* Cathedrals;
        Communicating by color
Star Wars, 43
Statues. *See* Images
Stereo. *See* Catechesis, stereo

Story, 171-72, 201-2
Structures. *See* Destructuring
Sunday schools, 25
Symbolic
    actions, 35
        begging, 18
        fasting, 155
        pilgrimages, 18, 146, 155
        prayer repetition, 18
        traditional feasts, 18
        vigils, 155
        yoga, 155
    experiences, 161
    knowledge, 60
    language, 146, 149-52, 183
        and conceptual language, 151, 185
    way, 2, 110, 146-67, 183-84
        an activity, 155
        and religious education, 163-67
        scheme of faith in, 166
Symbols
    to create freedom, 154
    cult of living, 63
    gestures as, 22
    of light, 154
    living, 206
    need for, 146-48
    numbers as, 22
    promote unity, 153
    public, 177
    unite knowledge and healing, 153
    See also Faith, communicating; Images;
        Love
Systems law, 9

Taizé community, 68, 82, 128, 137
Technology, 17, 62
    and religious identity, 25
Television, 193
    church's use of, 198-202
    and family, 174-75
    illusion of relationship, 177
    illusion of satisfaction, 178
    image dominates, 58, 183
    and imagination, 62-63
    medium, 57
    power of, 62

purpose of, 41
self-identification in, 201
shaping values, 176
strategies for use, 178-81
Temptation, language of, 149
Teresa, Mother, 63, 143
Teresa of Avila, 97
Testimonies, 201-2
Thomas Aquinas, 28
Time, meaning of, 173
Toffler, Alvin, 11, 50
Tongues, gift of, 82
Tradition, oral. *See* Culture, oral
Transcendence, 60, 116
Translucence, 124-25
Transparence, 120-21, 215, 216-17
Trent, Council of, 25, 26, 28, 33, 187
Turin, Shroud of, 127

Unconscious (collective)
    primitive images of, 30-31
Unity, church/ecclesial, 185, 197, 198, 201
    by image, 38
    of opposites, 135

Vibration, 31, 58-59, 121, 122, 174, 206, 215
    audible and visible, 62
    in art, 124. *See also* Modulation;
        Reverberation
Video cassettes, 35, 192, 195
Video clips, 150
Video recorders, 193
Vigor, 136-37
Voice, 121-22
    inner, 60, 61

Way
    of illumination, 110
    purgative, 110. *See also* Beauty;
        Catechetical way; Symbolic way
Welles, Orson, 50
Word, of God. *See* God, word of;
        Modulation, as word
Writing, collective experience in, 19

Zeffirelli, Franco, 63, 130, 152